# THE
# NEW
# MINISTRY
# OF TRUTH

## Combat Advisors in Afghanistan
## and America's Great Betrayal

## MAURICE L. NAYLON IV

Hellgate Press          Ashland, Oregon

# THE NEW MINISTRY OF TRUTH

Published by Hellgate Press

(An imprint of L&R Publishing, LLC)

Hellgate Press

PO Box 3531

Ashland, OR 97520

email: info@hellgatepress.com


Interior & Cover Design: L. Redding

Cover Photo: Maurice Naylon IV


Cataloging In Publication Data is available from the publisher upon request.

ISBN: 978-1-55571-945-6 (paperback); 978-1-55571946-3 (e-book)


Printed and bound in the United States of America

First edition 10 9 8 7 6 5 4 3 2 1

*To the warriors on our left and right –*
*may their voices be heard.*

If you're a veteran coping with your own anger and frustration,
writing can help. Share your story at *www.newministryoftruth.us.*

# Praise for *The New Ministry of Truth*

*"A solid, down-to-earth, honest narrative that shows the skills an adviser must learn. On top of that, Chipp has the insight and sense of humor to describe the whackiness of our endless mission in faraway and fractured Afghanistan."*

—Bing West, author of *The Wrong War* and
*One Million Steps: A Marine Platoon at War*

"THE NEW MINISTRY OF TRUTH *is an honest, gut-wrenching account of Chipp Naylon's service in Afghanistan as a military adviser. Written clearly, cogently and bluntly, it is the kind of no b.s. memoir one expects from a United States Marine. But it is also a thoughtful, analytical and intimate account of America's longest war—and the challenges and frustrations endemic to it."*

—Professor Bruce Hoffman, Georgetown University,
author of *Inside Terrorism*

*"Naylon grinds down to the grain describing the turbulence of being a military advisor during The Long War—written in plain speak with no punches pulled. If there was a military decoration for, 'telling it like it is,' Naylon's award citation is already written."*

—Major Scott A. Huesing USMC (Ret), bestselling author
of *Echo in Ramadi: The Firsthand Story of
U.S. Marines in Iraq's Deadliest City*

*"For nearly two decades, America's leaders have told us that we will only succeed in Afghanistan 'by, with, and through' our local partners. With this refreshingly unvarnished and unglamorous account of his service, Chipp Naylon has succeeded in exposing the fatal flaws in our counterinsurgency conceit."*

—Gil Barndollar, Center for the National Interest,
former Marine combat advisor

# CONTENTS

·················

# PREFACE

·················

T HIS IS NOT a traditional war story or combat memoir; if
you're looking for the daily grind of battle that so many
Marines and soldiers faced during their time in Afghanistan, this
isn't it. For those stories, read about Marines fighting in Sangin
District, soldiers in the Korengal Valley, the battle for the Shahi-
Kot Valley, and countless other accounts of truly heroic combat
actions. For us, things were actually pretty good. Tasked with
defending the largest coalition base in Afghanistan, we had plenty
of amenities, more air support than we could hope for, and, all-
in-all, a pretty "country club" deployment. Frankly, if we weren't
in the middle of Afghanistan, Bagram Airfield may as well have
been thrown down in the middle of any military town in America.
This reality begs the question, what's the point of writing this?
Why is this book important?

On one hand, selfishly, writing this has been an exercise in
catharsis for me. Country club or not, seven months in a combat
zone can be a stressful experience. More specifically, seven
months of sending guys out on security patrols and deliberate
operations round-the- clock, selecting the villages that become
their objectives- and potentially the places they're killed- wears
you out. For seven months, you can never "turn off," regardless
of the Pizza Hut and Green Beans Coffee a few hundred meters

away, as you always have someone outside-the-wire, someone in harm's way. And, as combat advisors working with forces from both the Republic of Georgia and Afghanistan, culture clash proved another recurring source of stress.

On the other hand, the above stress was significantly compounded by realities and decisions unrelated to the individuals outside of Bagram trying to kill us on a daily basis or the forces we were advising, which leads to the primary purpose of this book. As the combat advisors to a battalion of Georgians charged with securing the interior and exterior of America's largest base in Afghanistan at the end of 2014, we found ourselves in a unique situation. Broadly speaking, the war in Afghanistan included two categories of service members: those making decisions within the confines of a base, and those executing those decisions and fighting outside of a base. Our position and role on Bagram Airfield placed us at the nexus of the highest-level generals in the former category while conducting the security operations outside-the-wire at the lowest level of the latter category. On one day, I found myself eating lunch with the 4-star general in charge of all coalition forces in Afghanistan, on another day conducting a deliberate operation searching for IED caches in an Afghan village. Consequently, as 2014 rolled into 2015, and we saw the "end of combat operations" and beginning of the Resolute Support mission, I had keen insight into both A) the operational-level decisions being made by the generals, and B) the tangible and direct impact those decisions had on the guys fighting day-in and day-out to secure a base.

This proximity to the decision makers in Afghanistan, and the effects their decisions had, is why this book is so important. I am neither a smart man nor an eloquent writer, but I have a story that, in my opinion, needs to be told: the development of America's new Ministry of Truth in Afghanistan, and our country's betrayal of the servicemembers sent to carry out its whims.

# A NOTE ON NAMES

· · · · · · · · · · · · · · · · · · · · · · · · · · ·

A T THE END of the day, this is my story, written from my perspective; recognizing this, it will have all the biases, flaws, and misperceptions associated with a first-person narrative. Furthermore, there are individuals in my story I paint in a particularly negative light. My intent is not to ridicule these individuals in a public arena, but to expose the broader context of flawed decision-making and distorted priorities that Afghanistan circa 2014-15 became.

Having outlined the above, I will use the convention of referring to the people in this book by first names, call signs, or military titles; they know who they are, and lacking explicit permission to do otherwise, I'd like to honor their privacy. For the readers, if this system disrupts your appreciation for the story, I apologize in advance.

# PART I

# THE WORK-UP

*January-May 2014*

# I-1

# THE RIFLE RANGE

......................................

S URPRISINGLY, THE START of my time as a combat advisor began in the footsteps of the *Top Gun* cast, that is, hanging around the air station in Miramar, California. After filming epic "we were inverted" and shirtless beach volleyball scenes at what had been Naval Air Station Miramar, the early nineties Base Realignment and Closure (BRAC) hearings saw a transfer of the base from the Navy to the Marine Corps. In some Jedi mind trick that I certainly don't understand, Congress decided that it would be more cost effective to call the base *Marine Corps* Air Station Miramar, as opposed to *Naval* Air Station Miramar. Same base, same pot of money, different name—the logic and cost savings are infallible.

But, my story isn't about Miramar (though it's a fitting place to begin my path towards the boondoggle that Afghanistan 2014-15 would be). In January 2014, I was serving as an infantry company executive officer (XO) with Weapons Company, 1st Battalion, 5th Marine Regiment, a unit based a few miles up the road from Miramar at Camp Pendleton, the sprawling Marine base along the Pacific Ocean and I-5 between San Diego and Los Angeles. In this capacity, my company commander and I were down at Miramar with the whole company using the air station's rifle range to conduct our shooting qualification, an annual requirement for Marines.

Hanging out with Chris, the company commander, at the end of a day's shoot, he received a call from our battalion's XO (I was a company XO responsible for roughly 150 Marines, whereas the battalion XO is a more senior officer responsible for five individual companies and closer to 800 Marines). Listening to Chris's side of the conversation, I heard something along these lines: "Yes, sir. I'm sitting right next to him, sir. Aye, sir, I'll have him see you in your office when we're back to Pendleton tomorrow, sir." Regressing to the mindset of a high schooler who's been caught doing something wrong, my immediate reaction to the side of the conversation I heard was, "Shit, what did I do?"

Fortunately, I wasn't being court martialed for something I'd done. But, I was being offered an opportunity to go to Afghanistan. Apparently, our battalion's higher headquarters, 5th Marine Regiment (in practical terms, my boss's boss's boss) had been told by some general further up the food chain that the regiment needed to provide some infantry officers to support an individual augment, or IA, mission to Afghanistan. Most military deployments consist of an organic unit, such as my battalion, heading overseas to complete some mission; but, at least in the Marines, another deployment path exists, more the red-headed-stepchild approach: temporarily formed teams of IAs thrown together to complete some mission that doesn't fit within the standard deployment cycle or job description of an infantry battalion. And, my mother's opinion aside, we IAs are typically not selected as a result of our outstanding performance, more often chosen for having the bare minimum requirements to meet the manpower tax imposed (no one wants to give up their unit's rock stars). Take me, for instance: I happened to be the most junior captain in the battalion, which, as I'd find out, made me a prime candidate for either A) this requirement, or B) staying back from our next deployment to be in charge of the

Marines with medical and legal issues preventing them from deploying- the two options I'd soon find out lay ahead of me.

Pressing Chris for more information, all he could tell me was that, yes, the XO had asked if I'd be interested in this upcoming IA deployment to Afghanistan, and no, he didn't provide any other details. I'd have to wait until the next day, when, returning to Camp Pendleton, I could swing by the XO's office to get the whole picture.

# I-2

# GEORGIA (NOT THE STATE)

·················································

T URNS OUT WHAT I thought would be the "whole picture" was actually a small sliver of something resembling a picture. Arriving back to the 5th Marine Regiment area of Camp Pendleton, isolated in the far northern reaches of base and nestled in the rolling hills of southern California, I walked up the hill from the Weapons Company office to our battalion headquarters to meet the XO.

If you've never served in the military, popular culture makes it seem as if the Marine Corps (and every other service) runs on motivational speeches, epic assaults, and hell-or- high-water last stands. In reality, the Department of Defense runs on e-mails and PowerPoint slides. Fittingly, the power on our portion of base happened to be out the afternoon I returned from Miramar, grinding all staff work to a halt as no one could access e-mail accounts. So, rather than get a full run down of the IA job I'd been offered, the conversation with the XO went something like this:

*XO*: "Capt Naylon, the battalion needs to provide an infantry officer to an upcoming IA, and we think you'd be the perfect candidate." (As I've already stated, "perfect" should have been replaced with "convenient".)

*Me*: "Sounds good, sir. What're the details?"

*XO*: "Well, I have some info in an e-mail, but, since I can't access that right now, I'm fairly certain it's going to involve some time in Georgia and then a deployment to Afghanistan."

*Me*: "Any options, sir, or am I being tasked with this?"

*XO*: "We're not going to tell you that you have to do it, but the alternative is staying back from our Australia deployment to be in charge of the RBE (remain behind element)."

I learned two things from this exchange. First, I would definitely not be deploying to Darwin, Australia with our battalion as planned, so I either could A) go to Afghanistan, or B), serve as the designated cat herder responsible for a bunch of Marines who, for either legal issues, medical issues, or some combination of the two, would not be deploying. To an outside observer, this wouldn't seem like much of a decision at all: stay in sunny southern California for six months babysitting, or go halfway around the world to some country full of a bunch of people trying to kill Americans? While somewhat tongue-in-cheek (but not completely), anyone who's worked with an RBE will likely agree, six months of trying to get a bunch of people with no fucks to give to care just a little bit would prove far more detrimental to one's health than deploying to a combat zone. So yeah, I sure as shit wasn't going to do that.

That leads to the second thing I learned: the IA I'd be doing was part of the Georgia Deployment Program. While the XO didn't know the background, coincidentally, I had a pretty good idea of what I'd be doing, at least conceptually. A few years before my meeting with the XO, a good friend of mine served as the logistics officer for a small group of Marines that went to the Republic of Georgia to embed with a battalion of Georgian soldiers, train, then deploy with the battalion as combat advisors to Afghanistan.

Yes, this is the small country of Georgia, not the American state of peaches, peanuts, and the Braves. Located in the stretch of land known as the Caucasus, Georgia's in a region that connects Europe and Asia, and is wedged between the Black Sea and Caspian Sea.

Specifically, Georgia is bordered to the west by the Black Sea, to the north by Russia, and to the south and southwest by Turkey, Armenia, and Azerbaijan, respectively. To the best of my very limited knowledge at the time, Georgia had been committing troops to Afghanistan for a while now. So, what does this tiny, former Soviet country have to do with Afghanistan? Well, cynically, and I offer the disclaimer that I certainly was not part of any national strategy discussions conducted by the Georgian Ministry of Defense and president, I'd say that Georgia's commitment to Afghanistan has little to do with that central Asian nation. Rather, this has everything do with its neighbor to the north, the Russian Bear that walked all over the country in a brief 2008 war with Georgia. By offering its soldiers to fight in a conflict that really has nothing to do with its national interests, Georgia sought to build support for accession into NATO and, ideally, a hedge against future Russian hostilities.

But, I digress. Stepping off my speculative soapbox and returning to Camp Pendleton in January 2014, I still had no idea of any timelines for what I'd be doing. The only real details the XO had were that I'd need to report to some place called the Advisor Training Cell the following Monday.

Not knowing whether I'd be leaving for Georgia in three days, weeks, or months, I headed home to digest these new developments.

# I-3

# LEAVING 1ST BATTALION, 5TH MARINES

·················································

$A$FTER A WEEKEND mulling over how things with this IA gig were going to unfold, things started rolling the following Monday morning. Fortunately, the power was back on at our portion of Camp Pendleton, so, with Microsoft Outlook accounts flowing, I got a little more info. Touching base with the battalion XO again, he printed some specific instructions he'd tracked down for checking in at this Advisor Training Cell (ATC), an organization down on the south part of Camp Pendleton that, from my powers of deduction, likely trained advisors. Basically, I needed to get my medical and dental records, rifle and pistol, and night vision goggles and drive my happy self down there by the end of the week.

Technically, I'd remain a part of 1st Battalion, 5th Marines, but, for all intents and purposes, I'd be "OFP," that is, on my own fucking program.

Now that I knew the short-term timeline, I could focus on wrapping things up with the battalion and transferring my responsibilities as the Weapons Company XO. To anyone willing to listen, I describe the role of company XO as the most valuable job you'll never want to have again; in a non-stop firehose of overseeing a multimillion dollar armory, coordinating the logistical requirements for three platoons, planning training, running the company's day-to-day operations, and just generally putting out fires, life sucks. But, in balancing these disparate responsibilities, you learn a couple valuable skills: 1) managerial organization (sink or swim...), and 2) how to FITFO (figure it the fuck out). Essentially, serving as an XO is like acting as the oil in an engine; you're not making the car move, but the engine sure as shit can't get things going without the oil lubricating it. Though I didn't know it at the time, these skills- often learned through screwing things up and trial and error- would be crucial moving forward as a combat advisor.

So yeah, I wasn't sorry to leave the XO job itself, but I was certainly sorry to leave the dudes I worked with- particularly the platoon commanders and non-commissioned officers (NCOs), two groups that formed the heart and soul of the company. Fortunately, the battalion XO, a driving force in manpower management for the whole battalion, sought my feedback on who should replace me. Through the shared misery and suffering of serving together in an infantry unit, leaders develop intense pride in both their unit and the Marines in it, and it meant the world to me to recommend a close friend, my buddy Josh, with whom I'd gone through most of my Marine Corps training and the last deployment, to replace me. While he certainly took a lot of time "mother-fucking" me about throwing him under the bus, as he had to leave a platoon commander gig he loved, turning over my XO responsibilities to him, a guy I significantly trusted and respected, eased the burden of leaving Weapons Company.

After spending a few days turning over my XO responsibilities to Josh, I made my first trip down to ATC. Unlike San Mateo, 5th Marine Regiment's infantry camp tucked into the inland hills and rugged terrain of northern Camp Pendleton, I'd be conducting my advisor training in the picturesque Del Mar area on the south side of base, a palm tree lined area nestled between I-5 and the Pacific coastline. On the first Monday I arrived, step 1 was finding the armory. The Marine Corps is particularly anal retentive about its weapons and gear accountability, so very strict procedures and paperwork requirements exist for moving weapons and optics from one armory to another. So, with paperwork, weapons, and optics in hand, I found the ATC armory and turned in all of my gear, freeing me up to start exploring my "home" for the next several months.

# I-4

# ADVISOR TRAINING CALL

·················································

U NLIKE NORMAL NEIGHBORHOODS, most military
buildings and centers on a base don't have typical street ad-
dresses; rather, building numbers are used that indicate A) the
broad area on base (the first two digits), and B) the specific location
within that area (the last two or three digits). I'm pretty sure that
somewhere out there, a Marine or administrator exists that under-
stands the details of this location system, but that Marine's certainly
not me. Armed with a building number for ATC and not much
more, I drove around Del Mar's grid system of streets and military
command headquarters looking for this advisor place.

After a few false starts / questionable directions from random
Marines on the street (e.g. "Yeah I think I've heard of that place—
head about three blocks that way, turn left at the chow hall, and
stop before you get to the water"), I arrived at my destination.
In retrospect, that first impression of ATC would foreshadow
our whole experience as advisors.

Surrounded by beautiful headquarters buildings, military recre-
ational bungalows on the Pacific shores, and palm trees, ATC
was a clump of trailers and a hodgepodge of generators surrounded by chain link fence; though the location was beautiful-
top of the escarpment that descends towards the ocean- the ad

hoc nature of the place, especially relative to its far nicer surrounding commands—seemed to scream that advisors were sec-
ond-class citizens in the eyes of "Big Marine Corps."

Despite my initial, negative impression of ATC, this advisor
schoolhouse would prove me wrong, embodying one of the
mantras that keeps a chip on the shoulder of underfunded and
undersupplied Marines everywhere- "do more with less." Walking
up the ramp of the trailer labeled ATC, I was surprised to find a
buddy of mine from college and fellow Marine, Sam, sitting inside. After the standard round of catch-up pleasantries associated
with not having seen someone in five years, he told me he was
the new operations officer for ATC, having just returned from a
deployment with the Georgians himself. With only a few months
remaining on his time in the Marine Corps, it didn't make sense
to send Sam back to a battalion, so he'd worked out a deal to
wrap up running the day-to-day operations at ATC, putting his
real-world lessons learned as an advisor to good use training us
bright-eyed and bushy-tailed newbies.

Having Sam at ATC would be a godsend over the next few
months. For one, he was the consummate professional in terms
of taking ownership of ATC training and operations. And, more
importantly, he possessed a wealth of knowledge on Georgian
culture, military, and the realities of Marine-Georgian coexistence,
as he'd just spent the last eleven months of his life embedded
with one of the country's battalions. Sitting down to shoot the
shit with him that first day, Sam filled in a bunch of my unknowns
regarding the upcoming deployment.

The full name of our mission was the Georgia Deployment
Program—International Security Assistance Force, or GDP-ISAF,
and our advisor team would be the 14th group of Marines conducting the mission, designating us Rotation, or ROTO, 14.
Within GDP-ISAF, two separate teams existed- the Georgia Liaison Team (GLT) and the Georgia Training Team (GTT). We

would be the former, a small team of active duty Marines tasked with embedding with a Georgian infantry battalion, conducting three months of training side-by-side in Georgia, a culminating mission rehearsal exercise at a US base in Germany, and a seven-month deployment as combat advisors in Afghanistan.

While we as the GLT would focus our efforts on developing relationships and training side-by-side with our partnered battalion, the other half of the GDP-ISAF mission, the GTT, was composed of a mix of active and reserve Marines tasked with training the Georgian military's own cadre of instructors, the Georgians overseeing the training of our partner battalion. These Marines would spend five to six months on a training base in Georgia, mentoring and developing the country's resident military instructors while building the Georgian military's resident training expertise. At the end of their time in Georgia, the GTT Marines would hand over their responsibilities to an incoming GTT and return to the States.

Having broadly outlined our mission, Sam explained how the next four months of training at ATC would work. Over the next week, the remainder of the GLT Marines would make their way down to Del Mar from their parent units to check in with ATC. We'd then conduct a pre-deployment training program, or "work-up," tailored to preparing advisors for combat. Some of the wickets we'd need to hit as a team would be combat life-saving ("first aid," in non-military speak), combat marksmanship ("shooting rifles and pistols," in non-military speak), training and licensing in armored vehicles, counter-improvised explosive device (C-IED) training, and some sort of month-long basic advisor training out in Virginia Beach (still needed some more details on that). During the talk with Sam and our review of the upcoming work-up, one thing was apparent- as a small team, we'd all be doing everything, lacking the manpower luxuries that would allow for any one individual to not become "brilliant in the basics" of combat patrolling.

# MEETING THE TEAM

······································

A FTER TALKING WITH Sam, I had a much better sense of our upcoming mission with the Georgians and what we'd be doing to get ready for it, at least the broad strokes. The other major piece of the puzzle he provided was the actual make-up of our team of advisors by job type. Personally, it's nice to know who you'll be working with for the next almost year and a half. Professionally, understanding the different types of specialties composing a team gives you a much better sense of what sort of capabilities that team will have.

For the GLT, the guys going to Afghanistan with the Georgians, three sub-groups existed: the core group of advisors, a group of maintenance and communications enablers who'd meet us in Afghanistan, and a group of fire support specialists who'd also meet us in Afghanistan. The core GLT would include seventeen Marines and one Sailor, all of whom would be responsible for both executing their specialties and advising the Georgians in their respective fields: nine infantry Marines, two military intelligence, two logistics, one Navy corpsman, two communications, a senior enlisted advisor, and, responsible for all of us, our officer in charge (OIC), the Boss. Within each one of these groups, there'd be a mix of junior officers, staff non-commissioned officers (SNCOs), and non-commissioned officers (NCOs), making the GLT fairly senior in rank relative to your standard Marine unit heavy on privates and lance corporals.

Over the next week, most of the generic job descriptions outlined above changed to actual names, as day-by-day Marines made their way down to the ATC trailers in Del Mar to join the team. The Boss would end up being the last to arrive, a couple weeks after the rest of us due to some other commitments with his prior assignment. So, due to pretty much no other reason than the fact that I was the first captain to check-in with the GLT (followed shortly thereafter by our intelligence officer, Captain Mike), I anointed (read, defaulted) myself into the temporary OIC job, setting priorities early on for the team.

At the time, I didn't know much about advising or, as mentioned, the specific details of our mission. But, I did have the benefit of having some other buddies like Sam who had experience as combat advisors, and I leaned heavily on their advice in those initial days. In particular, I knew that as a small team, each of us would have to do far more than whatever our primary job was—just too much work to go around and not enough people to do it.

With that said, I felt confident enough declaring a single rule to guide our training: whatever training we were doing, the whole team would do it, regardless of specialty, as this would ensure A) proficiency across the board, and, ideally, B) the bond of mutual suffering throughout the team, with no individual, from lowest to highest ranking, appearing to "have it easy." Having set this initial priority, it was refreshing when, a couple weeks later, the Boss, a major soon to be promoted to lieutenant colonel, arrived at ATC and concurred with the philosophy that everyone would participate in training and meet the standards.

Sitting down and chatting with the Boss that first afternoon, he set the stage for a great relationship. In the Marines, at least on paper, we emphasize the value of "mission tactics," which boils down to providing subordinates overarching guidance of what they need to do and why they need to do it, then stepping back to supervise and allow them to use their own initiative to figure out the how of getting it done. In reality, we often fall back on overly micromanaging subordinates, frustrating initiative, and dictating the specifics of how something should be done. The Boss was very clear from the start, he'd provide his guidance and, within those broad guidelines, expect us to FITFO. Outstanding. This is absolutely what Marines crave- the responsibility and top-cover to go out and make things happen, an environment of mission tactics that would prove critical to success in both Georgia and Afghanistan, places where uncertainty would necessitate creative problem solving and initiative. And the cherry on top? The Boss was a Buffalo guy, so we got to commiserate about the Bills together.

# I-6

# RADIO DRILLS AND TRAINING

······················································

A S MENTIONED PREVIOUSLY, I didn't know much about
advising when I checked in to ATC, but I had the good
fortune of having a couple buddies who'd recently completed
advisor tours. Actually, my two roommates had, within the past
year, wrapped up gigs in Afghanistan, one advising the Afghan
National Army (ANA) and one the Afghan National Police
(ANP). Cody, who'd spent seven months in the hinterlands of
Afghanistan with the ANP, provided two pieces of advice that
would significantly shape our approach to training.

First, the Advisor Training Cell will facilitate training you develop, but it's not going to do it for you. In other words, you get
out of ATC what you put into it. Okay, so that became clear very
early- if we wanted high-quality training, the support staff at
ATC would jump through hoops to get us the gear and training
areas we needed so long as we put in the effort planning it; if we
wanted to fuck off for the next few months and end each day at
noon, we could do that, too. We chose the former. The second
piece of advice Cody provided dealt with skillsets we'd need as
advisors. Out on a small team, largely alone and unafraid, we'd
have too few Marines to hide incompetence; everyone, regardless
of job specialty, would need to be proficient in a few core skills.

1) *Communications*: Typically, Marines depend on specially trained "comm" Marines to manage radios and the encryption necessary to protect radio transmissions. We wouldn't have the luxury of comm Marines supporting each of our infantry patrol advisors, so we'd all have to know the ins-and-outs of preparing, operating, and trouble-shooting comm equipment.

2) *Fire Support*: Similar to comm, conventional units typically have multiple Marines whose primary role in life is to provide close air support, that is, attack aircraft supporting ground troops. While we would be augmented by a group of Marines specializing in fire support, they couldn't become single points of failure, and we would all need a solid grasp on fire support procedures.

And finally, 3) *Combat Life-saving*: This is the military jargon term for "first aid." While our core team had one Navy corpsman, a trained trauma medic, we still didn't know how many corpsmen would be joining us in Afghanistan. And, the previous years of America's fights in Iraq and Afghanistan had clearly illustrated the dangers of improvised explosive devices (IEDs). Supporting both Georgian and Afghan soldiers on patrol with only a handful of Marines, we knew that each of us could be called upon to apply a post-blast tourniquet to prevent someone from bleeding out, and, if we wanted to keep people alive, we wouldn't have the luxury of relegating that duty solely to trained corpsmen.

Though still largely shooting in the dark with respect to the specifics of our mission, identifying the above three skills provided unity and focus to our training. Regardless of how we'd be employed as a team, which was largely out of our control, we could control our preparation. For the rest of the time training on Camp Pendleton (and continued through Georgia, Germany, and Afghanistan), we'd integrate our own "white space" (that is, free time) training into our daily routines, holding everyone on the team, from comm chief to officer in charge, to standard.

To me, the most memorable example of this training, and one

that truly set the tone for our team, involved radio races; basically, four Marines would line up on one side of a field, sprint to a radio and crypto loader on the other side of the field, load the secure crypto "0s and 1s" into the radio, and conduct a "comm check," making a radio transmission to ensure they'd done all the radio procedures properly. As a major, the Boss certainly could've been doing other things while the rest of the team ran around, racing each other and loading radios, and no one would've thought anything of it; instead, he joined the first group of Marines racing, busting his ass across the field and talking shit when he won the race. For the rest of the work-up and deployment, no one would get a free ride; regardless of job or rank, you'd do all the training the rest of the team would do.

# I-7

# VIRGINIA BEACH AND BUILDING THE TEAM

.........................................

A FTER A MONTH training in Camp Pendleton, our team headed out to the east coast for a few weeks of work in Virginia Beach, the first travel we'd be conducting together. While the ATC included the word "advisor" in its definition, it remained a temporary, ad hoc solution to the need to train combat advisors for Iraq and Afghanistan. Conversely, the Marine Corps Security Cooperation Group, MCSCG, represented the Marines' effort to establish a permanent command for both A) training advisors for advising other nations' militaries, and B) building regional teams organic to MCSCG to take responsibility for leading security cooperation missions with other countries. Looking into the tea leaves of Department of Defense funding, the Marines recognized the increased emphasis on advising foreign forces, vice shouldering the burden of nation building alone, and forming MCSCG helped ensure the Corps' piece of that budgetary pie.

At MCSCG, the core GLT members would go through the school's Basic Advisor Course, a three-week crash course on the fundamentals of combat advising. This training focused on 1) the "soft skills" of advising (e.g. communicating via interpreters, cross-

cultural communication, influencing counterparts without destroy-
ing rapport, etc); 2) language and culture training specific to the
Republic of Georgia; 3) foreign weapons skills (as the Georgians
still used many Soviet-style small arms); and 4) a more rigorous
course of instruction on combat life-saving (CLS) than we'd had
to date.

I'm not going to discount any of the above training, as all of it
in some way, shape, or form assisted us both in Georgia and
Afghanistan. But, the real value of flying across the country for a
few weeks of training wasn't the training itself, but the environment
in which we lived. In California, despite the emphasis we put on
forming a cohesive team, life had a habit of getting in the way.
Guys had wives and children to go home to at the end of every
day, medical appointments pulling them out of certain things, the
inevitable calls from their old units with different questions, and
countless other minor distractions that, as a whole, detracted from
our ability to build the team. This all changed once we arrived in
Virginia Beach. From corporal (junior-most Marine) to major (the
Boss), we all moved into the barracks. At MCSCG, we'd focus on
nothing but building our team's cohesion.

Professionally, we continued to emphasize our "white space"
training, working to build combat patrolling skills across the team
after each day's formal instruction concluded. Though more work
than just wrapping things up when the MCSCG instructors ended
their training each day, this extra effort started establishing what
would eventually become an attitude of fierce pride across the
GLT in our ability to work our asses off to get the job done, regardless of the obstacles in our way.

Personally, that is, outside of our daily training environment,
we truly began to mesh as a team. I'm a huge believer in the value
of bonding via two shared experiences: 1) suffering, and 2) a few
drinks. While calling life in the barracks "suffering" is certainly
overstated melodrama, going from living at home with our families

in California to sharing barracks rooms on the other side of the country at least provided us a little good discomfort to drive the bonding process. And, we certainly made the most of the "sharing a few drinks" mantra; whether through team bowling night over pitchers of beer, weekend trips to D.C., or a couple late night altercations out in town, we had plenty of opportunities to bond outside of work, building tight-knit relationships that would carry through deployment. While I don't explicitly condone bar fights, the team's "extra-curricular activities" during our time in Virginia Beach put in very concrete terms a necessary trait of any team: we could count on each other.

# I-8

# WE'RE TEAM GUYS (COUGH), GEORGIA LIAISON TEAM...

......................................................

T HROUGHOUT OUR ENTIRE training work-up and deployment, a "Bad News Bears" theme seemed to stick to
us. For better or worse, the conventional Marine Corps (and, as
we'd see in Afghanistan, the Army) often views advisors as the
red-headed step children of the military community, a sometimes
necessary evil that should be tolerated, never fully embraced.
And, though indicative of broader funding inconsistencies,
nowhere did we more clearly see our place in the proverbial
pecking order than while at a range on the SEAL base in Dam
Neck, Virginia.

As mentioned above, one of the topics we covered during our
advisor training was foreign weapons. Essentially, the logic goes
that, working with foreign forces, we may at some point in time
be expected to either A) train other soldiers on how to use these
weapons, or B) use them ourselves. So, we spent a week at MC-
SCG in a classroom environment learning the ins and outs of
old, Soviet-style weapons, and the plan was to head down to one
of the ranges at Dam Neck at the end of the week for a day of
live-fire training with the PKM medium machine gun. Looking
forward to this shoot, the little boys in all of us Marines thought,

"this is going to be some badass, Rambo-like, shoot-from-the-hip machine gun shit." Entertaining and good cinema? Absolutely. Good training? Not so much.

Basically, our problem was, how do we ensure that, with the limited time and resources we were given, this machine gun shoot would be quality training, not just an "ammo dump?" Ideally, we would find some way to get actual target feedback, that is, a sense of whether we were actually hitting targets or just sending a lot of rounds into a dirt berm. While it may seem like, "hey, you're shooting a machine gun—you'll know if it hits something," this isn't usually the case with a lot of the flimsy (though cost efficient) targetry we use, with rounds punching through without much indication of whether or not you actually hit the target.

Tackling this problem, one of our grunts, using a little Marine ingenuity and embodying the Corps' ability to do more with less, suggested balloons. While shooting balloons with a machine gun seems ridiculous at first, it's actually a brilliant solution. By blowing up balloons and taping them to targets on a range, you get immediate feedback—either the balloon pops or it doesn't, that is, you either hit the target or you didn't. So, with our cost-effective feedback plan outlined, a couple guys went out the night before the range and bought a bag of balloons.

Naturally, the only balloons our guys could find were some sort of "Little Princess" ones, all of which were pink, purple, or red- nice. This color scheme became even more entertaining the morning of the shoot when we realized that the range immediately adjacent to ours was being used by some of the SEAL "team guys," you know, the cool, bearded dudes. Backed by small numbers and a seemingly unlimited budget, these special forces operators had the benefit of automated, dynamic targets, providing them a constantly changing and fully responsive shooting scenario. So yeah, it was a pretty entertaining dichotomy: On one side, special forces guys with the best training equipment money can buy; on the other side, a group of Marines chasing pink, purple, and red balloons up and down a range anytime a nice breeze picked up...

Embracing the absurdity of our situation, so began a recurring joke among the team, self-deprecatingly referring to ourselves as "team guys (*cough*), Georgia Liaison Team." But, self-mockery among a team drives a particular benefit: cohesion. This range became another milestone pulling us closer as a unit, building the bonds that would sustain us for the next year. Yeah, we were shooting a bunch of "Little Princess" balloons next to a force the President appeared to have on speed dial, but A) it was great training, and B) it reinforced the theme that, regardless of situation or lack of support, as a team, we'd be able to FITFO (Figure It The Fuck Out).

# I-9

# SETTING THE TONE FOR GEORGIA, PART I

..............................................

B ACK IN CAMP Pendleton and the Adviser Training Cell after a month on the east coast, our team was certainly better trained and a tighter unit, but we still only had a vague idea about what to expect dealing with the Georgians. Fortunately, I knew we could lean on Sam here, pumping him for information about his time with the GLT. Yeah, we'd be working with a different group of Georgians, but he'd still be able to provide pretty solid insight into the ins and outs of Georgian cultural idiosyncrasies and what our expectations ought to be. With that said, we carved a little time out of our schedule for a Q&A session led by Sam for the eighteen core GLT members.

The first point Sam emphasized, something that would be critical to maintaining our sanity over eleven months of working side-by-side with the Georgian military, was expectation management. Georgian soldiers aren't Marines, and, while this point may seem self-evident, its importance cannot be overstated. Many good Marines will never make good advisors- not due to lack of effort or motivation- but because they fail to grasp the differences between advisor and advisee. If we went into our time in Georgia envisioning a partner battalion of Marines, not only would we fail, we'd lose our minds in the process.

Georgian differences in military training deviated too much from our own. Whereas the Marine Corps emphasizes months of formal indoctrination and military skills training, transforming civilians into professional Marines before they ever arrive at their units, the Georgian approach (as they build capacity), is much more informal and ad hoc, leading to Georgian units composed of soldiers with limited military indoctrination and formal training. Expecting Georgian soldiers to function as Marines just wouldn't work.

Even more significant than training disparities, our differences in cultural acceptance of empowerment (or lack thereof), would prove a huge sticking point in relations with our Georgian counterparts. In the Marines, we take immense pride in delegating authority and empowering leaders at the lowest levels, thriving as a service on the initiative and hard work of our corporal and sergeant non-commissioned officers. As we'd come to see first-hand, Sam harped on the realities of dealing with a post-Soviet force, one that places more value on centralized control than junior initiative.

Rather than push decision-making and initiative to the lowest level, a pervasive "zero-defect" mentality existed in the Georgian (and many of the world's) armed forces. This mentality translates to an environment where junior leaders fear making a decision on their own, paralyzed by concern for retribution if anything goes wrong. Instead, the process for doing everything is just slowed down, with the common solution to any problem or obstacle being, "I must ask higher [headquarters]," a refrain that would put many grey hairs on my head over the course of our deployment.

After dwelling on the above potential pitfalls of working with the Georgians for a while, Sam wrapped up by stressing the true key to success as an advisor- rapport. Over the course of a single deployment, we weren't going to change years of ingrained cultural and structural differences between two nations' militaries, but we could build relationships that would let us transcend those differences. By embracing expectation management and accepting our inherent differences, we could focus on building relationships and rapport with our counterparts. By knowing when things got shitty, we could fall back on the mutual trust that, regardless of situation, we would watch each other's back, all the other differences became ancillary. Bottom line, our time in Georgia should be spent building relationships, choosing very carefully our military-specific "hills to die on," as those hills would be far more significant once in Afghanistan.

# I-10

# "EXCUSE ME GENTLEMEN, DO YOU MIND KEEPING IT DOWN?"

••••••••••••••••••••••••••••••••••••••••••••••••••••••

O UR NEXT MAJOR training event would be a week-long combat marksmanship program (CMP) range, Marine-speak for going out to fire thousands of rifle and pistol rounds. In addition to this being just great training, developing weapons muscle memory and proficiency, a week in the field had two major, ancillary benefits. First, despite the fact that a primary element of our mission in Afghanistan would be patrolling, we had no allocated block in our work-up devoted to this combat skill; using the afternoons and nights at the range when not shooting, we could incorporate patrolling skills into our white space training. Second, and arguably as important, a week living out at the range- as opposed to going home every night- reinforced the notion that we're in this fight as a team, further building camaraderie.

As a team, we had two areas of focus for our patrolling work. On the one hand, the staff Marines (intelligence, logistics, and communications) would be serving inside of our combat operations center (COC), tracking patrol positions and requesting external support for Marines outside the wire (e.g. casualty evacuation helicopters, fire support, quick reaction forces). On the other hand, the infantry Marines would actually be out on partnered patrols with the Georgians, needing to be absolutely rock solid in the core skills of combat patrolling. This reality was further complicated by the fact that our three infantry advisor NCOs all came from the Light Armored Reconnaissance community, making them extremely proficient in armored vehicle movements and patrolling, but limited in "green-side skills," that is, dismounted, walking-around-with-all-your-kit-on- your-back field craft.

To hit the above two training targets, both the COC battle tracking and the infantry skills portion, we put together a "full mission profile," basically building a scenario to replicate planning for and executing a combat patrol. To make this happen, we wrote a notional operations order from a higher headquarters and briefed it to the infantry NCOs, each of whom then planned his own patrol. After going through the learning process of putting together these plans, we then picked one of the three to actually execute, requiring the Marine who planned it do all the necessary pre-patrol coordination with the staff who'd be battle tracking it from our mock COC (table with some radios, maps, and status boards).

The above pre-patrol coordination- routes, communications plans, casualty evacuation procedures, etc, served as a critical link between COC and executors, providing the watch standers battle tracking a patrol the key information they would need to support the guys outside the wire. And, for us, this served as our first opportunity to give the team some reps at this work. So, coordination complete, we conducted our patrol, with the NCOs serving as the patrol leaders, and the more senior staff NCOs and officers acting as the riflemen. While not necessarily pretty, roughly two hours after "departing friendly lines," we "took contact," completed some notional fire support missions, and coordinated the evacuation of a simulated casualty. We now had our first team rep doing something we'd be doing every day for seven months in Afghanistan - conducting and supporting combat patrols

Skills wise, I can't overemphasize the value of both this patrolling exercise and the CMP shoot we conducted this whole
week. But, the bonding element of this training really played the
critical role in making us a more effective unit, and I can point to
one moment that truly catalyzed this process, pulling us together
as a team, and it proved to be the first of many instances of fucked
up priorities we'd face over the rest of our time together.

Mid-way through our week-long shoot on a beautiful, sunny
day in Camp Pendleton, we were paused behind the firing line, re-
loading rifle and pistol magazines for our next set of CMP drills.
As we were about to head to the line, a sergeant walked up behind
us, explaining that he'd been sent up from a sergeant major's retirement ceremony a few hundred yards down the road to ask us
to stop shooting so as not to interrupt the ceremony. I was dumb-
struck to the point of silence—surely this Marine wasn't asking us
to stop shooting and training for the sake of a ceremony? In what
world did preparing for combat play second fiddle to some retirement? (In fairness, this request was definitely not the sergeant's
idea, he just had the misfortune of being the messenger).

Before I could even begin to overcome the absurdity of the
situation and respond, the Boss interrupted with a booming laugh
followed by a, "Hey, Sergeant, why don't you get the fuck off of
my range?" As this unfortunate messenger walked away, our
whole team erupted in laughter. About two minutes later, we
were on the firing line shooting.

This anecdote (and yes, I feel mildly bad for the sergeant who
took one on the chin from the Boss) illustrates how minor experiences can set the tone for an entire deployment. Not only did
the "us versus them" reality of such a ridiculous request pull us
tighter as a team, but in one interaction, the Boss one hundred
percent solidified the team's priorities—preparing for and, ultimately, conducting our combat mission.

# 1-11

# KANGAROO COURT AND THE GODSONS

........................................

A FTER A FEW months training together—a relatively short Stateside work-up period—we were quickly approaching our departure to Georgia. But, keeping with a long-held military tradition, we had one more team-internal wicket to hit before heading out to Georgia—the kangaroo court and designation of call-signs.

Merriam-Webster defines a kangaroo court as, "1: a mock court in which the principles of law and justice are disregarded or perverted, [or] 2: a court characterized by irresponsible, unauthorized, or irregular status or procedures." Bottom line, we needed an opportunity to get the guys on the team together, drink a little more than we should, and formalize some radio call-signs for the deployment. Now I recognize that any aviators reading this will question the legitimacy of a non-pilot kangaroo court, what with the aviation community claiming ownership of all things call-sign. I'll answer this, though, by pointing once again to the inherent lawlessness of the above definition, which would provide us ample procedural leeway.

In practice, this type of kangaroo court falls somewhere between a christening and a roast, with the Boss overseeing and playing the role of judge, jury, and executioner. Specifically, each of the team leaders would have formal "charges" brought against him relating to general misdeeds and absurd behavior from the previous few months together. As the other guys generally pile on mockery, eventually someone would suggest a fitting call-sign relating to these past transgressions (unlike the *Top Gun* fallacy of "cool" call-signs like Maverick and Ice Man, most monikers are of a much more self- deprecating nature). With a potential call-sign suggested and seconded by the group, the Boss would use some faux legalese to formally confirm, solidifying a guy's radio handle for the remainder of the deployment. Some examples:

*Bane*: Infantry team leader built like a brick shithouse who A) regularly did an outstanding Bane impression, and B) at several times while out with the team in a social setting acted as if he may in fact be the *Batman* villain: "It would be extremely painful… for you."

*Claymore*: Another infantry team leader—call-sign referenced the claymore anti-personnel mine, which, when detonated, projects a wall of ball bearings at everything in front of it (similar to his activities on liberty, hence, liberty claymore).

*Derby*: Logistics officer who was also the archetype of the small town, all-American boy—derived from the Boy Scouts' Pinewood Derby event.

*Sleepy*: Call-sign somewhat speaks for itself—intelligence officer who had an "off button on his ass," that is, inevitably nodded off once we sat down for a brief.

*SloMo*: Communications officer who asked, in all seriousness, if a video of a rocket-propelled grenade shown frame-by-frame, slowly moving across the screen, was actually in slow motion, as he was pretty sure he'd be able to "dodge" it.

After a lot more beer and mockery, we'd formally anointed

each of the team leaders, but we still didn't have a name for the team as a whole (besides our official GDP-ISAF ROTO 14). As these things go, one quickly fell into our lap. During the whole process, the Boss sat on an elevated platform, lording over the proceedings, so it made sense when one of the guys announced, "Sir, you look like the Godfather" (that is, the Mario Puzo version), to which another guy responded, "Oh shit! We're the Godsons!" And with that, the Boss had his call-sign, and the team had its own: "The Godsons."

Was all of this ridiculous and mildly immature? Absolutely. But, a week out from the first leg of our deployment, we felt like a team.

# I-12

# THE FAMILY BBQ

....................................

M AINTAINING MILITARY PROTOCOL, we organized a family BBQ as our final official team event before catching the flight to Georgia. In battalions and other large deploying units, these "mandatory fun" gatherings are typically put together by the Family Readiness Officer (FRO), a civilian responsible for ensuring, as the title suggests, solid communication and relationships between a deployed unit and the families left behind. As an eighteen-man team, we didn't have our own FRO, so planning fell to our logistics officer and chief.

Derby, our logistics officer, and our logistics chief (*Derby Bravo* in military parlance) did an outstanding job putting this event together together—lake-side pagoda on Camp Pendleton, hot dogs and hamburgers, photographer to take family pictures, etc.—good stuff. But, while all of these BBQ elements were great, it was the families and friends who made this so worthwhile. Joining the eighteen guys on the team, we had moms and dads, sisters and brothers, wives and children, girlfriends, and childhood friends come in from all over the country to spend these final hours with their loved ones.

I'll admit, I initially viewed this BBQ as a necessary check-in-the-box prior to deployment, a view I realized very quickly was extremely self-centered. While I'd always paid lip service to the importance of family readiness events, I'd lacked any real sense of empathy. These events aren't about the guys deploying. They're about the loved ones staying behind, something readily apparent at our BBQ.

As a Marine, it's easy to fall victim to the facade of an emotionless hard ass, someone immune to feelings. But, it was very clear at our event how concerned all of our family and friends joining us were, and I watched an incredible transformation over the couple hours we all spent together. Though it may have just seemed like idle chit chat and perfunctory introductions at first, spending this time together provided an unbelievable level of comfort, that is, family and friends now knew the guys their loved ones would spend the next year of their lives with. While nothing can eliminate the stress and heartache of knowing your husband, or brother, or father, or friend is in harm's way, at least the people at the BBQ could take comfort in meeting the guys on the left and right of their loved ones, seeing the strong bond we'd already formed.

While the above provides a somewhat abstract overview of the good that came from this BBQ, one specific example will always stay with me. Our team corpsman, aka "Doc," had been around the block by the time he checked in with our team. By extension, his wife had been through her fair share of deployments, both with and without children. As I wandered around the BBQ, I watched Doc's wife talking with a couple girlfriends (mine included), a young wife, and a mother of a guy on the team. While I'm paraphrasing, she essentially told these worried women: "Yeah, it'll suck at first, but you get through it. You focus on your routine and take comfort knowing that your loved one is surrounded by guys who would go to hell and back for him. Before you know it, he'll be back home." Listening to Doc's wife, and clearly seeing the solace her words provided, I knew I'd never view these types of events as merely checks-in-the-box again.

# PART II

# DEPLOYMENT, ROUND I
## (The Republic of Georgia & Germany)

*May - September 2014*

# EARLY LESSONS AND "HOW DO I GET TO YES?"

··············································

A S THESE THINGS tend to go, our deployment began be-fore dawn, with about forty-eight hours of travel ahead of us. From Camp Pendleton, we would drive north to Los Angeles, where we'd fly from LAX to Atlanta to Munich and, finally, to Tbilisi, the capital of Georgia. But I'm getting ahead of myself; before we started flying places, we first had to make sure we had everyone with us at our "muster site," a parking lot on base where we'd load up on the bus to LAX.

By 5am, the time we were supposed to be leaving for the air-port, we were one short. Now, in a 1,000-person battalion, this is a pretty common occurrence before deployment, with a handful of Marines either deciding to go AWOL or just going on a bit too much of a pre-deployment bender and missing departure time. For our fairly senior and small advisor team, I definitely had not anticipated having to put out fires this early in deployment (that is, before it even started). But, such is life, so we started calling house phones and cell phones, trying to track our guy down. After a few minutes, we made an executive decision—he lives on base on the way north to the airport, so we'll just wheel the bus up in front of his house and knock.

If you have a wife and multiple kids in the military, you're probably going to be stressed before an eleven-month deployment. But, you know what makes you even more stressed? Getting woken up at dawn to someone pounding on your door, a tour bus parked in front of your house in a nice residential neighborhood, wildly confused because you stayed up late with your little kids then fell asleep on your couch and forgot to set your alarm. So, after many "holy shit!" and "I'm so sorry, don't know happened!" exclamations, the Boss imposed calm on the situation.

*Paraphrasing the Boss*: "Relax, we're still on time, and I'm not letting you leave your wife and kids for eleven months, upset and frustrated for not waking up. Go inside, give them a kiss and hug, then come out and get on the bus."

Lesson learned: Sometimes emergencies only become emergencies because you treat them as such.

So, after a slightly inauspicious start, we were on the way to LAX, just barely behind schedule, having seen the value in another important lesson: whenever possible, factor buffers into tight timelines. But, despite already getting some knowledge bombs thrown our way, the most important lesson I'd learn during our travel to Georgia came from watching the Boss interact with the airline attendants at the check-in counter of LAX.

As a team of combat advisors, our luggage contents didn't necessarily look like most of the bags being checked in that morning. Beyond the body armor and other tactical gear, we had hard-shelled Pelican cases holding a team's worth of rifles, side arms, and optics. So, it wasn't surprising when the airline attendant told Derby that she couldn't check our weapons, as it was against airline policy (as team logistics officer, it made sense that "bag duty" fell within his purview). After a few minutes of back-and-forth, Derby realized he wasn't getting anywhere, and he knew that the Boss would have to get involved. This is where experience kicks in, as the Boss, after hearing the situation, approached the counter:

*The Boss*: "Excuse me, ma'am, I've been told you're not able to check our weapons."

*Attendant*: "Yes, sir, I'm afraid it's against policy."

*The Boss*: "Okay, since you clearly can't get me to 'yes,' I'm going to ask you to please go get a supervisor, and we'll eventually find someone who can."

In this fashion, the Boss went through several echelons of airline management, until a supervisor ultimately arrived, recognized that we were, as active-duty military members on deployment, fully within compliance, and instructed the attendant to promptly check-in our weapons.

Though the Boss's methods may appear mildly condescending, the "how do I get to yes" approach would prove invaluable to our entire team, but especially Derby, over the course of our deployment. As a small team, we would not be able to use "no" as an excuse for failing to accomplish our mission and any critical tasks. In one brief interaction, the Boss further emphasized the FITFO mentality of the team. One way or another, we would get the job done.

# II-2

# SETTING THE TONE FOR
# GEORGIA, PART II

······································

WITH THE WEAPONS SNAFU resolved, we were one step closer to Georgia, but we still had a lot of travel ahead of us. From LAX, we flew to Atlanta for a brief layover then on to the longest leg of our travel, Atlanta to Munich. Due to the quirks of flying into Tbilisi, a large number of international flights into the city arrive well after midnight. For us, arriving in Munich mid-morning German time, this meant we had a roughly twelve-hour layover at the Munich airport.

Now, the best way to approach twelve hours in the Munich airport is certainly up for debate. After waking up at the crack of dawn California time and traveling for the past twenty-four hours or so, I was exhausted by the time we touched down in Germany. Fortunately, I'd heard rumor that there was a Hotel Kempinski attached to the airport with pool access for a few dollars; so, for me, the appeal of napping poolside far outweighed any other Munich options. After a quick snack at an airport cafe, I checked into the hotel's spa, threw on shorts, and passed out in a bathrobe by the pool for the next eight hours. Perfect. However, as I said, there isn't only one way to approach twelve hours in the Munich airport. And, while I certainly don't regret my relaxing time at the Hotel Kempinski pool, my decision wasn't the one that would set the tone for our time in Georgia; the lieutenants assumed that mantle.

In a previous life, that is, prior to the Marine Corps, Bane had logged some time backpacking around Europe, to include a stay in Munich. Naturally, once we landed, he suggested catching the train from the airport into Munich proper for a liter or several at the *Hofbrauhaus.* In my head, I thought: *On one hand, drinking beers and crushing bratwurst in Munich would be an absolute riot. On the other hand, all of the junior officers on a team of Marine combat advisors getting drunk and disorderly in another country may not be the best way to spend the first day of an eleven-month deployment.* Short of explicitly telling the guys they couldn't go into Munich, I left them with a "might not be the best idea," then continued on my merry way to the pool, thinking that was that.

Shame on me for not explicitly saying "no." We have a common saying in the Marine Corps, that, when you give Marines an inch, they'll typically take a mile. So, I guess yeah, I knew in the back of my head that, as I nodded off at a hotel pool, Bane, Claymore, Derby, and SloMo—the hard charging lieutenants on the team—would be slamming German beers at the cyclic rate out in town.

All I could do was smile when I finally got to the gate an hour before taking off for Tbilisi and saw the guys—three of the four passed out at odd angles, and Bane looking at me with a glazed-over, shit-eating grin on his face. *Okay fellas, well played.* There's a reason I titled this story "Setting the Tone for Georgia, Part II." In the Part I story during our time at ATC , Sam emphasized to us how critical building rapport with our Georgian partners would be to success in combat. Part II set us up for a central pillar of how we'd build that rapport: drinking heavily.

# II-3

# WELCOME TO KTA

.....................................

A FTER THE LONG Atlanta to Munich flight, the brief hop
across the Black Sea to Tbilisi felt like nothing at all. And,
despite arriving around 3:00 a.m. Georgia time, the strange scheduling of the airport's international arrivals made it feel like rush
hour in the terminal. Fortunately for us, we received the VIP
treatment. Immediately upon deplaning, we were met by some
US Embassy personnel and a group of Georgian military police
(MPs). With the MP escort, we picked up our bags and were
whisked through a passport control line that, without Georgian
assistance, I'm pretty sure I'd still be waiting in today. Outside
the airport, the MPs had a few vehicles lined up for us, so we
loaded up and began the final leg of our journey, a twenty-minute
or so ride through the dark, Georgian countryside to our home
for the next three months, Krtsanisi Training Area (KTA to us,
as *Krtsanisi*, like many words in the Georgian language of Kartouli, is far too difficult for non-native speakers to utter smoothly).

As chance would have it, we arrived at the front gate of KTA
just as the sun was coming up, giving us a clear impression of
our new home as we drove up the long drive from the gate to the
actual garrison (living and office space) area of the base. Located
on the high plateau between the Greater Caucasus mountain

range to the north and Lesser Caucasus to the south, KTA had the windswept and grassy look of the rolling foothills of the Rocky Mountains—very few trees as you left the shelter of the river valleys that criss-crossed the country. Running east-to-west and roughly parallel with the southern boundary of the base, there's a long ridgeline that serves as the impact area for all of the base's live-fire ranges (terrain features like this prevent bullets from traveling further than intended during training). To the north of the base, rolling hills and farmland unfold towards Tbilisi, located along the sheltered confines of the Mtkvari River Valley. But I'm already ahead of myself.

At this point in time, I had no sense of this tour guide-y description of the area around KTA. Rather, I was still extremely disoriented from a darkened drive in the back of a van through unfamiliar countryside.

Back to the ride up KTA's long drive. About a half mile from the base's front gate, we arrived at the garrison area, divided into two separate, fenced in zones. In the eastern zone, there was a large field and concrete parade ground bordered on two sides by a series of one-story, concrete buildings. Apparently, this area housed all of the base's classrooms and the barracks of the Georgian battalion we'd be advising, the 51st Georgian Light Infantry Battalion (51st GLIB). For these soldiers, life at KTA was life away from home, too, as their battalion was based out of the city of Gori to the east, but the unit was required to move to KTA for its pre-Afghan training.

We would be living in the western zone of the base, which was comprised of more low-slung, concrete buildings and neat rows of prefabricated, "trailer-esque" buildings separated by a grid system of gravel paths. In addition to housing the GLT and GTT Marines (who had arrived about two months prior), this side also held a large motor pool of armored vehicles for training Georgian drivers and the offices of the permanent staff at KTA, the Georgian soldiers tasked with training the battalions that came through KTA on their way to Afghanistan.

As our convoy of vehicles parked along one of the gravel roads on our side of base, we were met by one of the GTT Marines for a quick orientation. We spent about fifteen minutes walking along the gravel paths of our zone, taking a quick look at the key places. *Chow Hall*: old Georgian ladies prepare three meals a day, and what they make is what you get (but quite delicious). *Morale, Welfare, & Recreation (MWR) facility*: trailer with ping-pong, a pool table, darts, and a TV with dozens of DVDs. *Gym*: small, but enough free weights and equipment to keep the meat sticks on our team occupied. *Civilian interpreter ("terp") Hut*: where the contracted civilian terps hung out during working hours, enabling the Marines to communicate with our Georgian partners. *GLT Office*: located across a gravel road from the GTT office and with enough computers and white boards to handle our daily work and long-term planning. And, the highlights of the base, *LBD and Jack*: the two base dogs, one a little brown dog, hence LBD, and the other a mangy, spotted white and brown old-timer, Jack. Not sure which previous rotation of Marines had named these guys, but the monikers stuck, and they were welcome additions to the base.

Our living spaces, the last stop on our brief tour, proved to be the most welcome after our travels. Though certainly not spacious, our roughly 7' x 7' "cans" had everything we would need to be comfortable—air conditioning for the hot Georgia summer, wi-fi access, and communal bathroom/shower access. We all left our bags in the rooms, headed to the just-opened chow hall for a quick breakfast, then passed out for some much needed rest. We'd take the remainder of this first day on base to sleep off the travel and, for some, the hangover.

# II-4

# LAUNDRY, COLLECTION, AND MY "SWING ZONE"

·············································

I DIDN'T FIND out about one place near, though not on, our side of base until a few days after our initial orientation. Recognizing that A) US service members typically have money to spend while deployed, and B) young Marines probably don't enjoy doing their own laundry, some enterprising old ladies set up a laundry trailer just outside of the base perimeter. For a few *lari* (Georgian currency), we could bring out a mesh bag of laundry, drop it off, and pick it up cleaned and folded a couple days later. We foster local entrepreneurism, and someone else does our laundry. Win-win.

For me, in addition to the laundry perk, I enjoyed my trips to the laundry trailer for another reason: language practice. The old ladies who ran the place all spoke Russian (and I'm pretty sure, were Russian). So, much to the amusement of the other guys on the team, I'd try making small talk in my very broken Russian whenever I was over there, inevitably leading to fits of giggling from the old ladies. Apparently, despite never fooling myself into thinking I had any charm with young, beautiful Georgian girls, I could clean up with the 70+ crowd in Georgia, leading the guys to dub this age range my "swing zone."

Now, when topics of conversation with the laundry ladies shifted away from small talk, things got interesting. Here's a typical conversation (I've attempted to demonstrate in English the very broken nature of my Russian):

*Me*: "Good afternoon to yous on this finest of days."
*Laundry lady*: "Hi! How are you doing?"
*Me*: "I am doing best. I have requests for yous to clean laundry."
*Laundry lady*: "Of course! Anything for the handsome Marines! *So, how many Marines live on the base?*" [italics added for emphasis]
*Me*: "Big thanks to yous. It is now I must going."

Yep, those old Russian ladies were pretty sly. Play up the US pride a little bit, then casually slide in a little intelligence collection. I guess you don't have to wear a tux, drive an Aston Martin, and down martinis to act like a spy

# II-5

# THE TRAINING AREA AND INDY 500

......................................................

A FTER A FEW days at KTA, we still hadn't met our Georgian counterparts. Rather than try to organize a bunch of one-off introductions, the Georgian battalion commander scheduled a formal introduction the Friday after we arrived between the GLT and the key members of the 51st GLIB. While this would certainly be an effective way to conduct introductions, it led to a few days of open schedules for us.

For the infantry advisers on the team, the ones who'd be doing the bulk of the "field" training with the Georgians, this free time served as a great opportunity to tour the rest of the training areas in and around KTA. While we were all now pretty thoroughly familiar with our zone in the garrison part of base, we still hadn't spent any time (minus our initial drive from the airport) seeing the broader base environs. Not opposed to ducking out of their day jobs for a couple hours, a few GTT Marines volunteered to play tour guide and show us around the area. Step 1: Grab one of the contracted drivers and a van. As I'd find out shortly, there's a compelling reason for not allowing American service members to drive themselves in Georgia, instead relying upon contracted drivers. Any time we needed to drive somewhere, be it for work or weekend liberty, we relied upon a group of local drivers and small fleet of vans and SUVs.

After piling into a van, we made the short drive out towards KTA's main gate, the route we'd followed coming from the airport a few mornings prior, and stopped at the base's "range control" tower. On any base, range control functions as the gatekeeper for any training activities, especially live-fire ranges. Before reserving a range, you first need to have range control review your plan, making sure that all required safety procedures are adhered to and your training doesn't conflict with anything else on base. And, before actually beginning to shoot, you need explicit permission from range control to make sure that it's safe, that is, no one's "down range" in the impact area.

Relative to US military bases, the live-fire requirements imposed by KTA's range control weren't overly cumbersome. Here, we really just needed a couple planning products to put together a range. We'd build a basic scheme of maneuver diagram, depicting the geometries of where we'd be firing from and where our targets would be located (this ensures that our bullets don't inadvertently travel somewhere they shouldn't, which is never a good thing). With this diagram, we'd include a one-page word document covering some of the additional details like timeline, type of ammunition we'd be using, and brief narrative of our training to amplify the diagram. Lastly, and absolutely critical to any live-fire training, we'd outline our casualty evacuation (CA-SEVAC) plan in the event of injury. Having a corpsman on our team, Doc served as the on-scene first responder, and we always had further evacuation contingencies. For non-life threatening injuries, we'd use a HMMWV (*humvee*) to drive to the base clinic. For life-threatening injuries, we kept a radio and interpreter to communicate with range control, who could then request a CASEVAC helicopter for movement to the nearest base hospital.

All in all, the range control requirements were enough to ensure safe execution, but not overly onerous enough to prevent creative training. Good combination.

From range control, we took the van out KTA's main gate to drive to a training area not technically part of the base, but frequently used. Upon turning onto the road outside of base in the middle of the afternoon, it became immediately apparent why we were not allowed to drive here. While technically a two-lane road, we really turned from the base entryway onto a five-lane superhighway. Both shoulders, the middle line, and even the opposite side of the road—all seemed to be fair game for Georgian drivers. Pulling into this chaos felt like entering the Indy 500, but with the added twist of two-way traffic. As an outsider thrown into this chaos, the best survival mechanism was simply looking down or closing your eyes. Watching the road in front of you caused nothing but panic.

Somehow, we made it through the gauntlet of Georgian traffic to our destination, an urban training facility known as Arashenda, which means "unfinished" in Kartouli. Apparently, sometime in the nineties there'd been a housing boom in Georgia, and developers began to build a neighborhood. Something happened, and the plan was scrapped, leaving the skeletal remains of a half-built neighborhood. While I'm sure unfortunate for some investors, these unfinished houses were a boon to the military, providing KTA access to a top-notch, extremely realistic facility for conducting urban operations training. And, in addition to getting a tour of Arashenda, this trip also provided us our first view of the 51stGLIB conducting training, as the battalion scout platoon was in the middle of an urban patrolling exercise when we arrived. It's tough to get a comprehensive sense of a unit's proficiency by a brief snapshot into its training, but, if nothing else, seeing the scouts in action made us all the more eager to actually embed with our Georgian partners and get to work.

# II-6

# TBILISI IMPRESSIONS

.........................................

S TILL NOT HAVING met our battalion, our days the first
week at KTA remained open. While not truly necessary, the
day before meeting our counterparts, a few of us took the roughly
thirty-minute ride into Tbilisi to tour a couple of Georgian hospitals
with the US Army medical officer temporarily assigned to KTA's
clinic. Ostensibly, these tours were meant to provide us an understanding of the civilian hospital infrastructure around KTA. In
reality, all that research and vetting had already been conducted
by US Embassy personnel. For us, this was really just an excuse
to check out Tbilisi for a day. In the military, these types of ex-
cursions are affectionately known as "boondoggles."

Fortunate to be driving into Tbilisi on a beautiful, sunny day,
we got a great overview of the city. From KTA, we drove northwest, descending from the rolling hills of KTA's high-plain environment down into the Mtkvari River Valley, which we wound
along, tracing the river from the outskirts of Tbilisi into the city
center. The outlying districts of the capital were about what
you'd expect in a former Soviet-bloc country: decrepit, gray concrete structures. However, as we approached the historic center
of Tbilisi, it's hard to overstate the beauty of the historic buildings,
churches, and homes spanning both the gradually sloping south

side of the river and the towering escarpment on the north, all under the shadow of stunning, wooded mountain peaks.

Eyes glued on our surroundings, we zig-zagged through the narrow side streets and along the river boulevards of old-town Tbilisi. I actually became so engrossed in seeing the city, I was surprised when we pulled up in front of the hospital. But, we did our token tour and, in all honesty, I came away feeling far more comfortable about local trauma care than I anticipated. And, it's refreshing to know that if, worst case scenario, we had to air CASEVAC someone from any training, I could at least visualize where they'd be going for immediate care.

But, boondoggles being what they are, we had to do something a little less productive than a trauma facility visit to really round out this excursion. A stop at a local supermarket for some snacks fit the bill. The medical officer had been at KTA for a while, so she knew a good place to stop. For the next hour or so, we wandered the aisles of a Georgian grocer, picked up a bunch of snacks with no English-language descriptions, and pretended we were actually fluent in Russian with a couple promotional girls serving up samples of local wine. Certainly not the worst afternoon I've had.

## II-7

# MEETING THE 51ST

······································

B Y THE TIME our first Friday at KTA rolled around, we
were all pretty eager to finally meet our 51stGLIB counterparts. Adhering to military formality, the Georgian battalion
commander organized a "meet & greet" session that would begin
with words from both him and our officer-in-charge, the Boss.
So, Friday afternoon, the GLT got together and walked across
the KTA garrison from our zone over to where our counterparts
were living and training, ready to meet the guys we'd be working
with for the next eleven months.

When we arrived at KTA's largest training classroom, which
also served as an event venue of sorts, the 51stGLIB battalion
commander and sergeant major (the senior enlisted adviser for
the unit) stood at the front of the room, with the battalion's key
staff members in chairs up front and dozens of other Georgian
soldiers filling up about ninety percent of the rest of the space.
Filling in the couple rows that appeared to be allocated to us, we
took seats as the Boss and our senior enlisted advisor walked up
to greet the 51stGLIB battalion commander, Maj Koba, and his
right-hand man (while "Koba" is a first name in Georgian, that's
actually how he introduced himself to us, recognizing the American difficulties with pronouncing many Georgian last names).

Once we were all settled in, Maj Koba began his remarks. Though he spoke basic English, in most official settings dealing with the GLT or other Americans, Maj Koba spoke via his personal interpreter, Levan, an absolute rock star who had spent enough time in the States to speak English fluently. And, as I'd come to appreciate, he was skilled and militarily savvy enough to translate intended, not literal, meaning when bridging the Kartouli-English divide, a trait that would serve us all well moving forward as stress and frustration levels frequently peaked.

Both Maj Koba and the Boss gave remarks one would typically expect in this sort of setting: "We look forward to working with you....It's an honor being part of the Georgian-American team.... We know we have much to learn from each other," and so forth. Then, as each leader wrapped up his introductory remarks, he turned to introducing his respective staff and subordinate leadership to the group. For me, this meant keeping my eyes out for two key Georgians: the 51stGLIB's operations officer and A ("alpha") Company (A Co) commander. While I'd be acting as the GLT's operations officer once we reached Afghanistan, working primarily with the 51stGLIB's operations officer, my focus of effort in Georgia would be working with the A Co commander, helping prepare his rifle company for combat patrolling operations.

Following the introductions, we broke out into small groups, with the Marines tracking down their counterparts for face-to-face introductions. As I approached the A Co commander, who was surrounded by his three platoon commanders, I realized how foolish I'd been not properly preparing for this. Specifically, it dawned on me as I said "hello" and got some blank stares, I had assumed that the whole interpreter thing would just work itself out, not actually heading to the "terp hut" prior to the introductions to grab an interpreter. So, we were able to do some basic Charades-type introductions, and I learned his name was Shalva. But, beyond that, we just kind of spent a few moments standing awkwardly in a circle until parting ways with a "Welp, see ya later!" type exit. Great start. Fortunately, things went a little better with the operations officer, Major Nik, who spoke pretty good English. From our brief exchange, I got the impression of a Georgian version of Santa Claus—a big, red-cheeked, and jolly guy with a constant smile on his face.

I walked away from our introductions with another important lesson beat into my head: interpreters can never be assumed, but must always be planned for. In retrospect, this lesson is patently obvious, but a lesson that we all nonetheless had to learn the hard way at one point or another. For the rest of our time in Georgia, Germany, and Afghanistan, interpreters, for better or worse, would be a make-or-break asset to whatever task needed to be completed.

# II-8

# LIB-O! (TBILISI)

.............................

WITH THE OLD promo, "Join the Navy and See the World," people aren't thinking about "seeing the world" from inside the bowels of a grey-hulled ship in the middle of the north Atlantic. Rather, the mystique of travel with the military revolves around port visits in far- off, exotic lands—places you could never fathom seeing outside of the movies. We call these occasional respites from the grind of daily military duty "liberty," a temporary sense of freedom from the otherwise authoritarian lifestyle of a service member. So yeah, you can bet getting into Tbilisi our first full weekend in Georgia for a little "lib-o" (liberty, for short) was high on our list of priorities.

Liberty, as one would expect, doesn't mean complete freedom from the rigid structures of military life. Our first night in Tbilisi, we required escorts from the GTT, guys who had been there for a few months, for "guided liberty." Naturally, it was mandated that we be shown all the "off-limits establishments," those places deemed problematic for one reason or another. As the three in- fantry officers on the GLT, Bane, Claymore, and I linked up with a couple of the infantrymen on the GTT, hopped into one of the contracted vehicles, and got dropped off in Shardeni Square, the heart of old-town Tbilisi and a bustling hub of foot traffic, bars, and restaurants. For the first hour or so, we wandered through Shardeni and the surrounding neighborhoods, seeing the strip clubs, "massage" parlors, and Iranian clubs to avoid. In essence, frequenting places with a high-likelihood of Russian mob and/or Iranian intelligence involvement was frowned upon.

After this obligatory review, we grabbed a table at a traditional Georgian restaurant for our introduction to an absolutely delicious cuisine. For the next couple hours, we drank Georgian beer and ate a gluttonous amount of national staples: *khatchapuri* (a delicious flatbread covered with piping hot, melted cheese with an egg broken in the middle of it); *kingali* (meat dumplings of sort-hard knot of dough at the top that you hold onto while biting into the actual body, drinking the hot broth inside the dough and, when finished, eating the rest of the dough and spiced meat filling); *mts'vadi* (also known as *shashlik*-seasoned chunks of pork, beef, or lamb skewered with onions and slow cooked over coals).

After eating our fill (then surpassing it), a waitress finally removed the plates from in front of us. But, to properly wrap up a Georgian meal, we had one more box to check: *chacha*. This grape-based liquor is the rocket fuel of the Georgian drink world, a high-octane spirit that I'm pretty sure could clean an engine block. And, this is not a country for ordering single shots, so we got a bottle, drank to Georgia, and, with the bottle empty, wrapped up our introduction to life at the Georgian table. A perfect first night in town.

# II-9

# LIB-O! (RUSTAVI)

····································

AS TO BE expected, we all woke up somewhat groggy after our first Friday night in Tbilisi, and, night out or not, began an outstanding Saturday/Sunday morning routine. With the exception of times when we were out on longer field exercises in Georgia, the weekends were our own. The 51stGLIB soldiers went home, and we got some free time to relax and explore the country. So, when not traveling, I embraced the weekend morning routine in KTA's chow hall: eggs-to-order, some greasy potatoes and bacon, an industrial-sized serving of French press coffee, and a good book. I'm nothing if not a creature of habit, and those quiet weekend mornings hanging out in the chow hall as people began to stir remain some of my fondest memories from KTA.

Alright, that was a bit of a rabbit hole. Back to our first Saturday in Georgia. While Tbilisi was about thirty minutes away from base, Rustavi, a smaller city, was only about ten minutes down the road from KTA in the opposite direction from the capital. Still feeling that new-to-a-foreign-place excitement and need to get out and see things, we rallied that Saturday afternoon to check out Rustavi.

As we approached the city, I was immediately struck by the contrast between the historic beauty of central Tbilisi and the Soviet-bloc feel of Rustavi. Whereas you saw old, concrete block architecture on the outskirts of the former, this barren design comprised all of the latter. Rustavi had the feel of a planned, industrial city—perfectly laid out grids of Soviet apartment complex after Soviet apartment complex.

Despite the less-than aesthetically pleasing look, Rustavi had a real local charm to it. Our driver, surprised that we'd asked to go to Rustavi at all, dropped us off at a central market. Radiating out from a main square with a grocery store on one side were streets lined with tent-style stalls, with locals selling everything from flip-flops, to cell phones, to Georgian sweets. For a couple hours, we just aimlessly wandered, enjoying the sites and sounds of a city off the tourist beaten path.

Eventually, we made our way back to the central square, where we found a big Georgian restaurant around the corner from the grocery store. Drawing some strange looks as we walked in (as I said, Rustavi isn't really a tourist destination), a young hostess seated us. Apparently, I said something or other in Russian, leading her to bring me the Russian language version of the menu. Armed with a false sense of my own proficiency, I proceeded to order in Russian, thinking that I'd ordered us a few dishes of *mts'vadi*, as I understood *shashlik* in the menu's Cyrillic script.

Fast forward thirty minutes, and the waitress, shit-eating grin and all, placed a massive, pickled pig's face on a platter surrounded by pickled vegetables on our table. Did I intend to order this? Certainly not. Did the waitress likely know I didn't intend to order this? Most likely. Did she clearly get a laugh out of the looks on our faces when we saw this pig's face slammed down in front of us? Absolutely. But, pride being what it is, we ate every last piece of that face.

Between the laugh we all got from my pig's face SNAFU and the complimentary bottle of vodka the owner brought us, our loyalty was solidified. For the rest of our time in Georgia, every Sunday night a group of us would head over to Rustavi for dinner here. We just made sure to order from the English menu.

# II-10

# TRAINING WITH A CO

EARLY ON IN our pre-deployment work, the GLT decided that during training, everything our Georgian counterparts did, we would do, seeking to build as much rapport as possible while still in Georgia. The Monday following our initial introduction with the 51stGLIB, we all finally got that opportunity. As I mentioned, on our eighteen-man team, nine of us were infantry Marines slated to advise the three rifle companies of the Georgian battalion. These nine were broken into three teams of three, each of which had a junior officer (lieutenant or captain), staff non-commissioned officer, or staff NCO, (staff sergeant or gunnery sergeant), and non-commissioned officer (corporal or sergeant). The intent was to be able to have similar ranks mentoring their respective rank counterparts in the Georgian company.

Due to a last-minute medical emergency, my infantry advisor team's staff NCO became non-deployable about a week prior to leaving for Georgia, so we brought in a replacement. Fortunately, Staff Sergeant (SSgt) Johnny (first name), the new guy, was in my company in 1st Battalion, 5th Marines, so I knew he was solid. But, because the change was so last-minute, he wouldn't arrive in Georgia for a couple weeks. Down a man, Sgt Curtis (also a first name) and I embedded with A Company, 51stGLIB, excited to finally kick things off.

That first week, we gained insight into an interesting dynamic in the Georgian Armed Forces. For the entire week, the battalion and company leadership were all involved with a combat operations center (COC) simulated training event. A COC is the nerve center of combat patrolling, coordinating and providing support for patrolling units while ensuring everyone "outside-the-wire" remains deconflicted with other friendly forces in the accomplishment of the unit's overall mission. In this capacity, understanding proper COC procedures is certainly critical, but, strange to us Marines, while the A Co company commander, executive officer, and platoon commanders all were inside for this training, the rest of the company was conducting a live-fire attack range with the KTA staff.

If you asked one thousand infantry Marines if, over the course of their careers, they ever went to a live-fire range as a company without a single officer from that company, I would wager you wouldn't find one Marine respond in the affirmative. As we would see, the level of "leadership from the front" so pervasive in the Marine Corps didn't always exist here. As such, that first morning, we grabbed an interpreter (yes, lesson learned), and observed a couple hours of the COC training—good excuse to more formally (and effectively) introduce ourselves to the A Co staff.

Following our requisite observation of the COC training, we ducked out to actually get to the range. For us, the handful of Marines who would be patrolling day-in and day-out with the Georgians, our primary concern was if they could shoot, move, and communicate, that is, fight. And, while COC operations were important, a Marine back-up would always be present in these command and control centers (more on that later), but, outside-the-wire, we would have to fully rely on the Georgians to our left and right if we got in a bind. Bottom line, we belonged out at the range.

That first afternoon, we observed the attack rehearsals that the company would be doing live the next day. As the 51stGLIB was still in the early stages of its pre-deployment training, this range was a fairly canned, "right-up-the-gut" attack. Six to eight soldiers would be arrayed in a line facing targets down range, and one of the KTA staff would call "contact," simulating contact with the enemy. At that point in time, the intent was for these soldiers to work as buddies, bounding forward towards the targets, with one shooting and providing cover as the other moved, gradually leap-frogging forward as a unit to close with the enemy.

The second day at the range, a cold and rainy morning, the two of us drew our weapons from the armory, signed out some ammo, and headed out to the range. Sticking with our philosophy of leadership by example, we figured we'd hop in a few of these shoots. And, what builds camaraderie better than being cold, wet, and muddy together? At the end of that day, caked with mud, we'd definitely taken a step forward in terms of bonding with the guys, pulling closer through that wonderful glue, shared suffering with smiles on our faces.

## II-11

# SOSO MAKARIDZE

......................................

I MET SOSO Makaridze at the above live-fire range, my first time training with A Co, 51stGLIB. When he introduced himself, I was blown away, as he spoke English like a native. Who was this Georgian soldier who was more fluent than any of the interpreters we'd met so far, and who sounded like he grew up in the States? Soso solved the mystery for me later that week when we were hanging out after some training, shooting the shit. Apparently, he received a nomination by the Georgian Ministry of Defense to fill an appointment to the United States Coast Guard Academy, where he would be entering his senior year the fall following our time in Georgia.

Each year, a handful of international students are selected to attend the different US service academies. Upon graduating, these newly commissioned officers return home to serve in their armed forces. The fact that Soso received one of these prestigious and selective appointments speaks highly of his work ethic, intelligence, dedication, and commitment to service—traits that jumped out in all of my interactions with him.

For the next couple months in Georgia, Soso remained with A Co, both learning and observing the ways of the Georgian Armed Forces and greatly helping the Marines bridge the linguistic and cultural gaps with our counterparts. Rather than take his well-deserved summer leave, Soso decided he'd rather spend that last college summer working at KTA, getting to know the Georgian service members he'd soon lead. Absolutely selfless young man.

As we parted ways at the end of the summer, Soso and I exchanged e-mails and promised to stay in touch. Soso had excelled academically to the point that, following his time at the Coast Guard Academy, the Georgian Ministry of Defense wanted him to stay in the States to receive a masters in engineering prior to returning home. Related to this honor, below is the last e-mail I received:

> *Firstie year is definitely great, it is exciting and I am so close to graduation. Just submitted my graduate school applications and now I have to wait for response. I hope to be accepted in one of the universities. I wish you best of luck and great mission.*
>
> *Kind regards,*
>
> *1/c Soso Makaridze*

In March 2015, a few months after I got this note, I found out that Soso and a younger Georgian exchange student at Coast Guard, Bersarian Gorjoladze, were killed in a car crash back in the States. Six months into our time in Afghanistan and dealing with significant frustration, this news nearly pushed me over the edge. Soso represented the best, not just of Georgia's or America's youth, but of youth in general, and he will be missed.

## II-12

# PLAYING THE MOMMY VS DADDY GAME

......................................................

D URING OUR PRE-DEPLOYMENT time spent in Virginia Beach at the Marine Corps Security Cooperation Group, we met and worked a bit with our counterparts in the GTT, the Marines tasked with training the Georgian Armed Forces KTA training cadre. In essence, these Marines had a "train-the-trainer" mission. As such, there would be an underlying friction between the GLT Marines, whose sole focus in life was preparing the 51stGLIB for combat operations in Afghanistan, and the GTT Marines, whose mission was to build Georgia's organic military training capability. Though plenty of overlap existed between these missions, we had significantly different time horizons. While the GTT could take the long look and seek incremental progress, we needed results now, as the success or failure of the 51stGLIB's training would directly translate to performance in combat.

Despite this inherent friction between the GTT and GLT missions, we ultimately established an extremely positive working relationship with our counterparts, largely a product of the phenomenal support the GLT received from both the GTT officer-in-charge and operations officer, support that would trickle down through the entire GTT. This support enabled us to continue focusing on building that critical component of combat advising, rapport. My buddy Sam back at Camp Pendleton's ATC had emphasized this to me, but the presence of the GTT let us play a game of mommy vs daddy with our 51stGLIB partners. From the beginning of our time in Georgia, we emphasized to the best of our ability that there were two groups of Marines: the GTT (part of the "them"), and the GLT (part of the "us"). Down to the detail of both groups of Marines wearing different uniforms, we strove to show the 51stGLIB that we were in it with them, shoulder to shoulder, while the GTT Marines were the outsiders.

The "mommy vs daddy" dynamic let us "back door" training of the 51stGLIB. Basically, if our partners were consistently screwing something up, we could take one of two options to correct it. Option 1 would be addressing the discrepancy and correcting it ourselves. From a practical perspective, this would be the quickest form of remediation. However, if we corrected our partners, at best we'd build a trainer/trainee barrier that's certainly not conducive to trust in combat. At worst, we'd irreparably rupture rapport with the 51stGLIB by correcting them too frequently (the Georgians are an extremely proud people, but more on that later). On the other hand, Option 2 was to take an issue and, rather than address it ourselves, explain the situation to the GTT. Then, the GTT Marines would stress this training priority with their counterparts in the KTA training cadre, who in turn brought the hammer down on the 51stGLIB.

Was this an inefficient, convoluted method of training? You bet. But, it let us correct deficiencies while still building a level of "we're in this shit together" with the Georgians that would not have been possible otherwise.

# II-13

# TACTICAL TERPS

..............................

I'VE MENTIONED THE civilian interpreters ("terps") employed by KTA a few times, but, they're a unique enough group that they definitely warrant their own entry. While I'm not sure exactly how the contract works, and who funds it, somehow KTA keeps about a dozen civilian interpreters on staff to facilitate training and coordination between the Marines, the Georgian instructor cadre, and the Georgian battalions training at the base. From what I gathered chatting with them, working as an interpreter at KTA was a pretty good gig—good pay, decent hours, you get to practice your English all day, and you don't have to deploy—so, many of these terps had been there for years.

For continuity's sake, the guy in charge of assigning responsibilities to the individual terps tried his best to link them up with the same Marines regularly. This let us build solid working relationships, and it helped significantly when we tried explaining things to our counterparts in the 51stGLIB. For Sgt Curtis, SSgt Johnny, and me with A Co, we worked most closely with a young lady named Christina—Tiko, for short.

Tiko, a petite, fashionable Georgian girl, had been at KTA for a few years, so she'd worked closely with at least six different groups of Marines and their partner Georgian battalions. And, in working with these different rotations, Tiko had also sat through all the classes on military tactics KTA had provided these units, and listened to the GLT Marines work with and mentor the Georgians day-in and day-out. Consequently, and almost by osmosis, Tiko possessed a level of tactical proficiency in military operations surpassing most of us!

This led to some cognitive dissonance, nowhere more so than one afternoon going over a military training scenario with some of the Georgians on a whiteboard in one of the classrooms. As a bunch of camouflage-wearing, sweaty, and foul-smelling Marines and soldiers stood around debating the merits of different tactical approaches to this particular problem, Tiko, dressed in her designer jeans and blouse, matter-of-factly stated, "Your machine gun support-by-fire position should be on that hill." All I could do was smile. Tiko, a civilian with no formal military training at all, had slowly but surely become a tactical expert, just by translating for and putting up with the bullshit of Marines and Georgian soldiers for a few years.

As stated, and unfortunately for us, these civilian terps would not be deploying. This put us in a tough situation. On one hand, because they were so proficient, we wanted to work with Tiko and her co-workers as much as possible in Georgia, as it made communicating with our partners far easier. On the other hand, by relying too heavily on the civilians, we failed to develop relationships with the military interpreters, or MILTERPS, who'd actually be deploying with us. This failure to work with MILTERPS throughout the time in Georgia caused some serious problems for previous GLTs, problems that we hoped to avoid.

While the Georgian Ministry of Defense has its own language school to train MILTERPS, not all of these individuals graduate fluent in English (or, in some cases, not even barely conversant). Due to this reality, some past GLTs had relied solely on the civilian terps in Georgia, then got to Afghanistan with the MIL-

TERPS assigned to their battalions realizing, "Holy shit, we can't communicate with our Georgian partners any more."

Seeking to avoid the above situation, Claymore assumed the mantle of "Terp Assessor." As the MILTERPS who would be deploying with us weren't officially part of the 51stGLIB yet, they would come over to KTA Tuesday through Thursday each week to work with the Marines. Hoping to influence which MIL-TERPS actually deployed with us, Claymore set up a rotation. Marines would link up with different MILTERPs each day they were on base, and, at the end of the day, we'd sit down for a few minutes as a group to assess the English proficiency levels of each MILTERP.

In theory, we would, towards the end of our time in Georgia, make recommendations based on these reviews to Maj Koba about who the best MILTERPS would be, setting us up for success in Afghanistan. As we'd soon find out, this idealism reflected our tremendous naivete regarding politics and nepotism within the Georgian Ministry of Defense.

# II-14

# THE SUPRA

...................

E VER SINCE MY buddy Matt had done a GLT deployment back in 2011, I'd heard legend of the Georgian *supra*, a feast to end all feasts. In Georgian culture, the *supra* is a traditional feast held as either a celebration for something, or, in a more somber setting, a memorial meal following a burial. Early on in our time at KTA, the 51stGLIB officers hosted a welcome *supra* for the GLT officers and senior enlisted at a restaurant in Gori, the battalion's home city (and, coincidentally, Stalin's home-town—an unrelated but interesting historical tidbit). While I was pretty light on details going into the night, I did know that, however things unfolded, there would be much food and wine consumed.

When we arrived in the parking lot of the Gori restaurant, I felt an immediate flashback to a middle school dance, with boys against one wall and girls along the opposite. Lacking an inter-preter, we dumped out of our contracted vans and, with the Geor-gians on one side of the parking lot, we kind of shuffled around on the other side. After twenty minutes or so of this awkwardness, Maj Koba arrived with Levan, the doors opened, and we all headed inside to kick off the festivities.

On one side of the restaurant, there was a high-ceilinged, church-like banquet hall. Inside, there were five or so tables spread along both walls, with a wide aisle between both rows of tables. Immediately upon seeing the amount of food on the tables (to say nothing of the massive carafes of wine), I knew that the legend of the Georgian *supra* had not been overstated. So, naturally, I was blown away when I found out the massive servings of meat, cheeses, salads, and breads on the table were simply the *starters*.

As a quasi-formal ceremony, *supras* are emceed by a *tamada*, or toastmaster. Throughout the meal, the *tamada* makes a series of toasts, with all in attendance downing their glasses of wine after each one. As I'd learn over the next ten months with him, it made sense that Major Nik was the battalion's designated *tamada*, what with his great sense of humor, loud voice, and deep laugh.

After we all got settled (I sat with the A Co officers, one of whom spoke a little English and could help me translate), Major Nik kicked off the toasts. Over the next two hours, with multiple waves of ever more food and a bottomless supply of Georgian wine, we toasted everything imaginable: country, brothers-in-arms, family, the women in our lives, and, ultimately, devolving into plenty of inappropriate yet hilarious toasts (e.g. "to fucking Putin!"—raw wounds of the 2008 invasion were still fresh).

Following the meal, things really kicked off. With traditional Georgian music and dancing came the wine horn. This massive (not sure what type of animal), curved horn was designed in such a way that it couldn't be put down with any wine still in it, which meant one had to finish the horn to pass it on to the next person. I suppose this makes it roughly analogous to a "beer bong" with a long tradition at the Georgian *supra*.

Things devolved quickly. In brief moments of clarity, I'd smile looking around at Marines and Georgians, deep into drunken heart-to-hearts, despite the fact that neither spoke the other's language. Didn't matter by that point in time.

At the end of the night, dragging all the Marines out of there and into the vans was an adventure, to say the least—plenty of guys ducking back in for more wine, throwing up in the parking lot, and just general drunken belligerence. But, even with all this absurdity, the *supra* accomplished its aim. While we all woke up with raging hangovers, the barriers of formality between the GLT and the 51stGLIB had been shattered. We were one step closer to actually being a team.

# II-15

# SUSTAINMENT SHOOTS

· · · · · · · · · · · · · · · · · · · · · · · · · · · · · · · · · · · · · · ·

I N KEEPING WITH the team's training approach established
back in Camp Pendleton of all guys, regardless of military
specialty, training for combat operations, we scheduled four "sustainment shoots" during our time at KTA. These were opportunities for everyone on the team, not just the infantry advisors, to
rehearse live-fire rifle and pistol drills in two- and four-man
teams, as we would rarely have more than that number of Marines
operating out on patrol at any given time. Despite the fact that
we'd had a lot of time at the range during our Stateside training,
fire and movement as a small team, and combat marksmanship
in general, are perishable skills. And, with the combination of an
abundance of both rifle and pistol ammo earmarked for training,
proximity to the KTA ranges (we could walk there), and the
aforementioned, straightforward procedures for scheduling and
executing a range with KTA staff, it would be stupid not to get
out and shoot a few times.

Looking at the Georgian training schedule, we found four afternoons during our time at KTA that the 51stGLIB didn't have
any field training, so those would be the days we'd do our GLT
sustainment shoots. In a building block approach, each of these
times out at the range would build on the foundation of the previous one, working up in both numbers and complexity, culmi-

nating in a four-person ("fire team"), dynamic assault and "break-contact" range. Knowing that, with a significant training and language barrier between us and our counterparts, there may be times when the handful of Marines out on patrol would have to depend solely on each other in a tight spot, we wanted to ensure that our small-unit procedures were as rehearsed and proficient as possible prior to actually getting to Afghanistan.

Additionally, as the sole English-language speakers (minus questionably fluent MILTERPS) on most of our patrols, our radio communication would be the primary means of linking outside-the-wire Georgian patrols with external support (fire support aircraft, CASEVAC helicopters, and quick-reaction forces).

To prepare for this, in every training we did, to include these live-fire shoots and all other field time with the Georgians, we incorporated radio reporting procedures. From corporal to captain, you rotated through sending fire support and CASEVAC requests on the radio over and over and over, and then doing it some more, until these procedures became second nature. While these reporting exercises seemed monotonous and redundant, that was the intent, to imbue us all with the ability to, without thinking and regardless of surrounding chaos, pass up an accurate radio report. I would watch this emphasis help save a Georgian life in just a few months.

## II-16

# THE BASEBALL AND FOOTBALL EMBARRASSMENTS

··················································

O N A LIGHTER note, but an entertaining aside, apparently the Republic of Georgia has a national baseball team—really just a small group of kids who fell in love with the game and try playing anyone willing to side another nine. Seeing some good community relations potential, the US Embassy organized an annual game between the national team and a hodgepodge of Marines from the GTT and GLT. To the Georgians, every American is basically Cal Ripken, Jr. In reality, we fielded a team of baseball rejects that either A) had never played the game competitively, or B) hadn't played in more than a decade. So, despite a couple informal practice sessions on the embassy's makeshift diamond, we knew that we'd be at a marked disadvantage playing against the Georgians.

The day of the game turned out to be an absolutely gorgeous, sunny Saturday afternoon. Lacking an actual baseball diamond, the Georgians converted a soccer stadium, building an infield on the pitch. I don't know how they promoted it, but the stands were absolutely packed with locals (and a few Marines, eager to laugh at our soon-to-be embarrassing performance). I think we ended up only playing about five innings, I pitched a couple of them (hadn't done that in years, and I couldn't move my arm for about two days), got absolutely shelled, and the Marines ended up losing a whole lot of runs to one (at least we didn't get blanked…).

But, despite the embarrassment, the day was an absolute success. We had a blast, hung out in the sun for an afternoon, drank some beers, and, most importantly, all the proceeds from the game's ticket sales went to the Georgian Wounded Warrior Project.

Fast forward a few weeks, and we found ourselves in a similar situation. A group of Marines got roped into playing the Georgian American Football Federation's flag football team (yes, that's a thing, too). It was another surreal experience, hanging out at a soccer stadium in the middle of Tbilisi, with the stands full of fans waving Georgian flags, playing American football. And, once again, we got crushed by the Georgians in one of our own sports.

So, there were two parallels between the baseball and football experiences: 1) the Americans were embarrassed by the Georgians, and 2) I woke up the mornings after each feeling like I'd been hit by a truck, a solid indicator of my waning athleticism.

## II-17

# THE HELMAND HANGOVER
# AND BINARY PROBLEM

········································

L IKE CULTURE SHOCK in general, serving as an advisor
to a foreign military force inevitably has its ups and downs.
For me, my first day of extreme frustration with the Georgians
came a few weeks into our time at KTA on the day of the
51stGLIB's "patrol package." Despite the fact that ninety-five
percent of our outside-the-wire operations in Afghanistan would
consist of combat patrolling, only a single day out of the entire
51stGLIB work-up had been allocated for formal instruction in
this critical skill (the lingering result of some uninformed, unimag-
inative administrator from the Marines advising the Georgian
Ministry of Defense on pre-deployment training, but that's a
whole other story). While we'd get plenty of time to practice patrolling later in the training, without establishing proper fundamentals, the battalion would be set up for failure.

Already frustrated with the lack of patrolling instruction integrated in the training design, my outlook only worsened once
we left the classroom and A Co platoons began to "prac app" the
patrolling skills just taught on PowerPoint slides. And, to truly
understand one of the root causes of my frustration, it's necessary
to understand the history of the Georgia Deployment Program.

The first eleven GLT rotations deployed to Helmand Province, a region of southwestern Afghanistan home to some of the country's highest levels of poppy growth. And, due to the cash value of this crop as the source of opium and heroin, Helmand was (and remains today) a hotly contested region of the country, with the Taliban fighting tooth and nail to control the province's poppy fields that help finance the organization.

As the fourteenth GLT rotation, we still didn't know where we'd be assigned, but we knew we would not be going to Helmand Province, as the Marines had recently withdrawn from there. Despite this knowledge, the Georgians' prior time in Helmand had left a deep mark on the Georgian Armed Forces. Having sustained significant losses in that province, largely from pressure-plate improvised explosive devices (IEDs), which are pervasive in Helmand, Georgian soldiers now had imbued in their collective psyche the belief that there would be an IED under every rock and patch of dirt in the country.

Without minimizing the devastating effectiveness of pressure plate IEDs (they're terrifying and brutally efficient), this Georgian belief of omnipresent IEDs just wouldn't be the case outside of Helmand. Yet, when we went out to the training area to practice patrolling, the Georgians insisted on walking in a straight line right down the middle of the road. While this technique was used in Helmand to minimize the area needed to sweep for pressure plates with a mine detector, walking down the middle of any path is extremely dangerous, and, as British, Soviet, and American experience had shown, a surefire way to get ambushed. Fearing that the Georgians would head into deployment believing that roads would serve as safe havens, I grabbed our terp and had the following exchange with a Georgian soldier:

*Me*: "Why don't you get off the road, where it's safer?"
*Georgian soldier*: "It's safer on the road, because we can use our minesweeper."

*Me*: "Yeah, but it's also where you're going to get attacked."

*Georgian soldier*: Smiles and shakes his head as if to say, "Silly Americans," then explains, "There are IEDs in cover, and the Taliban is trying to get us to move there."

This interaction perfectly represented the Georgian binary problem. If something happened once (in this case, an IED planted behind a berm along a road during a previous deployment), it would happen every time. That is, because a Taliban ambush had lured Georgians off a road once, driving them towards an emplaced IED, every piece of cover in Afghanistan would now hold an IED, making the roads a safer bet. There's no assessing the terrain and your environment, every situation boils down into a binary, yes/no situation.

So, try as we all might, we couldn't convince the Georgians that walking along roads and trails was far more dangerous than taking advantage of moving over rougher terrain that would provide us cover from ambushes. Unfortunately, it would take a couple of suicide attacks to drive our point home.

I left this training significantly dejected.

# II-18

# GOLF ANALOGIES, CENTRALIZED COMMAND, AND "THAT'S ONE WAY TO DO IT..."

..........................................................

A S EMBEDDED TRAINING with the Georgians continued, it dawned on me that military advising is a lot like being a shitty golfer. Ninety-five percent of the time, it's an awful experience, but it's that five percent of the time that brings you back for more. I'll start with a little more of the ninety-five percent.

Recalling my talks with Sam back at Camp Pendleton's ATC, I knew going into this that, as a post-Soviet military, the Georgians embraced a very centralized command model. While an outside observer may think, "Well yeah, it's the military, of course it's centralized," this approach is actually counter to the Marine Corps' philosophy of decentralized execution. Specifically, the Marine Corps prides itself on empowering subordinates to, in a decentralized fashion, use their initiative and understanding of the situation to make decisions. Rather than having to ask "Mommy may I?" in every situation, the Marines have learned over the years that, within the left and right lateral limits of a commander's intent, it's far quicker and more effective for a subordinate leader to make his or her own decision in a complex environment.

Decision-making is the complete opposite in the Georgian model, where many young leaders seem almost paralyzed by indecision without a clear directive from their higher-ups. Whether it's from a fear of making a mistake or just lack of confidence, this inability to make independent decisions proved a huge frustration to the Marines on the GLT. This centralized approach became abundantly clear while A Co conducted platoon-sized attacks supported by mortar fire.

In this sort of live-fire range, the general flow is as follows: 1) mortars fire on targets, which provides the "suppression" necessary for machine gunners to begin firing on those same targets; 2) once the machine gunners are suppressing the targets, rocket launchers can expose themselves to destroy enemy bunkers; 3) once the bunkers are destroyed, the riflemen can actually close with and destroy the individual targets.

In the Marines, each one of these individual steps offers clear, on-the-ground metrics of effectiveness, that is, if machine gunners look over a ridgeline and see mortars dropping on enemy targets, they know the enemy's suppressed. In this fashion, each ensuing step in the platoon-attack process begins when clear "conditions have been met" in the previous step, allowing each one of those separate elements to execute responsibilities without needing to be explicitly told to do so. The machine gunners just know to start firing once the mortars provide effective suppression.

With the Georgians, the notion of "conditions" is laughable. Rather, each individual step of the above platoon attack must be centrally directed "on order" by a platoon commander. Before the machine gunners fire, they must be ordered to fire. Before the rocket launchers destroy the bunkers, they must be ordered to do so. Before the riflemen conduct their final assault, they must be ordered to do so. This is a wildly inefficient and frustrating level of centralization that completely inhibits initiative, and, for the rest of our time with the Georgians, it would remain an uphill battle trying to get young leaders to make decisions on their own.

The above frustration fell smack-dab in the middle of our ninety-five percent. But, like I said, we had a few five percent situations that made it all worth it. For one, volleyball became one of our prime bonding opportunities with the Georgians. Looking for ways to continue building relationships outside of work, we started playing volleyball in the evenings over on the 51stGLIB side of base. These games started as Marines versus Georgians, but, when the competition got a little too heated, an A Co soldier suggested playing mixed games, with three Georgians and three Marines on a team. This was perfect, because, when one Marine acted like an asshole, the Marines on the other team would call him out (and the same with the Georgians). Through these intermingled teams, we showed we could put the team before the uniform.

Another five-percent situation involved the notion of working smarter, not harder. I remained frustrated with a lot of the things that the KTA instructors were teaching the A Co soldiers, but this frustration collided directly with Georgian pride. If I saw some instruction that just wasn't right, the standard Georgian response was, "Well, this is how we do it, so it's right." So, rather than fight this fierce pride, I embraced it and subtly shifted my approach. Instead of explicitly saying something was wrong, I prefaced each of my observations with, "Hey, that's one way to do it, but here's another way, how we do it." This allowed me to provide some guidance to the Georgians within the context of how Marines do things, while avoiding the mistake of explicitly saying something's wrong. And, throughout our time in Georgia, as the 51stGLIB soldiers began to embrace the notion that we're in this fight together, they started listening more and more.

# II-19

# KAZBEGI, GEORGIAN HOSPITALITY, AND IRANIAN TOURISTS

·············································································

T OWARDS THE END of our time in Georgia, the Boss, Sleepy (intelligence officer), Derby (logistics), SloMo Bravo (communications chief), Maj Koba, and other key members of the 51stGLIB staff would fly over to Afghanistan for a pre-deployment site survey (PDSS). These trips are key tools in building a unit's situational awareness and understanding of a mission prior to the whole force showing up. Essentially, by conducting a PDSS, we would be able to more thoroughly plan for the initial stages of our time in Afghanistan. With that said, the weekend before the PDSS would be the last opportunity to have the whole GLT together in Georgia, so we figured we ought to do something to celebrate.

On the northern fringes of Georgia up in the Caucasus Mountains, and only a few miles from the Russian border, there's a beautiful mountain town, Kazbegi, that we decided on for our weekend trip. After coordinating with the GTT guys, we locked on two of our contracted vans to take us up to Kazbegi. Friday afternoon, we loaded up and began the few hour drive up the mountain, traveling along a steep and treacherous road seeming to switch back-and-forth every quarter mile—thousands of feet dropping off one side, and sheer mountain on the other. Fortunately, we'd made a booze stop leaving Tbilisi, negating what should've been significant concern over the speed with which the Georgian driver took some of these turns.

By the time we pulled into Kazbegi it was dark, and the driver had to spend some time on the phone with the owner of the hostel where we were staying to successfully navigate us to our destination. Eventually, we pulled up in front of our place and were welcomed by the proprietors, a mother and son who rented bunkrooms to backpackers. Despite the late hour, the owners put out a great spread of fresh bread, cheeses, cucumbers, and tomatoes for the group, which is a perfect segue into Georgian hospitality. As fierce (and at times, frustrating) as Georgian pride can be, equally passionate is the Georgian sense of hospitality. Speaking to one of the civilian terps on base, he actually criticized the extremes of this hospitality, saying that a Georgian family would prefer to miss a rent payment than fail to put on an extravagant enough feast for a guest. This was an interesting dichotomy working with the 51stGLIB. On one hand, the soldiers' pride could make them the most stubborn individuals in the world. On the other hand, if you needed something, they wouldn't hesitate to take the shirts of their own backs.

The next morning, we woke up to an absolutely stunning view. While it was tough to tell the night before, our hostel was far up the western slope of a beautiful mountain valley, with high, rocky peaks on each side and the village of Kazbegi straddling the rushing river winding beneath us. For the rest of the day, the guys went about on their own adventures, planning to reconvene for a team dinner that evening. The other junior officers and I spent the day hiking up into the mountains to explore a mountaintop monastery and, further into the high ground, a glacier. Despite some whining during the ascent, the view of the glacier (and a good bottle of Georgian brandy) were well-worth the effort.

After a long day of hiking, we made it back to our hostel,

showered, and headed into town to meet the whole GLT for our final team dinner. Anticipating a significant language barrier, I'd had Tiko (our civilian terp) call the restaurant from KTA earlier in the week and order for us, ensuring we would have more than enough delicious Georgian food. In a nod to our Georgian counterparts, we held our own modified *supra*, with epic proportions of *kingali, mts'vadi, khatchapuri*, Georgian beer, and *chacha* spread across our outdoor table, and, though lacking a formal tamada, toasts throughout the night. By the time we left, I didn't know whether I was drunk from the chacha and beer, or delirious from eating what felt like ten pounds of food. Either way, this was a great culminating team event for the Georgian portion of deployment.

Sunday, our last day in Kazbegi, we all woke up a little groggy to a drizzly Sunday morning. Excited to have a relaxing morning with nothing to do, Claymore and I walked to town and posted up at a café in the town square, where we struck up a conversation with a young couple sitting near us. Turns out, Hussein and his wife (unfortunately I did not catch her name), were Iranian and on a long weekend vacation away from Tehran. Hussein worked at a laser cutting factor while his wife pursued her doctorate in French literature, ultimately hoping to settle in Quebec and become Canadian citizens.

After some small talk and buying them each a cup of coffee, we conceded that, yes, we are Marines (tough to pretend otherwise with the haircuts...). The next part of the conversation unfolded like this:

*Hussein's wife*: "Our state media brands you all as barbers."
*Me (fairly certain that Iran's state press doesn't claim all Marines cut hair professionally)*: "You mean barbarians?"
*Hussein's wife*: "Yes! Barbarians! But you're not!"

It's always great shattering some preconceived notions, and we spent the rest of the morning talking about the joys of American culture and swapping stories of our childhoods, concluding (seemingly logically) that, just because governments don't like each other, it doesn't mean we can't hang out, laugh, and drink coffee (though I'm sure there are some counter-intel "spooks" rolling in their graves as I come to this conclusion). And—the ultimate irony to the situation—as we were sitting there chatting, a tour group of Israelis entered and took up the rest of the tables in the café, literally surrounding us. I couldn't have made this up: two US Marines talking with an Iranian couple surrounded by a busload of Israeli tourists.

## II-20

# OUR INTRO TO "VISTA"

·············································

F OR OUR CULMINATING exercise in Georgia, we would conduct a company- and battalion-level field exercise (FEX) at one of Georgia's other large military training areas, Vaziani South Training Area (VSTA, pronounced "Vista"). For the first few days, we'd focus on operations at the company level, so I'd be working with A Co, and the KTA training cadre would guide us through training exercises and assessments. For the second half of the training, the training would be focused on the battalion actually commanding and controlling its three individual rifle companies (A Co, B Co, and C Co) during twenty-four-hour operations, attempting to replicate our future in Afghanistan.

As we'd be using all of our armored vehicles for the training, the battalion conducted a massive tactical vehicle movement through Georgian cities and countryside, travelling in a mile-long column from KTA to Vista. As we rolled through the decrepit Soviet architecture of Rustavi's outlying districts and into the barren, rolling hills of Vista, I felt like I was part of an actual invasion force rolling through the old Soviet Union. Surreal.

Moving slowly with dozens of massive vehicles, it took us a few hours to get to Vista, a sprawling training area tucked in the hills just north of the Azerbaijani border (close enough that we could see the guard towers separating the countries off in the distance). To access the base, we drove through a cut in a massive ridgeline, winding our way through the draw and coming out on the eastern side at the base of the windswept hills rolling upwards towards another massive cliff face miles away to our east. At the base of these hills was the central training complex, a walled in compound replicating a forward operating base, or "FOB." As a lingering side effect of the former Georgian mission in Helmand Province, the battalion and one rifle company would occupy this FOB, while the remaining two rifle companies occupied two smaller bases, known as combat outposts, or "COPS." With A Co, I found myself at one of these COPS.

As most of the column pulled off the dirt trail to move into the battalion FOB, the A Co vehicles and GLT one continued on up into the Vista hills to our COP. Located out on a finger jutting over a long, winding valley, our home for the next week had four dirt walls, guard towers at each corner, a single vehicle entry point, about a dozen tents, and a line of hole-in-the-ground toilets, affectionately, if inappropriately, known as shitholes. The perfect place for a week of solid infantry training.

For the company FEX portion, the KTA instructors guided A Co through "lane" (station) training focused on dismounted foot patrols, mounted vehicle patrols, and cordon and search operations (surrounding a building with security and searching that same building for weapons or individuals). However, it became readily apparent how woefully unprepared A Co (and the whole battalion) was for actually executing these types of operations. Going back to my previous rant about the shortcomings of the KTA cadre's instruction on patrolling, we were seeing the results now. How can you expect a unit to plan and execute a combat patrol, which is not easy to do well, after a only a few hours of PowerPoint instruction? Answer: you can't.

From a training development perspective, a major shortcoming of the KTA instructional model, aside from just the limited time allocated, proved to be a lack of demonstrations. By not showing "what right looks like" in any of their instruction, the KTA staff set the 51stGLIB up for failure. They provided lectures, but they never took the next, critical step in adult-learning theory: demonstrate how that instruction looks in the real world, providing the bridge between lecture and successful execution.

But, despite the frustrations, I felt some little victories during the company FEX time at Vista. Going back to my golf analogy, we had a few "five percent" situations that kept my morale up, bringing me back for more. For one, the company FEX was my first opportunity to jointly plan an operation with the A Co commander. The two of us, struggling with communication via a MILTERP, planned a cordon and search of an old Soviet housing complex used for military exercises. And, while the execution of the plan was absolutely awful, this was a step in the right direction.

And, speaking of MILTERPS, this turned out to be the second little victory of really our whole time at Vista. At KTA, we always knew we could fall back on the reliable, contracted civilian terps if things got bad. Out at our COP with A Co, we only had MILTERPS. Though frustrating, this is how we'd deploy, and we learned some great lessons. Bottom line, we'd need to use some trial and error, very specific language, slow and deliberate speech, some good charades, and approach topics from multiple angles, but we started to get the hang of communicating via MILTERPS.

After the few days of company FEX work, the Marines were tighter both as a team and with our 51stGLIB counterparts, and the Georgians were more tactically proficient, if only incrementally so. I was seeing more and more that this would be a deployment of *little* victories.

# II-21

# VISTA, PART II: MILITARY TOURISM, PIZZA, AND "PITCH PERFECT"

·············································

I NITIALLY, THE PLAN was for the company FEX to flow seamlessly into the battalion FEX, transitioning from lane training into the twenty-four-hour operations of the battalion-level exercise. But, in a uniquely Georgian situation, the Ministry of Defense made a last minute decision to pull all the soldiers from the field for twenty-four hours between the two events so they could return home to vote in a recently scheduled national election. However, as one would expect if a bunch of Marines were given an overnight furlough from field training, most soldiers came back fairly hung over. Democracy's great, but, for young grunts in any country, booze is pretty nice, too.

Despite the disruption to training, the day and a half we had off while the 51stGLIB returned home was a nice way to relax before the battalion FEX. While most of the GTT Marines who were out at Vista headed back to KTA to work, it didn't make sense for the GLT guys to do the same. So, the morning the A Co soldiers left our COP, we decided to take our armored vehicle out for a little joyride through the training area for some military tourism. On the far eastern border of Vista, nestled into the cliffs in the distance, was an ancient, Georgian Orthodox monastery. Were this religious site, carved directly into the cliffs, not on a military base, it would absolutely find itself featured in Georgian travel guides. Standing in the shadow of this beautiful monastery, next to an armored vehicle and covered in dirt and sweat from the past few days in the field, was surreal, to say the least.

After about an hour exploring, we loaded into our vehicle and drove through the hills back to the "good life" of the main FOB to link up with the rest of the GLT. I say good life because, once life's conveniences (e.g. electricity, air conditioning, running water, toilets, etc) are taken away from you, little things take on far more relative significance. For us, after a few nights sleeping in tents in 100 plus degree heat, heading down to the main FOB to spend an afternoon relaxing in an air-conditioned "can" with the other guys on the team felt like a day at the Ritz Carlton. What could make the afternoon better? Ordering a dozen pizzas, watching *Pitch Perfect* projected up on the back wall of the can, and singing along like a bunch of giddy school girls. Yep—a perfect break in the action.

# II-22

# VISTA, PART III: KTA FRUSTRATIONS AND MORE GOLF

· · · · · · · · · · · · · · · · · · · · · · · · · · · · · · · · · · · · · · · · · · · · · · · · · · · · · · · · · · · · · · · · · · · ·

WITH THE GEORGIANS back at Vista, we rolled right into the battalion FEX. Whereas the company-level training had focused on limited duration lane training, this culminating event was supposed to replicate twenty-four-hour operations in Afghanistan. Within the context of a training scenario and with the use of role players from the KTA staff, the 51stGLIB would conduct round-the-clock patrolling and security operations out of its main FOB and two outlying COPs for the next several days. In practice, these twenty-four-hour operations looked a lot more like eighteen-hour operations, with the recurring question from our counterparts of "Why do we need to patrol at night?" We'd be fighting that question for the next eight months.

The first patrol A Co launched from our COP reinforced my despair from the company FEX. For one, no real planning had gone into this patrol. From an outsider's perspective, it seemed like the patrol was sent out more to appease the KTA staff than actually practice good patrol planning and execution. And, my frustration with this lack of planning and guidance for the patrol was exacerbated by KTA staff injects. In a training environment, you have to rely to some extent on the "I believe button," that is, the controllers running the exercise "painting" a scenario around you. In the case of KTA, these "paints" directed the A Co guys to do some pretty unsafe stuff. From setting up vehicle checkpoints in the middle of a street without support from their own vehicles to patrolling away from a village down the middle of a road without any "overwatch" covering movement from threats in that village, things were, in military parlance, more fucked up than a football bat.

My mom will probably tell you that I have many great qualities, but even she wouldn't be so blind to my imperfections as to pretend I handle frustration with external events well. And, this last part of an overall frustrating patrol, strolling away from a village like we were just walking to the corner store, finally put me through the roof. I took my helmet off, walked up to the KTA instructor overseeing this patrol, said, "You're out of your fucking mind if you think this is okay" (in English with no interpreter, but I think he probably got the gist of my exclamation), and walked directly back to the A Co COP to talk to the company commander and executive officer.

Was this little temper tantrum of mine a mature response to the situation? Absolutely not, but, there was a positive that came from it. After venting to the A Co leadership about my significant concerns over unsafe patrolling practices, I got my point across. I'd still spend the rest of my time with the Georgians fighting bad-practice, but following this exchange, the two Georgian leaders seemed to finally grasp why the Marines were there in the first place. We embedded with the Georgians as tactical *advisors*—we couldn't actually order them to do anything. And, as advisors, we had the same goals as the 51stGLIB, namely to accomplish our assigned mission and bring everyone home alive. But, to do our job, the Georgians needed to actually listen to our advice.

Making some strides in the whole working together thing, my above heart-to-heart led to the company commander and me jointly planning a cordon and search of a local "village" (really just a few tents set up with Georgian role players acting as Afghan locals). This would be the final golf situation of the battalion FEX, that is that five percent situation that would bring me back for more. The two of us, with the help of a MILTERP, planned the operation on a whiteboard. And, in addition to the planning, the commander asked that I lead the security element, the group of soldiers that would actually establish the cordon around the village, a huge coup for an advisor with no formal authority.

I took two major things away from this joint planning and execution. First, it was an opportunity to not only explain, but actually demonstrate, acceptable execution of a cordon and search (I say acceptable because, with most military operations, there isn't one right way to do things, but there are definitely plenty of wrong ways to do them). And second, more importantly, this cooperation set conditions for the marionette approach I sought in Afghanistan; that is, the Georgians running the show with the Marines planning and driving operations from behind the scenes. This may seem selfish, but I could really care less about building the overall capability of the Georgian Armed Forces. As a combat advisor, I had one driving concern: ensuring the GLT did everything in its power to set the 51stGLIB up for success in Afghanistan.

# II-23

# PIECES OF THE PUZZLE

......................................................

A S STATED, DUE to unfortunate scheduling constraints with the pre-deployment site survey (PDSS) to Afghanistan, the Boss, Maj Koba, and some key staff members missed all but the last day of the Vista FEX. But, despite the obvious drawback of not having these players at the final training event in Georgia, their trip provided us some critical information about our upcoming deployment. Most importantly, we now knew where we would be going and, broadly speaking, what we would be doing.

While the first eleven GLTs deployed to Helmand Province, the Marine Corps area of operations in southwest Afghanistan, we knew we wouldn't be going there, as responsibility for that region had been turned over to Afghan Security Forces. Additionally, the previous two GLTs had been in Kandahar Province, in southeastern Afghanistan, supporting the Army. However, we'd been told we wouldn't be going there either. Process of elimination left us suspecting that we'd end up at Bagram Airfield, the largest US air base in the country, located just to the north of Kabul, the Afghan capital. But, in the fluid world of the military, where plans can change at the drop of a hat, it took the PDSS actually *going* to Bagram to confirm that yes, that's where we'd deploy.

When the PDSS itinerary was finally confirmed just prior to the bulk of our team heading out to Vista, we had one more piece of the puzzle, that is, we could say where we were going. We still lacked a clear sense of what we'd be doing there, though. So, in good military fashion, as we typically exist in a world of having only part of the picture, the guys staying back in Georgia compiled a laundry list of questions for the PDSS team to answer. First and foremost, what would our mission be?

Starved for information and eager to get the full "data dump" from the PDSS team, I spent a full day at the Embassy with the Boss when the guys returned. Wearing my hat as the team's operations officer (as opposed to A Co advisor), I needed to start planning the initial phases of the deployment. And, supported by graphics and files from the Embassy's secure communications, the Boss walked me through his understanding of our mission.

Broadly speaking, we'd own four key responsibilities at Bagram. First, we'd own a portion of the outside-the-wire patrolling mission, focused on disrupting rocket and IED attacks against the airfield. Related to this, we'd also be responsible for manning a quick reaction force (QRF), a vehicle-mounted unit within the base that could respond to contingencies throughout our area of operations at a moment's notice. Third, and also somewhat expected, we'd own a majority of the inside-the-wire security for the base. That is, we'd be responsible for securing Bagram's perimeter and access points. Lastly, and not anticipated, we'd have a secondary advising responsibility. In addition to the GLT's primary role as combat advisors to the 51stGLIB, we'd have to figure out how to train and advise an Afghan National Army (ANA) battalion, a task that would remain vaguely defined until we actually arrived in Bagram.

Beyond providing us more pieces of the puzzle in terms of our responsibilities, the PDSS also provided us a deeper appreciation for threats we'd be facing. While our team of Georgians and

Marines was in Bagram, a suicide bomber killed four soldiers from a Czech security force also stationed on the base, demonstrating quite clearly the realities of the upcoming deployment.

# II-24

# POST-FIELD ACTIONS AND CRUNCHING NUMBERS

....................................................

W HEN THE BATTALION FEX finally finished, we spent a half day cleaning up our spaces on Vista, doing our best to leave it in better shape than we found it. And, with that finished, we reversed the previous week's massive armored vehicle movement, rolling back through the Georgian countryside and outlying urban districts to KTA.

On base, we kicked off a pretty standard routine of post-field actions. Regardless of where in the world you were, the following would happen: 1) Post up in the GLT office to get some AC; 2) Someone turns on some music; 3) A couple guys grab drinks for the team; 4) Massive plugs of chewing tobacco get stuffed in faces; and, 5) Spend a couple hours bullshitting and cleaning your weapons. Once all weapons are cleaned, accounted for, and turned into the armory, guys are cut loose to put away gear, shower, and get some chow. There's definitely some catharsis to this seemingly monotonous routine.

After we all cleaned up, we headed into Rustavi for a bite at our local Georgian restaurant. Massive amounts of food, beer, and *chacha* unfolded into some pent-up debauchery.

Despite a fairly significant hangover, I woke up early the next morning for a day of crunching numbers at the embassy. Armed with both key information about our mission and points of contact for decision-makers in Afghanistan, we needed to put together a few options for how many Marines we'd actually bring to Bagram. In addition to the core GLT members, the guys we'd trained in Camp Pendleton and deployed to Georgia with, the full complement in Afghanistan would include two other detachments: 1) A team of Marines specifically focused on fire support, drawn from the Air Naval Gunfire Liaison Company (ANGLICO, pronounced "ang-li-coh"); and, 2) A group of Marines known as the "enabler detachment," comprised of a variety of maintenance, communications, supply, and motor vehicle specialists.

At the embassy, the Boss and I would need to put together three different options for numbers of ANGLICO and enabler Marines we would need to execute our mission. Recently, the Force Management Level (FML), a White House mandated cap on the number of US troops allowed in Afghanistan, was cut down to 9,800. This reduction had spurred cost-cutting across the board, and we expected the shit to roll downhill to our numbers. So, we spent the day looking at both our assigned tasks, as identified during the PDSS, and the risks to successfully accomplishing those tasks associated with three different levels of Marines.

After a day of coffee, aspirin, and putting together Excel spreadsheets matching available troops at different levels to assigned tasks, we had three different options, and their associated pros/cons, developed. At the top, we outlined the mission if we had all of the Marines initially assigned to the mission. Next, we cut twenty-five percent off that, and we outlined where we'd be stretched thin. Last, we showed the "nuclear option," that is, how we would execute our tasks with a forty percent reduction in forces, to include the significant risks associated with this option. After completing our work, we forwarded these products up the Marine chain-of-command and on to Afghanistan for approval.

A couple of weeks later, we got the final word. We'd need to take our "nuclear option" total and chop another ten percent. At the end of the day, Marines were going to figure it the fuck out, but these numbers spread us dangerously thin, and the Boss, as the guy in charge, would have to make some pretty serious decisions about where he was willing to assume risk with regard to advising the Georgians at this final number. On the positive side, we now knew for certain how many guys would be on the GLT, and we could plan accordingly. On the negative side, the effects of the recent FML reduction would be the first indicators that, for the rest of our deployment, political decisions would have serious, negative consequences on our abilities to operate effectively.

# II-25

# OFF TO GERMANY

........................................

I N THE FORMAL military support agreement signed between the United States and the Republic of Georgia, one of the latter's stipulations mandated a final, US -run mission rehearsal exercise (MRE) before actually deploying to Afghanistan. Essentially, Georgia wanted two things from this MRE. In the short-term, the Georgian Armed Forces wanted to confirm that, to the fullest extent possible, the battalions heading to Afghanistan were prepared for the fight. In the long-term, Georgia sought to build its own training capacity, further increasing the KTA staff's ability to, without outside support, train and assess a battalion before deployment. In this respect, despite being US run, our final exercise would have a high level of KTA involvement.

In theory, each year that the KTA trainers participated in a US -run mission rehearsal exercise, they would move closer and closer to actually hosting and leading this MRE themselves. Until that point, GLTs and their partner battalions would fly up to Germany for the final month of their pre-deployment training, where the US Army had a large base, Joint Multinational Readiness Center (JMRC) Hohenfels, designed specifically for this sort of foreign force training. So, in the week or so between wrapping up at Vista and leaving for Germany, we attempted to build some training priorities to get the most out of our time in Hohenfels. With the PDSS back, we now not only knew what our mission would be, but we knew how the unit we would replace was operating and, more importantly, what was and wasn't working for them. For the GLT, we saw our time in Hohenfels as an opportunity to address the shortcomings of the training in Georgia so far. Specifically, we knew we had to get as many reps as possible planning and executing patrols—in vehicles, on foot, and a combination of the two. We had to improve.

In addition to seeing our time in Germany as a great training opportunity, preparing to actually *go* to Germany had its own training value. That is, we viewed picking up and moving as a team to Hohenfels as a rehearsal for our movement to Afghanistan. With that in mind, the day of our departure to Germany, we briefed our plan for movement to the team, did final gear checks, loaded our kit into a flatbed truck, then piled into a bunch of contracted Land Rovers for the drive to the Tbilisi Airport. Thirty minutes later, our huge convoy of SUVs and military transport trucks carrying the 51stGLIB soldiers rolled out onto the airport's tarmac, pulling up next to our contracted 737 passenger jet. For a brief moment, I actually felt pretty "VIP" with this treatment, that is, except for the whole needing-to-load-our-own-bags-onto-the-plane thing.

Next stop, Nuremberg International Airport!

# II-26

# HOHENFELS: AN ORIENTATION

····················································

W E LANDED IN Nuremberg at night, were whisked through security, and took an hour or so bus ride to JMRC (aka "Jam Rock") Hohenfels. With essentially no ambient light in the rolling hills of the Bavarian countryside, it was tough to tell where we were going, leaving us with no real sense of our surroundings. We eventually pulled down a street lined on both sides with rows of one-story, barracks-like buildings, which, as logic would suggest, were, in fact, barracks.

To ease the chaos and confusion of a whole battalion's worth of soldiers moving into a bunch of different barracks at night, the 51stGLIB, KTA staff, and the GTT had each flown some guys into Germany ahead of the main body. So, when we unloaded the buses, we were met by guys who'd already laid out who would be living where, labeled the barracks buildings accordingly, and showed us where we needed to go. For the GLT, we had our own barracks, which was divided internally by a long, central corridor with about a dozen "squad bays" (military-style rooms with neatly arranged rows of bunk beds) on each side. After confirming we had all our gear and getting everyone situated in their bays, we passed out.

I woke up the next morning to a gorgeous, sunny day and was absolutely struck by the marked difference between the lush, wooded hillsides surrounding us and the barren, windswept hills of Vista and central Georgia. Enjoying being back in this sort of countryside, we spent that first full day figuring out the lay of the land at Hohenfels. Turns out, the fenced-in area where we were living was a camp within the broader Hohenfels base known as Camp Albertshof, which began as a German military facility in the 1930s, held POWs during World War II, and served as temporary housing for refugees and displaced persons immediately following the war. As the Cold War kicked off, the US Army retained possession of both Camp Albertshof and the surrounding Hohenfels training areas. Eventually, Hohenfels and its US 7th Army staff assumed responsibilities for training multinational partners in Europe, making it a logical fit for the Georgian / Marine MRE.

Up the road about a half mile from Camp Albertshof, Hohenfels had its "main side," the area of base with the commissary (military grocery store), mini-marts, gym, restaurants, offices, and a bowling alley with a great German-style *bierhall*—basically the facilities used by the soldiers stationed at Hohenfels and their families on a daily basis. The countryside surrounding Albertshof and main side was the actual training area. Known as "the Box," this massive area of wooded hills, replica villages filled with role players, forward operating bases (FOBs), combat outposts (COPs), and miles and miles of tank trails would be where we'd spend the majority of our MRE.

For the first few days in Germany, we'd stay at Albertshof, finishing up our orientation, checking out vehicles and other gear, and conducting specialty skills training (counter-IED lanes, driver training, and Blue Force Tracker (BFT) familiarization— basically a military GPS system). Next, we'd head out into the Box in a fashion similar to Vista, with one rifle company and the battalion staff at a main FOB, and the remaining two companies at outlying COPs. For the first half of our time in the Box, the

Army trainers—accompanied by KTA staff—would lead each company through squad- and platoon-size training. For the second half, known in Hohenfels lingo as the "X days," we'd actually conduct our evaluated, multi-day culminating exercise. It should be pretty apparent from this description, but the MRE would essentially be a longer, more robust version of the company and battalion FEX at Vista.

While we were all ready to get the training going, there were a couple benefits to having a few low key days on the front end of the MRE. First, we were able to play some pick-up basketball at an outdoor court on Albertshof—GLT Marine versus 51stGLIB. We played a couple nights in a row, and the Marines thoroughly thrashed the Georgians, which was a much needed boost to our collective morale after the football and baseball embarrassments back in Georgia.

These first few days also gave us an opportunity to build some new bonds and further mesh as a team, as the whole ANGLICO detachment and a few key players from our enablers joined us for the MRE. And, as chance would have it, we had a great opportunity to celebrate those first few days. On the first of the month, when new promotions are announced, we found out that three of our corporals had been selected for sergeant—a huge deal. To properly commemorate this occasion, we figured we'd take advantage of Hohenfels, and the entire GLT drove to the ruins of a mountaintop castle that happened to fall within the boundaries of Hohenfels. As the sun set over the tree-lined hilltops of the Bavarian countryside, the Boss promoted these three Marines on the crumbled walls of this castle—an absolutely incredible experience.

Naturally, to properly finish our orientation of Hohenfels, we'd have to take these newly promoted sergeants down to the *bierhall* for some celebratory drinks. Several hours later, after doing a full round of introductions with all the newly arrived Marines and drinking through the bar's stock of German beers, we made the drunken walk back to Albertshof, tighter than we'd been that morning (I suppose in two ways). Like our Kangaroo Court back in California and the *supra* our first week in Georgia, this night further reinforced my belief that, there's no better way to shatter barriers than by sharing a few drinks.

# II-27

# SPECIALTY SKILLS AND GEORGIAN "WINNING"

..............................................

D URING THE FIRST few days of specialty skills training at Hohenfels, the counter-IED training in particular provided outstanding insight into Georgian pride (and the frustrations associated with it). In a typical counter-IED training, soldiers first receive some formal instruction, typically a PowerPoint slideshow, followed by an actual demonstration of the equipment and skills taught. This demonstration then leads into practical application, with soldiers actually walking an "IED lane," using the equipment and skills from the lesson to identify replica IEDs.

Looking at the big picture, the goal of the above IED lane training is not to find a specific IED. Rather, the ultimate take-aways are meant to be the skills and familiarity with equipment that will keep you alive when dealing with an environment riddled with real IEDs. However, the Georgians saw things a bit differently. With the 51stGLIB soldiers, the first group would head down the IED lane, get notionally killed by an IED, and then return to the start and tell the next group of soldiers exactly where the IED was emplaced. In turn, the next group would walk straight to the IED without using any equipment or counter-IED skills from the lesson, point to the IED, and claim victory, not understanding what "winning" truly meant.

Due to the extreme pride of the Georgians, and a lingering post-Soviet zero-defect approach to the military, it was difficult to get the point across to the soldiers that this "game" wasn't about finding a specific IED. This training was about practicing and refining the skills necessary to find unknown IEDs while deployed. However, having dealt with similarly proud cultures in the past, the crafty US Army instructors at Hohenfels had a pretty good solution. After the first couple rounds of Georgians "gaming the game" by clearly knowing exactly where all the training IEDs were located, the instructors adapted. Between each turn, these explosive ordnance disposal (EOD) techs, guys who'd been dealing with improvised explosives in Iraq and Afghanistan for years, would seed the lane with new IEDs. Naturally, these new IEDs significantly fucked with the Georgian's dope.

You could almost see their thoughts when "killed" by an IED they hadn't expected: "But I couldn't have stepped on that IED; my buddies didn't tell me it was going to be there."

Whether with IEDs or placing opposition forces in different buildings during urban patrol training, "gaming the game" would be a recurring problem, and this backwards-logic approach offered good insight into the mindset of the average Georgian soldier. For such a proud culture, the idea of learning by doing, failing, and improving doesn't make sense.

Pride and saving face are the keys, and the GLT Marines would need to continue to find the best way to account for this reality during the MRE and our deployment to Afghanistan.

# II-28

# TERPS, NEPOTISM, AND LIFE AS AN ADVISOR

••••••••••••••••••••••••••••••••••••••••••••••••

I KNOW I'VE written about it several times, but we'd spent a significant amount of time in Georgia evaluating and ranking MILTERPs, as they'd be the ones deploying with us. While we got a taste of things to come at Vista back in Georgia, the Hohenfels MRE would really throw us into the deep end. For the two or so weeks we'd be out in the Box training, we'd solely be working with MILTERPs, making these guys linchpins of our success (or failure).

We were confident about the MILTERP situation heading into Germany, though. Prior to leaving, the Boss and Claymore had compiled all of our evaluations from KTA, ranked the interpreters, and presented recommendations to Maj Koba on the ones with the highest levels of English proficiency. Leaving this meeting, both of our guys were extremely optimistic, as the battalion commander both clearly appreciated our effort and recommendations, and, more importantly, he explicitly endorsed our conclusions, having seen first-hand the work of good and bad MILTERPs during our time in Georgia.

Despite the concurrence of both the GLT and Maj Koba, we

were in for a surprise. Upon arriving in Germany, we realized that many of the *tajimans* (Kartouli and Dari for interpreter, and something we'd yell countless times over the course of the deployment) that had been selected for the MRE were the least proficient of the group, the ones we'd lumped into the category of "Do not take—do not speak English at all."

While I won't go down a rabbit hole of every experience with bad MILTERPs, here's one example of what we were trying to avoid. At one brief back in KTA, a few Marines were waiting for a civilian interpreter to arrive to begin discussing something with the Georgians, leading to that awkward silence inherent to language barriers. Eventually, the terp showed up, out of breath from running to get to the meeting, and looked at a fat, grumpy Georgian major in the back of the room, someone I didn't recognize but assumed was part of the KTA staff. Apparently, that major was technically a MILTERP, but responded to the civilian terp's Kartouli inquiry of, "Hey, why didn't you help out since I was running late?" with a shrug of his shoulders. Holy shit, man! You're claiming to be a MILTERP, but you don't speak English!? Yep, he was waiting for us at the MRE.

When the Boss approached Maj Koba about our concerns with the final MILTERP list, we received a very clear lesson in Georgian politics and nepotism. Ultimately, the MILTERPs were chosen by the Ministry of Defense, and English proficiency had nothing to do with the selection process. Getting on this deployment, which would serve as a critical promotion milestone for many Georgian careers, was a matter of who knew whom at the Ministry. If you weren't a lackey or relative of a Ministry bureaucrat, you weren't going to Afghanistan, regardless of your English skills. As one might expect, this nepotism led to significant headaches for everyone, both Marine and Georgian, down the road.

## II-29

# OUT IN THE "BOX"

......................................

A FTER A WEEK of orientation and specialty skills training, we headed out into the Box. Though we received a quick drive-around when we arrived, it wasn't until we loaded up into our tactical vehicles and left Albertshof that I truly grasped the scale of the Hohenfels training area. Winding throughout the sprawling, wooded landscape of rolling hills were miles and miles of both paved roads and dirt trails. And, dotted throughout the countryside were numerous "villages" for training. While I'd trained in plenty of these replica towns on Marine bases Stateside, nowhere had I seen such money and effort put into the smallest details—all the way down to drapes on the windows. Having spent the majority of my time as a Marine officer living out of the back of the VW Jetta, these training villages looked downright luxurious in comparison.

In addition to the large staff of US Army trainers and evaluators on the base, Hohenfels employs a bunch of civilians as script writers for training. Depending on the unit involved and exercise purpose, nearly any context and backstory can be imposed on the generic map of Hohenfels. For us, and once again a hangover from the Georgian time in southwest Afghanistan, Helmand was superimposed on the whole MRE for us. Route names, FOBs, and COPs were all named after those in Helmand, which meant nothing for us, as we would not be in Helmand. But, organizational change is difficult, and some decision-maker had clearly deemed it not worth the effort to update the scenario for our upcoming Bagram mission.

With an outdated scenario, we took an outdated approach, replicating our time in Vista by using one main FOB and two outlying COPs. And, in line with this structure, the Boss and I once again decided that it would make more sense for me to focus on my role as A Co infantry advisor than team operations officer for this training. So, the day we left for the field, SSgt Johnny, Sgt Curtis, and I, along with the ANGLICO team working with us, loaded into two HMMWVs and drove out to COP "Ertoba" (a Georgian outpost in Helmand).

The COP, our home for the next two weeks, would be a pretty good place for training. Built with a trench-and-wall perimeter lined with security towers, Ertoba had semi-permanent tents for berthing, some wooden structures for setting up a COC and giving briefs, and, the crown jewel, actual porta-johns (to most Marines, "porta-shitters"—an inappropriate but apt description). After a week of the Vista hole-in-the-ground system, this final amenity turned COP Ertoba into a five-star resort for us. Once again, the little luxuries in life fall along a relative spectrum.

One hundred meters outside the COP's walls was a robust town that would soon be occupied by dozens of Afghan role players. Not satisfied with just some plywood structures, the Army went all out in building these towns—stocked stores, mosques, a police station, unique houses, a madrassa (Islamic school), and about twenty five other buildings—this place had it all. With utterly no experience in urban patrolling to date, training here would be an interesting experience for the Georgians.

Less than an hour after arriving at our COP, the Georgians had already broken out power tools (I have no idea where they found them). Apparently "carpenter" was a position required in every company, and it was a sight to see these guys work. Every inch of scrap wood in and around our base was gathered up, and, a couple hours later, we had new tables, wooden terrain models for briefing missions, parking dividers for the tactical vehicles, and small-scale plywood "buildings" to conduct walk-throughs. Unbelievable. But, as impressive as things looked, it remained to be seen whether this new construction was simply another Georgian tactic to impress "higher," or tools to actually facilitate training.

# II-30

# ARMY LASER TAG, AND ANOTHER ROLE FOR THE GLT

·················································

T HERE'S A JOKE in the Marine Corps that, once the Army is done with its equipment, it gets passed along to the Marines— the result of a chronic inferiority complex about funding compared with our sister service. And, we saw the reality of this joke in action at Hohenfels with the Army's "laser tag" system. Called MILES gear, the Multiple Integrated Laser Engagement System turns force-on-force training into something out of *Starship Troopers*. Each rifle and machine gun is equipped with a laser that's calibrated to the weapon's actual sites. So, when a weapon has blank ammunition in it, every time those blank rounds are fired, the vibration of the shot "fires" laser energy (harmless to human eyes). On the receiving end, every individual training wears laser reflective devices, and a loud noise is emitted when you're "shot."

For Marines, force-on-force training involves each Marine receiving a handful of blank rounds, and officers and staff NCOs follow each unit around, assessing casualties during each blank-fire engagement. Unfortunately, with no target feedback (like what the MILES gear provides), this Marine model often leads into arguments of "No man, I shot you!"

In theory, the Army's MILES gear overcomes this who-shot-whom deficiency of the Marine Corps' "on-the-cheap" training. However, for the Georgians, this high-tech equipment simply became a time-consuming detractor of training value. And, for the Marines, the Army's emphasis on MILES gear became a significant point of contention between us and the Hohenfels training staff, the "Timberwolves." In addition to spending an entire day at the motor pool signing out MILES gear and attaching it to our vehicles, we needed to spend an entire day once out at our COP issuing individual gear to the soldiers. Time is a finite resource, and we were already significantly concerned with the Georgians' lack of experience patrolling. The MILES sideshow exacerbated an already limited opportunity to train before getting to Afghanistan.

Once again, the use of MILES gear is a great idea in theory and in the right situation, but, with the Georgians, using this equipment amounted to putting the cart before the horse. That is, the Timberwolves placed so much emphasis on these high-tech training aids while failing to understand that the Georgian soldiers lacked a baseline understanding of the military skills those same aids were meant to assess. Despite telling the Army trainers multiple times that this MILES gear would simply detract from training, with Georgians spending more time screwing around with the gear than focusing on actual combat training, we pushed forward with laser tag.

Looking back on it, I don't know what drove the Army's insistence on using MILES gear more: A) the sunk-cost of having invested so much in MILES gear, maintenance, and contractor support; or B) a true love and commitment to the gear's value. The truth was likely somewhere in the middle. Either way, after spending a whole day at our COP passing out gear, calibrating lasers on rifles, and trying to unfuck the equipment, one of the Timberwolves told me that there'd be a contractor out at 0515 the next morning to troubleshoot gear. I adamantly tried cancelling this appointment. First, none of the Georgians would be awake. Second, even if they were awake, they'd have nothing to give to the contractor to troubleshoot, as they had no baseline for whether the lasers were even working or not.

As expected, at 0515 the next morning, the MILES contractor showed up at our COP, no Georgians asked for help, and the Timberwolves tried venting their frustration to me. So, when some Army trainer barged into my tent and tried yelling at me, he received a very curt: "Get the fuck out of my tent. I told you how this was going to unfold." This interaction led to another combat advisor "epiphany moment." I realized very clearly that, moving forward with training and our time in Afghanistan, one of the GLT Marines' most critical roles would be serving as cultural go-betweens with our Georgian partners and other US units—explaining, facilitating, and, where necessary, defending the 51stGLIB.

# II-31

# "OMEGA" LANES AND CENTRALIZATION GONE BAD

.............................................

W ITH OUR MILES gear as unscrewed as it was going to be, we were ready to begin the situational training exercise (STX) lanes. These lanes were designed to put squad-, platoon-, and company-sized elements of Georgian soldiers into realistic situations in which they'd need to apply different combat skills. For the Marines, this was exactly the training we'd been waiting to begin, as it would include tons of repetitions of patrolling fundamentals for the 51stGLIB.

The night before the STX lanes began, the lead Army Timberwolf trainer for A Co grabbed one of the civilian interpreters (a group of them came up from Georgia to support this sort of administrative work) and briefed all the company leadership on the plan for the next day's training: timeline, training events, locations, et cetera. Sitting in on the brief and discussing with the company commander afterword, I felt confident that everything would run smoothly the next day. Oh man, what a mistake on my part. It's a military aphorism to, "plan for and expect the worst, but hope for the best." I'd come back to this theme frequently over the course of the deployment.

The major point of friction turned out to be what the Army dubbed "Omega Lanes." During this training, all of the 51st GLIB's platoon commanders and platoon sergeants would conduct the same squad-sized STX lanes that their respective squads would be going through, but they'd be doing it separately. This is actually a great idea in theory, as it's designed to let platoon leadership learn and make mistakes without losing face in front of the junior enlisted soldiers in their platoons.

While the Omega Lanes were a great concept, and they did significantly improve the tactical understanding of the platoon leadership, these gains came at the initial cost of a day's fucked up training. As I've tried to make clear, in the centralized, post-Soviet mindset of the Georgian Armed Forces, notions of individual initiative and personal drive to train are not promoted among junior soldiers. Down to the most junior guy, individuals do everything in their power to avoid making decisions on their own, fearing repercussions from "higher."

The above mindset combined with a general confusion among A Co's squad leaders to significantly disrupt the first day's training. Without platoon commanders and platoon sergeants around to tell them what to do, not a single squad showed up to its assigned starting location for the first day of STX lanes. And, when asked what they were doing, not a single squad leader had any clue what they were supposed to be doing during the training. Apparently the platoon leadership, all of whom had sat in on the previous night's brief from the Army Timberwolf, didn't pass on anything about the first day's plan to their guys. Bottom line, that first day's training was essentially a wash by the time everything was fixed.

Significantly frustrated that first day, I did some self-reflection to try to figure out where things went wrong, and I settled on three main failures. First, platoon and company leadership failed to ensure their guys understood the plan for the day. Second, squad leaders failed to demonstrate any sense of initiative to confirm the plan. And third, the greatest one, I failed to foresee all of these easily anticipated problems. As their advisors, we were supposed to be the subject-matter experts on all things Georgian, anticipating and solving problems before they arise. In the future, I would need to do a far better job of this.

After talking through things with the other GLT Marines out at the A Co COP, we adjusted for Day 2. For each one of the STX events, we'd have one Marine assigned to "facilitate" that event. While the Timberwolves and the KTA staffs were the ones running the training, the GLT Marines would supervise the process and ensure the A Co soldiers were where they needed to be, when they needed to be there. We did this by spending each night of the STX lanes building graphic depictions of the next day's plans, and then briefing those plans to all key leaders the night before each event. This led to long days and nights, but things ran much more smoothly for the remainder of squad and platoon STX lanes.

And, there was an added, longer-term benefit to our handling of the STX lane plans. By building these plans and assuming the role of "all knowing" advisor, we further set conditions for playing the role of marionette in Afghanistan, that is, putting a Georgian face forward, but planning and making everything happen behind the scenes.

# II-32

# WORK SMARTER, NOT HARDER

......................................................

I THINK I'VE made it clear in my above words that, after three months of working with them, I had an open disdain for the Georgian trainers from KTA. To return to the political realities of the Georgian Ministry of Defense, the 51stGLIB leadership was significantly concerned with the feedback these KTA trainers would provide to their higher headquarters. As a battalion commander, Maj Koba would not be evaluated based upon the tactical proficiency of the 51stGLIB. Rather, the assessment results KTA trainers provided depended largely upon their relationships with those being assessed (once again, it's impossible to escape nepotism).

As a result of this situation, and the fact that all of the battalion's leadership readily understood how the Georgian system worked, 51stGLIB soldiers continued to do silly, tactically unsound shit the KTA staff told them to do. Apparently it was better to just not rock the boat and risk offending their KTA evaluators than actually try to do the right thing. In fairness, though, I can't blame them, as I have the luxury of being an outsider. I'd likely act in the same way if I existed in a system where relationships, not performance, dictated one's progression and jobs.

Regardless of why the situation existed, the reality at our COP in Hohenfels was that I had a very open and toxic relationship with the KTA staff assigned to evaluate A Co. In the Georgian Deployment Program design for the MRE at Hohenfels, the US Army Timberwolves would take point on planning and coordinating all the STX lanes and associated support. Concurrently, the KTA trainers, as part of the Georgian "capacity building" agreement with the United States, would actually take point on evaluating and debriefing each STX lane. Personnel-wise, this meant that out at A Co's COP, there were a half dozen KTA trainers led by a Georgian major for the duration of the STX lanes.

Still fuming and generally infuriated with the KTA staff from our time in Georgia, and particularly our time out at Vista, I went into the STX lanes with a pretty poor attitude. After playing the KTA game on their home turf, now that we were on a US base, I thought to myself, *We're on American soil now, so you can get the fuck out of my way.* Once again, in hindsight it's easy to see how toxic an approach this was.

Something changed in my outlook during the squad-size STX lanes, and I had an epiphany of sorts. Rather than being a stubborn asshole, I could work together with these guys from KTA and much more effectively get across my debrief points from each training event (this also seems readily obvious in retrospect). In my old approach, following each training lane, the Georgian squad or platoon conducting the training would receive feedback from one of the Marines and one of the KTA trainers. After the KTA remarks, I'd very dismissively provide my own feedback, frequently contradicting what had just been said and barely hiding my disdain. This approach proved extremely counterproductive, as it confused the 51stGLIB soldiers, who had to sort between multiple opinions on military tactics, and it caused unnecessary friction and frustration.

Enter my new *modus operandi.* During each lane, I started walking with a Georgian interpreter and the KTA evaluator for that lane, and the three of us would conduct an internal review of how the training went prior to talking to the soldiers. These conversations very quickly made me realize that the Marines and KTA trainers agreed on far more than I'd been willing to admit. Following these internal reviews, the KTA instructor would then lead the debriefs to the training unit, hitting the key takeaways we'd just discussed.

This new approach accomplished two key items. First, it got all parties on the same page and largely stopped the passing of conflicting guidance to the Georgian soldiers. And second, on a more personal level, my life got a whole lot easier. Turns out it's far easier to embrace and work within the system than try to overhaul it. Who'd have thought? And, while my change in approach seemed fairly self-explanatory, this adjustment served as a significant shift in mindset at the time vis-à-vis combat advising: *a Georgian solution with full buy-in by the Georgians always beats a US solution with partial to no buy-in.*

# II-33

# FINDING THE SWEET SPOT

...............................................

**B**EFORE MOVING INTO the evaluated "X days" of the MRE, we would have to complete a company-level STX training. Whereas the first week of STX lanes had focused on squad and platoon training, this culminating event would include all of A Company. Specifically, we'd need to plan and conduct an assault on what the Timberwolves dubbed an "out of sector village," that is, one of the other training towns located adjacent to another Hohenfels COP about 10km away from our own. And, while the mission was unrealistic for us (we would not be conducting full-scale assaults on villages around Bagram), I figured this'd be a good exercise in planning, coordination, and using the small-unit tactics we'd rehearsed during the earlier STX lanes.

With the confusion and frustration of the first day of STX lanes still fresh in my mind, I attempted to be more proactive with shaping this company assault. To account for the language barrier, and just because it makes sense to depict these sorts of things visually, I planned out the company assault on PowerPoint with imagery of Hohenfels, going slide-by-slide to demonstrate each phase of the plan. I figured this would be a good technique for both me to talk through things with the A Co leadership, and for that leadership to use to brief everyone else.

Shalva, the company commander, was thrilled with the product. Turns out, the battalion commander would be going to each of the rifle companies to receive briefs by his company commanders on how they would execute their respective assaults. The slides I put together became the "meat and potatoes" of Shalva's brief, and he got good feedback from Maj Koba. Another two wins: 1) further solidified Shalva's and my relationship and mutual trust; and 2) further reinforced my grand design of functioning as a marionette.

Another major benefit of this company-level training was that we'd been given a full day to get ready for it, which gave us an excuse to demonstrate to the Georgian soldiers some fundamentals of mission preparation, namely, the importance of rehearsals. In many respects, solid rehearsals were the "missing link" of the Georgian Armed Forces. Leadership grasped the importance of thorough, well-developed briefs. However, they saw these products as shiny things, an end in and of themselves. In reality, briefs don't exist for those building them. They exist for those executing the plan. A brief is only as effective as how well it sets the people conducting the plan up for success in execution, and that success hinges upon solid rehearsals.

Knowing how important rehearsals would be to pulling off this company assault, something A Company had not done before, I pulled Shalva aside after he briefed Maj Koba. We had the entire next day to rehearse before actually conducting the assault the following morning, but quality rehearsals would depend on clear guidance from him and his platoon commanders. He nodded in acknowledgment, but, with MILTERPS, you never quite know how much is going through. I passed out not entirely optimistic about the next day.

Turns out I had significantly underestimated the effort the company was going to put into these rehearsals. When I woke up, a sergeant from the A Co headquarters grabbed my attention with a "Cap-i-tan-i, Cap-i-tan-i," and pulled me out to the wide-open, vehicle-staging area in the middle of the COP. In typical Georgian fashion, the carpenters had been at it again, and a plywood replica of the village had been built. Shalva had a shit-eating grin on his face when we made eye contact, and I didn't need an interpreter to let me know what he was thinking: "How about this for your rehearsals, Marine?"

The whole day turned into one of those "five percent days" from my golf analogy. Spending the day briefing, rehearsing, and confirming our plan for the assault, complete with A Co small-unit leaders moving around the model village talking through their specific roles, I couldn't have been happier. I suppose this seems like a ridiculous thing to fill someone with euphoria, but this level of thorough preparation and military professionalism was the gold standard to advising, that is, a foreign force doing things the way the Marine Corps does them.

The next morning, the assault actually started pretty well. As the Georgians were still familiarizing themselves with the Blue Force Trackers and GPS devices, we moved Marines around into Georgian vehicles to help navigate all the elements of the company to their different rally points prior to commencing the assault—all went smoothly there. However, things fell to shit pretty quickly once the first force of Georgians made it into the village. Anyone who's ever played "Cowboys and Indians" on the playground would recognize how things unfolded, with unit discipline falling apart and guys running around shooting aimlessly in all directions.

As we would be conducting most of our Afghan patrols in urban areas, watching this "death blossom" of firing in all directions, albeit just MILES gear vice real bullets, was worrisome. However, you have to take the good with the bad, and I learned another important lesson about advising. I'd failed A Co by developing a plan that required too much detailed coordination. While they did a great job briefing and rehearsing it, the plan involved some things these guys just hadn't done before, and I chose to ignore this reality (hence the abortion of a performance in the town).

Moving forward, to be successful in both planning and executing operations, I'd need to find the sweet spot between the level of detail in the plan and mission accomplishment. Basically, ops would need to be detailed enough to be safe in execution (e.g. not having friendly forces shooting towards each other), but simple enough that the coordinating details wouldn't simply get ignored in execution. This is a reality for planning with any organization, I suppose, but I would just have to adjust my sweet spot to meet the needs of our Georgian partners.

# II-34

# THE MRE

..................

T HE STX LANES wrapped up following the company assault, and the battalion transitioned into its week-long, evaluated Mission Rehearsal Exercise (MRE). The "X days." Aside from the outdated construct of the 51stGLIB spread across one large FOB and two outlying COPs this evaluation would attempt to replicate what we'd be doing in Afghanistan as closely as possible. And, despite the many frustrations of STX lanes, the high-quality of training built by the Army Timberwolves and the Georgian effort led to a noticeable improvement in tactical proficiency across the battalion—still not where we needed to be, but much better than ten days prior when we first arrived in Hohenfels.

The kick-off event the night the MRE began was an attack on each of the 51stGLIB's positions and breach of our perimeters by the OPFOR (opposition forces, or "bad guys"). While some of the OPFOR actions were unrealistic (an incidental result of knowing you'll only be shot by a MILES laser), it was a good event. The situation became extremely chaotic, it was night, which further clouded people's full understanding of what was happening, but the Georgians actually responded pretty well to the breach. Despite OPFOR members scaling the outer wall of the COP, the A Co soldiers effectively isolated that part of base, prevented the intruders from reaking havoc throughout the whole outpost, and generally minimized damage.

Looking at this event from a trainer's perspective, I saw the OPFOR's unrealistic actions for what they were: an attempt to induce stress and chaos in the worst-case scenario of your base being overrun and see how the Georgians responded. Shalva, on the other hand, lost his mind with frustration at the lead Timber-wolf, and I had to break up a pretty heated argument between the two. It took me a while to calm him down, but eventually I was able to convince Shalva that no one can "win" this exercise. Rather, the breach by the OPFOR is meant to and will happen, regardless of the training audience's actions. The training value is A) understanding the risks inherent to a base attack; and B) gaining an understanding and appreciation of the chaos that will accompany one. These are both valuable lessons, especially with the history of catastrophic base attacks against Georgian outposts in Afghanistan.

The remainder of the MRE continued in a cycle of ups and downs in terms of activity, which I suppose would also replicate our deployment. In the A Co combat operations center (COC), Georgian watch officers communicated with A Co patrols outside-the-wire while also reporting back to the battalion COC at the main FOB. And, seeking to validate our vision for command and control on deployment, there was always a Marine in these company COCs who could serve as the English-language, parallel line of communication back to our Marine watch officer in the battalion COC. This redundancy would help ensure that, if guys out on patrol needed external support (casualty evacuation, fire support, etc.), we wouldn't have to rely on a MILTERP to get it there.

We quickly fell into a standard routine. We'd go out on a mounted patrol (the Georgians insisted on having the vics on all patrols), stand a few hours COC watch, grab a couple hours rest, then do it again. As part of the training design, the Timberwolves made sure each of the companies dealt with some "injects," stressful scenarios tied into the training to force the Georgians to act: recovering a crashed drone and evacuating civilians after an IED attack in our village, among others. These events drove us to hit training objectives, and they helped us avoid complacency, something we'd also face over seven months in Afghanistan. Bottom line, the training was far superior to our time in Vista. And, as an aside, I was extremely impressed with the professionalism of the Army captain in charge of A Co's Timberwolves and the sergeant first class who served as his right-hand man. Top notch.

As we wrapped things up, we still had some pending issues to resolve. First and foremost, we still had to figure out how we'd organize the teams of Marine advisors who'd accompany all the Georgian patrols and operations outside-the-wire. After our numbers were slashed, Plan A for this problem was taken off the table. But, the MRE gave us some ideas to work with, and we'd solidify our procedures as we turned over with the outgoing units in Afghanistan.

Despite these lingering issues, we were in a relatively good place as our pre-deployment training came to an end. Going back to my buddy Sam's initial advice, the rapport between the Georgians and Marines was still high, a good sign. And, while we weren't where we needed to be, after four months together, both the Marines and 51stGLIB soldiers were better trained than when we'd started, another good omen. Prepared or not, our formal training was now over. However, as I'd quickly come to understand, we'd need to make every effort to train and grow as a unit over the next seven months.

The Godsons during a team combat marksmanship program shoot on Camp Pendleton prior to deploying to the Republic of Georgia.

The team's three infantry advisor team leaders training in Camp Pendleton: (*L to R*) Bane, Claymore, and Anvil (the author).

The Godsons junior officers at the team's family BBQ prior to deployment: (*L to R*) SloMo, Claymore, Derby, Sleepy, Bane, and the author.

A view of the ridgeline and range impact area south of Krtsanisi Training Area (KTA) in the Republic of Georgia. This is the base where the Godsons would live and train with the 51st Georgian Light Infantry Battalion (51st GLIB) for three months prior to deploying to Afghanistan.

A view of the Mtkvari River running through the heart of Tbilisi, the capital of Georgia.

Bane (*L*) and author on an afternoon off in Tbilisi.

The first round of food and wine on one of the tables at the 51st GLIB *supra*, a traditional Georgian feast consisting of hours of eating, drinking, and toasts led by a formal *tamada*, or toast master. This was the first social event with both the Godsons and 51stGLIB staff—trust and camaraderie built with the help of copious amounts of wine.

The author on the ridgeline south of KTA following a conditioning hike in Georgia—uniform standards noticeably lax.

The Godsons spent their final liberty weekend together in Georgia on a team trip to Kazbegi, a mountain town in the Caucasus Mountains several miles from the Russian border: *(L to R)* Derby, the author, and SloMo.

Claymore (L) and the author with a young couple from Tehran, Iran at a café in Kazbegi also full of Israelis on a guided tour. Seemed like the start of a joke: "Two US Marines, a couple Iranians, and twenty Israeli tourists walk into a café..."

Anvil Charlie outside of the team's hooch in Vaziani South Training Area (VSTA), site of the final, battalion-level training exercise in Georgia prior to a month of training in Germany.

The author and a Georgian military interpreter (MILTERP) with the 51stGLIB's A Company commander and executive officer discussing a cordon and search exercise in Georgia.

"Military Tourism": Author on a day off from training while at VSTA in Georgia. The ancient cliffside monastery in the background is located in the training area.

A Company, 51stGLIB at the beginning of the battalion's US-run mission rehearsal exercise (MRE) at Joint Multinational Readiness Center (JMRC) Hohenfels, Germany. This would be the Godsons' and 51stGLIB's culminating training event prior to deploying to Afghanistan.

The Boss addressing the Godsons at the JMRC Hohenfels *bierhall* prior to kicking off a team social at the beginning of the MRE.

Three Godsons non-commissioned officers (NCOs) after being promoted in mountaintop castle ruins at JMRC Hohenfels.

# II-35

# TEA WITH THE AFGHANS

·············································

B EFORE MOVING ON, I wanted to write about another interesting experience during the MRE. Though outside of
my work as a combat advisor to the Georgians, this experience
would certainly prove relevant heading into Afghanistan.

In the "village" outside of our COP, Afghan role players went
about their daily lives as if they actually were Afghan police, shop-
keepers, farmers, etc. Hohenfels and, by extension, the US government, invested a ton of money in hiring these role players.
Short of actually being in Afghanistan, their presence and involvement in the MRE scenario allowed us to as closely as possible
replicate the daily interactions we'd have with locals while patrolling
outside of Bagram. And, as would be the case in Afghanistan, we'd
need to rely on Dari-language (the primary language spoken around
Bagram) interpreters to bridge the communication gap.

For A Co, we had two Dari/English terps, brothers it turned out,
who lived on our COP with us. Many of the "injects" from the Army
Timberwolves required us to link up with the Afghan police outside
our COP for combined patrols, and, naturally, our terps were integral
to these interactions. So, over the course of the MRE, I worked with
these guys a few times, and they both performed well on patrol.

Midway through the MRE, one of the two terps working with A
Co approached me and asked if I'd write him and his brother a letter

of recommendation, just something generic stating what they'd both done to help our unit during our training. I hadn't really gotten to know either very well, but, as stated, they both performed well while out in the village with us, so I drew up a couple "To whom it may concern" letters of recommendation praising the brothers' work ethic, attitude, and language skills.

After e-mailing the letters to the brothers, I stopped over to their tent to give them a heads up that I'd sent them. At the tent, the younger of the two invited me in for tea.

Despite being in a dirt-floored tent sitting on cots, the brothers' hospitality was incredible. With a tea kettle set-up on a carpet clearly brought in by the two to add an element of home to the tent, I felt like I'd temporarily left our COP.

For the next hour or so, over tea and a variety of snacks laid out by the brothers, we spoke about life in Afghanistan, Afghan traditions, and their family story. After the Taliban killed their father, the two brothers fled the country with their mother and four other brothers, gaining asylum status in Germany. Once in Germany, the whole family needed to start again from scratch, having brought little more than the clothes on their backs from Afghanistan. And, part of starting from scratch entailed learning German, something the entire family took to diligently.

While one of the brothers had been a medical student in Afghanistan and the other a professional engineer, they both needed to begin their educations and certification processes anew to be considered for German jobs in their respective fields (hence the contract work at Hohenfels to keep some money in their pockets). Despite these obstacles, and all they'd already overcome, I was struck by the brothers' optimism and drive, true testaments to their resilience. And, in addition to the practical benefits of this conversation (that is, better insight into Afghan culture), their story did something else: quite clearly made all of my "first world problems" seem quite childish and insignificant.

# II-36

# WRAPPING UP THINGS

··········································

TIME OUT IN the field in Hohenfels wrapped up in much the same way that time in the field anywhere wraps up. We had working parties clean up the COP, we turned in all of our vehicles and "laser tag" gear, and we cleaned our personal weapons. With those necessities out of the way, we caught some much needed showers and ate some real food.

In an awesome move, the GTT Marines at Hohenfels organized two end-of-MRE trips for the guys in the GLT. On our first night out, we were all shuttled into Regensburg, a beautiful cathedral town about thirty minutes from base, for a night of German beer, brats, and general unwinding. And, despite a fairly sizeable hangover the next day, we were given approval to take a weekend trip before flying back to Georgia. So, we piled into rental cars and spent one day touring the French countryside in the Marne River Valley, a beautiful region of rolling vineyards that was the site of the Battle of Belleau Wood, a major fight for the Marines during World War I.

With a local guide possessing encyclopedic knowledge of the battle, we visited the major sites in the area. Unbelievable experience. And, to make it even more significant, we used this battlefield tour as an opportunity to present a Purple Heart from a previous

deployment to Bane Bravo, one of our staff NCOs. Administrative
paperwork has a way of holding up many military awards, but the
timing of this couldn't have been better. Bane Bravo's great grand-
father had been a Marine and fought at Belleau Wood, so pinning
on his Purple Heart while standing in a trench from that era added
an even deeper meaning.

Next stop, Paris. Much to the chagrin of more than a few significant others back home, a bunch of GLT Marines spent their
first nights in the City of Lights not on a romantic weekend, but
with a group of Marines. As one would expect, our night let
loose in Paris turned out to be an outstanding evening of good
food, a lot of booze, and solid bonding with the guys. While
people may scoff at the suggestion, there's definitely something
cathartic about drinking with a group of guys bound together by
shared suffering and a common sense of purpose.

Back in Hohenfels the next day, we took another contracted
flight out of Nuremberg into Tbilisi, where we landed and made
the drive to KTA. For the next couple days, things were pretty
quiet around base. Guys were busy packing up their rooms, mail-
ing extra gear back home, and getting ready for a couple weeks
of leave before heading to Afghanistan. I was off to the Balkans
to propose to my girlfriend (surprisingly, she said yes), a few
guys set out to backpack around Europe, and the rest went back
to California to see their families (and, in the case of the Boss,
get promoted from major to lieutenant colonel).

On one of those days, I grabbed a civilian terp and walked
over to the 51stGLIB side of base to touch base with Shalva and
the other A Co guys. We spent a few minutes chatting about
leave plans, as the Georgians would get a couple of weeks off,
too. Before leaving, Shalva and Pavle, the company's senior enlisted leader, gave me an A Co "guide-on," the ceremonial pen-
nant bearing a unit's insignia. Naturally, I was honored by this
gesture. And, stepping away from the situation, I also realized I

was quite relieved. Despite the trials and errors of my initial advising attempts, and the times I just completely fucked things up, we'd built some solid rapport. Over the next seven months, the trust we established in Georgia and Germany would be a reservoir we'd have to dip into often, as the stress, tensions, and frustrations of a combat deployment would certainly run high.

In addition to the positive state of things with the Georgians, I couldn't have been more pleased with the chemistry and cohesion the GLT Marines had solidified. Every single person on the team carried his weight, and there wasn't a single guy, from corporal to lieutenant colonel, with whom I wouldn't enjoy grabbing a beer. I wasn't sure how things would unfold once in Bagram, but I was confident that there wasn't a better group of guys suited to confront the challenges ahead.

# PART III

# AFGHANISTAN, END OF
# THE ISAF MISSION

*September - December 2014*

# THE INTERNATIONAL SECURITY ASSISTANCE FORCE

·················································

B EFORE TALKING ABOUT our time in Afghanistan, I'm going to provide some context. Specifically, to avoid confusion and understand how things changed from 2014 to 2015, it helps to understand the nature of the International Security Assistance Force (ISAF) mission.

First, it's important to grasp that ISAF and Operation Enduring Freedom (OEF), the term most frequently used in the US media to discuss Afghanistan, are not the same things. OEF is the official designation for the United States' Global War on Terror that began shortly after the attacks on September 11, 2001. And, while OEF has focused mainly on Afghanistan, it also involves counter-terror operations around the world. Bottom line, OEF is a US-led mission.

ISAF, on the other hand, emerged from the Bonn Conference in December 2001 and would serve as an internationally-mandated security force tasked with fostering a secure environment for re-building Afghanistan. After a couple years of rotating ISAF command among different nations, the practice of completely over-hauling a headquarters every six months proved inefficient and impractical. As a result, in August 2003, NATO officially assumed command of the ISAF mission, making it a *NATO-led* mission.

So where did this divide leave us, the GLT Marines? Though informally called the Georgian Liaison Team, our team's official title in Afghanistan was the Georgia Deployment Program— ISAF, Rotation 14. As the Georgians supported NATO, not OEF, we too fell under the auspices of the NATO mission, that is, Commander, ISAF. And, how did this OEF versus ISAF split translate in actions on the ground? Basically, it provided two separate legal authority chains. In other words, US forces conducting the OEF counter-terrorism mission were allowed to do things that US forces supporting the ISAF mission were not.

Despite the above dual-mission construct of both OEF and ISAF in Afghanistan, the United States had a significant say in the conduct of both. Yes, NATO technically ran the ISAF mission, but, it would be naive to suggest that the United States, as the major force and monetary contributor to NATO, was not driving decisions in the background. As such, it was decided that, on December 31st, 2014, both the ISAF mission and OEF mission would end. On the NATO side, ISAF would become the Resolute Support (RS) mission. OEF, on the other hand, would become Operation Freedom's Sentinel. For both missions, this transition would involve a major reduction in direct combat involvement and force levels in the country. Moving forward, the focus would be on *training, advising, and assisting* Afghan Security Forces.

In September 2014, this was all abstract to us. But, in January 2015, we'd get a very clear sense of how the political decisions driving this arbitrary transition date would seriously fuck with our dope.

# III-2

# A POINTLESS ADVON

········································

A FTER RETURNING FROM leave, the whole team seemed to have shed an outer layer of frustration, replacing it with optimism and excitement about the upcoming deployment. Funny how just a couple weeks away from a situation can make you forget the bad and focus on the good.

As a country supporting the ISAF mission but working with Marine advisors, the 51stGLIB's movement into Afghanistan would be coordinated through US military channels, with a variety of Marine and joint headquarters commands taking part in the planning and execution of the movement (no small feat figuring out how to fly 750 Georgians into a combat zone thousands of miles away from their country).

Prior to departing on leave, seven of our team members had planned and coordinated an "advon" flight into Afghanistan. "Advon," military speak for an advanced party, describes a small group of people that go to an area before the arrival of the main body. The thinking being that this advanced party can grease the skids, making sure everything is organized for when hundreds of people show up in an unfamiliar place, usually in the middle of the night. Consequently, our tasks as the advon would be to make sure things like billeting (where people were living), transportation to that billeting, chow, initial "welcome-to-a-combat-zone" briefs, etc., are all confirmed. Basically, an advon makes sure that the first few days after a unit arrives in-country go as smoothly as possible.

We initially planned our advon flights to get us into Bagram about a week prior to the front end of the projected initial main body flight window, as this would give us plenty of time to conduct necessary coordination before the main body arrived. I emphasize "projected" here because, with strategic lift (US military cargo planes flying all around the world), a ton of moving pieces exist, and final itineraries aren't solidified until a week or so out from a flight. So, when we returned from leave and found out that our main body flights had been moved up, the advon became irrelevant. The value in sending people ahead of the main body depends on time, and, with these updated flights, the advon would only arrive about twelve hours before the main body—not the week we'd initially expected.

If our advon flight was as straightforward as the main body flights would be, that is, directs from Tbilisi into Bagram, I'd have said "what the hell, twelve hours is better than nothing." However, with only seven of us going, we certainly would not have our own cargo plane allocated. Instead, we'd have to take a circuitous route, flying civilian flights from Tbilisi to Romania, where we'd catch a MILAIR ("military air," a cargo flight) lift into Afghanistan. All told, we'd be paying thousands of dollars for civilian flights to Romania, only to gain the benefit of arriving at Bagram twelve hours ahead of everyone else. The costs clearly did not outweigh the benefits of this course of action, and we briefed our higher headquarters that, due to the new flight windows, we would no longer need the seven seats on the MILAIR flight out of Romania.

What transpired over the next day foreshadowed the absurdity, inefficiency, and waste inherent to the military and our involvement in Afghanistan, things that would prove recurring themes for the next seven months. Apparently, cancelling our seven advon seats on the lift into Afghanistan would have required GO-level ("general officer," pronounced *geo*) approval, as the seats were already confirmed. Yet, we made the mistake of applying logic to the situation, believing that, with our updated flight window and our advon no longer relevant, it would just make sense that we cancel our civilian airfare, save thousands of dollars, and just fly with the main body out of Tbilisi.

Nope. Because a staff member somewhere in the MILAIR approval chain wanted to avoid a potential ass chewing from a GO for seven seats going unfilled, we were informed that those advon seats out of Romania would have GLT asses in them—no room for discussion. Roger that. After arriving back from leave, seven of us were back at Tbilisi International Airport at dawn the next morning for flights into Constanta, Romania.

From a personal perspective, flying advon was a great gig. Rather than dealing with the cattle herding of flying 150 or so Georgian soldiers and Marines into Afghanistan, the seven of us got to fly civilian flights into Romania, which, flying Turkish Airlines, meant a free twelve-hour stop in Istanbul for a Turkish bath, some baklava, and a little sightseeing in the Sutanahmet District—not bad.

But, our little side trip certainly wasn't free. Looking back at my government travel charge card statements, my one-way ticket from Georgia to Romania cost $634 plus, having our whole kit for deployment with us, an extra $384 in excess baggages fees, for a total of just over $1,000 (roughly $7,000 for the seven of us). Clearly, $7,000 doesn't even qualify as a drop in the bucket with respect to Department of Defense funding, but seriously, this money might as well have been thrown away for what it accomplished. Our situation was a classic example of bureaucratic, military bullshit trumping common sense. Yet, fraud, waste, and abuse aside, two days after leaving Tbilisi and after a twenty-four-hour stop in Romania, our C-17 landed in the middle of the night at Bagram Airfield.

# III-3

# INITIAL IMPRESSIONS

··········································

T HERE WASN'T MUCH to see the first night we landed—
blowing wind and darkness outside the base perimeter.
After a brief "welcome aboard" video put together by the Air
Force (who, as one would expect, manage airfield operations), a
staff NCO from Task Force (TF) Top Guns, the Army unit we'd
be replacing, linked up with us at the passenger terminal. We
loaded all of our kit onto a flatbed and walked the quarter mile
or so to our billeting.

Whatever I'd imagined, this wasn't it. The place where we'd
be living for the next seven months was a two-story, concrete
structure that felt more like a college dorm than combat zone
billeting—bunk racks in rooms with full electricity, internet
drops, and showers inside on each floor.

After finding our rooms, we met the flatbed, brought our gear
upstairs, and headed down the street to the chow hall, or DFAC
("dee-fack," dining facility) to hit up the twenty-four-hour sandwich bar. Continuing the theme of luxury, after thirteen years of
war, the Bagram DFACs were more like college dining halls
than anything else—full-time contracted employees, great chow,
and big screen TVs piping CNN, Fox News, and ESPN into our
meal time.

We realized very quickly that this would be a "country club deployment," a tongue-in-cheek reference to the dichotomy we'd be living over the next seven months. We'd conduct security patrols and other operations in impoverished Afghan villages then return to a base with all the luxuries of any Stateside posts (minus a bar and golf course...). Our lifestyle would be drastically different than that lived by the thousands of Soldiers and Marines who'd spent their deployments spread throughout the country's rural areas, showering with water bottles, eating MREs (shelf-stable military rations), and laughing at the thought of air conditioning.

In addition to this odd juxtaposition between what we'd be doing on a daily basis "outside-the-wire" and the place where we'd be living, time on Bagram also provided us daily insight into the frustrations, inefficiency, and waste associated with the overarching failings of an Afghan war with unsustainable (and regularly changing) political objectives. Specifically, due to the size and importance of Bagram, the two-star commander of the base also played the role of deputy to the four-star general in charge of all operations in Afghanistan, putting us just one step away from ISAF headquarters.

Our initial, midnight impressions were reinforced our first morning on base. Waking up to a sunny day, I was blown away by the number of NTVs ("non-tactical vehicles," civilian trucks) driving down the main drag on our side of base. Once again, we may as well have been hanging out on Camp Pendleton. Due to the massive size of Bagram, the tens of thousands of service members, civilian contractors, and government employees working there, and the number of generals floating around with their associated staffs, the base was absolutely saturated with NTVs, to the point where traffic jams and speeding tickets (yep, a real thing) were daily occurrences (more to follow on that later).

# III-4

# BASE TOUR AND "ADVON BRIEF"

O UR FIRST MORNING on Bagram, and about a half day before the rest of the GLT Marines would arrive with the first
wave of Georgians, we took a base tour with the TF Top Guns staff
NCO we'd met upon arrival. From anywhere on the massive base,
the first thing you notice is the mountains. The foothills of the
Hindu Kush tower over three sides of the base, with the fourth side
a pass through the hills heading south towards Kabul. This ring of
mountains gives Bagram's surroundings the feel of a massive bowl,
with the Panjshir River flowing directly through it.

On the base itself, the dominant feature is the airfield, which
runs northeast to southwest through the middle of Bagram. This
line divides the base into two major sections, one to the northwest
of the airfield, and the other to the southeast. The base is surrounded
by a roughly twenty-five kilometer long perimeter. This perimeter
encompasses everything from high-tech, modern buildings to old
warehouses to Soviet minefields used during the time they controlled Bagram in the 1980s. Many of the older buildings remain
pockmarked with holes caused by bullets and shrapnel, legacies
of both the Soviet occupation and ensuing Afghan Civil War.

Another interesting aspect about Bagram, and one with which
we'd become intimately familiar, was the Afghan National Army

(ANA) side of base. In one huge portion, separated by internal checkpoints from the ISAF side of the base, the ANA ran a prison complex and a military court system. Over the next seven months, we'd spend a significant amount of time over on the Afghan side coordinating partnered patrols with our ANA counterparts.

Reflecting on our driving tour, one thing stood out to me: the staggering number of separate organizations on base. Air Force, Army, ISAF and Afghan partners, civilian maintenance contractors, and government employees were just a few of the major organizations, and, with our small team, we'd need to rely heavily on all these groups at one time or another. As our staff NCO escort from TF Top Guns eloquently phrased it, we'd have to work some serious "dude skills and drug deals" to get things done.

With our base tour complete, and feeling somewhat more comfortable with Bagram's layout, we headed back to the TF Top Guns command post, a two-story concrete building dubbed the "Pink Palace" for its salmon-ish color. Typically, an advon would receive a thorough "welcome aboard" brief upon its arrival, covering everything from the terrain and vegetation in the area to enemy threats and logistics concerns at the base.

However, both the TF Top Guns operations officer and the seven of us recognized the absurdity of spending a whole day in briefs when the rest of the Marines (and a bulk of the Georgian leadership) would be on base in just a few hours. Our primary role would simply be linking up with the Marines and Georgians when they landed and getting everyone and their gear to where they'd be living.

With that said, we did spend about forty-five minutes in the Pink Palace getting an initial map overview and talk-through of our area of operations and major concerns from some key TF Top Guns staff members. Key villages, routes, vegetation, and so forth. While not the in-depth brief we'd receive over the next few days, we now had a much more thorough understanding of what we'd be doing and where we'd be doing it.

# III-5

# "HIGHER"

··················

I N ADDITION TO our abbreviated advon brief clarifying some information about our area of operations, it also helped us get a better sense of who our higher headquarters would be. In conventional units like an infantry battalion, one's "higher" is fairly straightforward: platoons report to a company, companies report to a battalion, and battalions reports to a regiment. As we were discovering in the world of ISAF headquarters, things were a little more convoluted. Despite the previously discussed divide between the U.S.-led Operation Enduring Freedom and NATO-led ISAF missions, many commands "dual-hatted," serving roles in both OEF and ISAF. Fast-forward a few months into our time in Afghanistan, and it would take a one-star general drawing diagrams on a dry-erase board to try to explain the maze of command relationships stretching from our team of Marines up to the four-star general leading the Afghan mission.

I've discussed it a few times already, but a unit's higher headquarters is important for a few reasons. While operating outside-the-wire on patrols or other operations, higher coordinates all external support: CASEVAC aircraft, fire support, QRF support, etc. Furthermore, as a common higher headquarters between multiple units, higher command posts also keep units "deconflicted," that is, ensure that different forces out at the same time don't mistakenly or unintentionally shoot at each other.

While the above roles and responsibilities are positive, higher typically gets a bad wrap for its negatives. Specifically, from a legal perspective, higher also tells subordinate units what they need to do (tasks) and what they're allowed to do (rules of engagement). So, whenever a unit faces bullshit taskings with ridiculous restrictions imposed, "higher," whoever that may be, becomes the scapegoat, sometimes deservingly, and sometimes not.

For the Marines and Georgians, we had a fairly unique chain of command up through a series of higher headquarters. To begin, command relationships as a combat advisor are already unique. As I've stated, the Georgians had no legal authority to task us Marines, and we had no legal authority to task them. As a result of this dynamic, we set up parallel lines of communication, with every patrol having Marines reporting to a Marine watch officer in the 51stGLIB combat operations center (COC). Concurrently, the Georgian watch officer received reports from the Georgians out on the same patrol. In this fashion, we actually served as backdrops to each other, with the Georgian watch officers able to ask the Marine watch officers about information on patrol, and vice versa.

From the perspective of the dudes out on patrol, "higher" was this Georgian COC, the most senior, organic command post for the 51stGLIB. However, the next senior higher headquarters to us would be the Army task force (TF) in the Pink Palace, initially TF Top Guns, and soon to be turned over to 2nd Squadron, 3rd Cavalry Regiment's staff, known as TF Saber. This task force was only a headquarters element, and it manned what was known as the Joint Defense Operations Center (JDOC), coordinating all the units inside- and outside-the-wire responsible for defending Bagram Airfield.

Above the Army task force manning the JDOC things got strange.

Roughly 500 meters down the road from the Pink Palace was our next layer of command, our "higher's higher," a two-star general's staff that manned the Joint Operations Center (JOC) for the whole area of operations. This is where you start seeing ISAF and OEF start to blend. With respect to ISAF, this two-star general was titled Commander, Bagram Airfield (COMBAF). However, he also wore an OEF hat, serving as the US Forces–Afghanistan, Deputy for Support (USFOR-A, DS). As COMBAF, this two-star reported directly to the four-star in charge of NATO, Commander, ISAF (COMISAF). As USFOR-A, DS, he reported directly to the four-star in charge of the OEF mission, Commander, USFOR-A. The strange thing— COMISAF and Commander, USFOR-A were the same American four-star general. Confused yet? I *still* am.

So what did the above actually mean for us, the Marines and Georgians out on patrol? From the two-star COMBAF/USFOR-A, DS staff to platoon-sized security patrols, we were located within 500 meters of each other on the same base. This proximity would provide us keen insight into not only the low-level security operations we'd be conducting, but also operational-level decisions relevant to Afghanistan and, ultimately, the strategic-level decisions being pushed from inside the Beltway via COMISAF/Commander, USFOR-A. And, as the two-star closest to us, COMBAF/USFOR-A, DS became a target of our frustration, as his staff's directives would soon represent the very tangible manifestation of security operations intermingling with political decisions, leading us to dub the JOC, in a nod to Orwell, the "Ministry of Truth."

For better or worse, I'd have a very unique perspective on the "end of the war" as January 1, 2015 rolled around and America's and NATO's combat missions technically ended. Within 500 meters of each other, we'd be preparing for platoon-size security patrols while a two-star general staff dealt with COMISAF/Commander USFOR-A, decisions from the Beltway, and the confusion that inevitably entailed.

# III-6

# POPPING OUR ROCKET CHERRY

·············································

S O, YEAH, THIS probably isn't the most politically correct or appropriate title, but it feels right.

From our various briefs, bullshitting with the guys we were replacing on base, and the experiences of the Marines who went on the pre-deployment site survey, we knew rocket attacks would be the most frequent threat to Bagram. With essentially zero control of the main routes in and out of the Bagram Bowl, Taliban fighters and weapons facilitators could flow cheap, 107mm rockets into our area of operations with seeming impunity. And, once in the area, it's a pretty straightforward process to lean a rocket against a berm or grape vine, do some "Kentucky windage" aiming towards the base, set some incense or a cigarette as a fuse, and leave. That way, by the time the rocket finally launches, whoever placed it is long gone. If the rocket hits base, great. If not, no big deal—just launch one another day.

Due to the large number of rocket attacks against base, and the fact that using an airfield is somewhat difficult with rockets landing in the middle of it, our primary mission would be counter-rocket patrols. However, the other defense against rockets (more of a last-ditch effort than anything else) was the C-RAM system (counter-rocket, -artillery, and -mortar). Basically, the C-RAM used radar to detect incoming rockets then shoot hundreds of projectiles per second in an attempt to deflect it from its course. But, we didn't quite know how this system worked initially.

After a few nights on Bagram, a few of the Marines were at the rifle range on base, taking advantage of seemingly unlimited ammunition to shoot for a couple hours (in the penny-pinching Marine Corps, this level of "go ahead and let 'em rip" is unheard of back Stateside). Just prior to "going hot," that is, beginning to shoot, we all stopped, lowered our rifles, and stared up to the sky at what looked like a fireworks show paired with the roar of a thousand chainsaws streaking through the air.

Looking back on that night, I imagine seeing us at the range would've been a little bit like watching a scene from a cheesy movie to an outsider, with a filmmaker attempting to visually depict the delay in sight, understanding, and action of his cast. Standing at the range, we saw the C-RAM rounds, immediately became enthralled, and just stared for what felt like an eternity. After a few seconds, it finally dawned on us that we were watching a rocket streak through the sky towards base (or at least seeing the C-RAM tracers following that rocket). Not wanting to bear the brunt of a 107mm explosive, we all jumped behind some barriers by the firing line. What a bunch of fucking noobs.

Fortunately, that first rocket landed in an unoccupied area of base, not doing any real damage. And, it kicked off a process that would become second nature to us over the next seven months— IDF "accountability." Any time a rocket hit, we'd trigger a phone tree system, making sure that all the Marines were accounted for and not bleeding out in a ditch on base somewhere.

Cherry popped.

# III-7

# FIRST PATROL

..........................

D UE TO THE fact that the GLT Marines had arrived in
Bagram on either the advon flight or the first flight of the
main body, we had a couple weeks after landing when the Georgians would still be phasing their way into Afghanistan. With a
750-soldier battalion, you can't just snap your fingers and move
from Georgia to Afghanistan—it required a half dozen or so individual flights to deploy the entire 51stGLIB.

Within the first week of our being there, we'd knocked out all of
our initial, required training for entering a combat zone. Known as
Reception, Staging, Onward Movement, and Integration (RSO&I),
this training included the bare minimum of checks-in-the-box: brief
by a judge advocate on the rules of engagement, "zeroing" your
rifle (ensuring that your scope and rifle are aligned, so that where
you aim, the bullet goes), and an overview of the IED threat in the
area (this was an extremely poor excuse for a threat brief that we'd
need to improve down the line).

Done with this training, we were able to focus on familiarizing
ourselves with the Bagram area of operations, so we arranged to
start sending out one to two Marines at a time on patrols with the
Army unit we'd be replacing. While we'd conduct a formal left
seat/right seat (supervised turnover of responsibilities in a combat

zone) once the Georgians had all arrived and finished their RSO&I training, this initial familiarization would give us a leg up as advisors. Once we were out patrolling with the Georgians, having already seen a lot of the area, we could focus on advising, vice trying to familiarize ourselves with the terrain while also tactically assisting the Georgian patrol leaders.

The morning of our first patrol, Sgt Curtis and I got dropped off where Apache, the Army cavalry troop we'd replace outside-the-wire, prepared for its patrols. We had a chance to bullshit a bit with the Army patrol leader and his platoon sergeant, talking about their experiences to date, and what we'd be doing today. As they were conducting twelve- to fourteen-hour mounted patrols at that point, we'd have plenty of time to see the area outside base. So, after the pre-mission brief from the platoon leadership to the guys, we loaded up into MRAPs (mine-resistant, ambush-protected vehicles) and headed out. Here were the main takeaways from the patrol:

1. The terrain in the Bagram Bowl was incredibly topographically diverse for such a relatively small area. On one side of base, dried out *wadi* (dry creek bed) systems ran through desert plains, while a few miles away the lush green zones surrounding the Panjshir River low grounds were practically choked with vegetation. Surrounding it all were the towering Hindu Kush mountains.

2. From a population perspective, things were as diverse as the terrain. The area went from barren plains to extremely crowded and dense urban areas within the span of a few miles. The traffic on the roads—between pedestrians, cars, and motorcycles—was significant. This would be a force protection nightmare for us, and the suicide bomber who killed the Czechs a few months prior was not far from my mind that first patrol.

3. Kids can be pains in the ass wherever you are in the world. One of our main "threats" for the next few months would be rocks hurled by little kids as our patrols drove by—another reason to emphasize the need to actually get out of your vehicles.

4. The Afghan National Army (ANA) would be absolutely in-dispensable on patrol. We linked up with two HMMWVs of ANA soldiers outside the base, and they accompanied us for most of the patrol. These guys would play a key role in keeping the patrols safe (it was their culture, so they knew when something was off far more effectively than we did) and providing us legit-imacy during interactions with local Afghans.

5. Always watch where locals get the water for their chai pots. We sat and drank chai at a local police station for an hour or so, and, as we were leaving, I watched one of the guys fill up the hot water maker from a stagnant pool of gray water in the middle of their compound. Naturally, I had some digestive issues back on base that evening.

6. Finally, one of the most significant dangers we'd face over the next seven months would be complacency. When you're pa-trolling day-in, day-out, it's easy to become numb to threats. Apache Troop, after six months of not taking contact on any patrol, took a rocket-propelled grenade (RPG) in the side of one its vehicles on its last patrol in Afghanistan, a clear reminder that we'd needed to keep our heads on a swivel for the duration.

# III-8

# RIP ABORTION

·······················

A FEW WEEKS AFTER the first GLT members arrived in
Bagram, all Marines and Georgians were finally in-country.
Due to the Marines coming from three different locations and
three different units (core GLT in Georgia, ANGLICO in Camp
Lejeune, North Carolina, and enablers in Camp Pendleton), coordinating everyone's movement to Bagram took more time than
would've been ideal. However, with the closing of Camp Leath-
erneck down in Helmand Province, our team was now the largest
unit of Marines in Afghanistan, quite the change from the thousands
deployed over the previous few years.

With all of the Marines' and Georgians' initial RSO&I training
requirements complete, the turnover of responsibilities with outgoing units began in earnest. This replacement of one unit by
another in a combat zone is known as a relief in place, or RIP
(pronounced *rip*), and it is extremely difficult to do safely and
efficiently. Additionally, with our unique situation with the
51stGLIB, the RIP would be significantly more complicated than
a standard turnover due to three main reasons.

First, the 51stGLIB was not turning over with one unit. Rather,
the Georgian battalion was replacing two Army infantry companies, an Army cavalry troop, an Army task force command post,

and a couple of US Air Force security detachments. Essentially, the Georgians were taking each of these unit's separate missions and consolidating them into a single mission for both our battalion, and the Georgian units that would follow us. As a result, rather than conducting a single RIP, we really had to figure out how to relieve five separate organizations.

Second, due to the above consolidation of responsibilities (and the pesky Georgians-not-speaking-English thing), we needed to establish a whole new command and control structure to actually conduct our mission. Furthermore, we had to compile a single gear set from each of these disparate units, pulling accountability and ownership of millions of dollars of vehicles, communication gear, computers, weapons, and countless other pieces of required equipment. As grunts, we often take the non-infantry types for granted. But, successfully finding, inventorying, and keeping track of thousands of individual (and very expensive) items from a bunch of different units was an absolutely monumental task for our supply officer, and he knocked it out of the park.

Lastly, the language barrier proved a huge obstacle to the entire RIP process, far more so than we anticipated (poor planning on our parts, as this should've been a readily identifiable sticking point). In a typical U.S.-to-US RIP, small-unit leaders for the incoming unit link up with their counterparts in the outgoing units, and they're able to handle the turnover of responsibilities at their level. For us, we couldn't just send Georgian squad and team leaders to link up with their Army and Air Force counterparts. We did not have nearly enough Georgian interpreters to make this happen. Consequently, every aspect of our turnover had to be calculated and micromanaged in terms of our limited supply of interpreters. Every day, we had to look at a matrix of dozens of individual turnover responsibilities, and, by-name, assign interpreters to show up at a designated time and place to facilitate these turnovers. Nightmare—but hey, FITFO.

There's a tongue-in-cheek saying in the Marines that, "The two worst units in the Marine Corps are the one you're relieving and the one relieving you." The former seems lazy and complacent, and the latter seems naive and incapable of grasping the mission. In reality, TF Top Guns had prepared a solid U.S.-to-US RIP, but not a Georgian one. This situation re-emphasized our value as advisors, as the Marines needed to A) create a U.S.-to-Georgian RIP model from scratch, and B) serve as the driving force behind that model.

While this whole ordeal significantly strained our relationship with the 51stGLIB, we were able to fall back on the reserve of rapport built during our time in Georgia. And, despite the frustrations, we were now well on the way to taking over the mission.

# III-9

# KEY PLAYERS, PLANNING OPS, AND THE MARIONETTE APPROACH TO ADVISING

·················································

A S WE ASSUMED more and more responsibility, the week eventually arrived when the 51stGLIB took full responsibility for planning the following week's patrols. For the first couple weeks of our right seat/left seat with the Army unit we'd relieve outside-the-wire, those guys planned the patrols, and we rode along with them. Now, we'd be taking point on the planning, and the Army would start pulling back.

With the frustrations of patrolling in VSTA and Germany fresh in my mind, I knew patrol planning in Bagram would be an early source of friction between the Marines and Georgians. Through no fault of their own other than getting shortchanged by the KTA staff during their training, the Georgians tasked with planning the battalion's patrols bought into the notion of "patrolling for the sake of patrolling." To these guys, planning a patrol meant drawing some routes on a map, assigning a few checkpoints along the way, and having the guys on patrol report back to the COC that they'd passed those checkpoints. As I've tried to make abundantly clear, heading into this deployment my counter-insurgency and combat experience was limited to non-existent, leaning more heavily to the latter. But, I knew this Georgian approach of just driving around in armored vehicles wasn't right.

A saying exists among Marine planners that, "Intelligence drives operations, and operations feed intelligence." While I lacked any real experience beyond my own training, I did remember that quote, and I knew our patrols had to be intelligence-driven to have any real impact. The question now became, how could I convince the Georgians of this reality? As an advisor, I could not task or order the Georgians to do anything; all my leverage would come through rapport and trust built with the key players in the battalion.

Enter three Georgians for whom my respect is, though for different reasons, unparalleled: Lieutenant Colonel (Lt. Col.) Koba (like the Boss, recently promoted), Major Nik, and Captain Davit.

In some respects, Lt. Col. Koba fully embodied the post-Soviet, centralized mentality of the Georgians. Nothing happened without his say, as the practice of delegating major decisions was largely non-existent, and he ran his battalion with an iron fist accordingly. But, he was also an extremely intelligent and perceptive officer who both understood the limitations of his soldiers and their training and had significant trust in his counterpart, my boss, who could have "behind-closed-doors" conversations leading to increased operational influence by the Marine advisors. This increased influence fostered by the Boss led to a large number of planning responsibilities being pushed to me and my operations officer counterpart, Major Nik.

In addition to being an outstanding *tamada*, Major Nik continuously impressed my during our time together with his ability to understand the subtle balance between what *should* be done, and what *can* be done. If I had an idea for a patrol or operation that was outside the battalion's capabilities, I could count on Major Nik to give me a, "I don't know, Bro." Translation: better rethink things. On the other hand, if something both made sense and he knew it to be within the Georgians' capabilities, I'd get a "Why not, Bro?" Translation: go ahead and plan it. And then, as I planned something, I knew he'd provide me the back I needed with the Georgians who'd be out executing those plans with their Marine advisors.

Lastly, Captain Davit was the absolute glue of the battalion, the man who got things done. Due to his experience and English-language proficiency, Davit served as the interpreter for Major Nik and the 51stGLIB's operations section, which meant he and I worked together non-stop for seven months. With a great sense of humor and smile plastered on his face, Davit was a breath of fresh air whenever I felt like I couldn't deal with another Georgian issue. As soon as he saw frustration getting the better of me, Davit would laugh and give me a, "Fuck these guys, Man." For the past decade, Davit had been in and out of the Georgian Armed Forces, rotating between time in the military and time serving as a military contractor in Iraq. And, in this latter capacity, he'd worked with all sorts of forces and seen both what worked, and, more importantly, what didn't. Sharing an office with Davit and his common sense approach kept me sane for seven months.

So how did these three key players fit together from my perspective? With Lt. Col. Koba's implicit approval, Major Nik's top cover, and Davit's work ethic and language skills, I assumed the marionette role I'd been trying to build since arriving in Georgia, not having any formal role in tasking the Georgians, but pulling the strings behind the scenes to drive operations. Here's how it worked. I'd plan a patrol or larger operation, shoot the plan to Davit, he'd translate it, then Major Nik would disseminate it to the 51stGLIB company actually executing the plan. In this way, the Georgians would receive plans in Kartouli from their battalion operations officer ordering them to do something, vice getting plans in English from Marine advisors asking them to do something. And, I'd ensure that the Marines accompanying each one of these patrols received the English-language version of the plan, keeping everyone on the same page. Moving forward with this system established, we could now view operations as a continuation of training. Understanding that, as a Georgian-Marine team, we still lacked advanced patrolling skills upon entering Afghanistan, we could implement a phased approach to tactical complexity. Each week, I'd gradually increase the complexity of the operations we planned, ultimately working towards building the tactical proficiency of the battalion. By the time we left seven months later, we were conducting operations I wouldn't have dreamed of doing in a million years back at VSTA or Hohenfels.

# III-10

# THE INTEL PICK-UP GAME

...................................................

B Y FIGURING OUT the above procedures for the Major
Nik/Davit/me team planning of patrols, we'd successfully put
the cart before the horse. Yes, we now had the blessings and procedures in place to plan weekly patrol schedules and operations. But,
we also lacked a unified source of intelligence to drive this planning.

As I've said, I had shit for experience going into this deployment—had never done an Iraq or Afghanistan tour. Furthermore,
both our intel officer (Sleepy) and our intel chief (Sleepy Bravo)
had limited counterinsurgency experience. With that said, we
had a few things going for us. 1) I had no qualms admitting I
needed help, and I recognized that we were currently fucked up.
2) Sleepy had made tons of connections with different intel types
around Bagram during our few weeks there. And, 3) Sleepy
Bravo was one of the hardest working and smartest Marines I've
ever had the privilege to work with, and, through force of will
and critical thinking, he had a way of making things happen.

Unfortunately, upon taking over planning responsibilities from
TF Top Guns, it was readily apparent that no venue existed for
consolidating intelligence collection requests for the "grunts,"
that is, for the guys out everyday dealing with locals, having chai
with village elders and religious leaders, and bullshitting with

little kids. In essence, we knew we'd be outside the wire interacting with locals on a daily basis, but no higher headquarters helped focus our planning by telling us the information that it needed gathered from the area.

Basically, as units came and went on Bagram, each one turned over and reinvented the intel wheel, often letting great work they'd done fall to the wayside as the next unit unfucked things and learned the same hard lessons.

With that said, we knew that we needed to get some of the key intel players on Bagram in the same room on a weekly basis. We could be the eyes and ears for the actual smart people, but we needed to know what they needed to know (in order to focus our patrols) and what the best way to compile that information would be to ensure it wouldn't be lost when we left. The former requirement got worked out in the first meeting, but the latter would be a moving target we'd work on for the duration of the deployment.

To make things happen, Sleepy and Sleepy Bravo reached out to a hodge podge of different intel agencies and players on base, convincing people to add one more meeting to their weekly schedules. When we finally got everyone in the same room for our "sales pitch," it went something like this: "We're here to work for you. With the way things are, we're not a 'finishing agency' tasked to capture/kill individuals. But, you can use us to put together the intel products you need to hand off to the organizations that are. Just tell us what you need from us." Basically, as one of the few remaining US units operating outside-the-wire at the juncture of the war, we were offering our services to be the eyes and ears of any and all intel agencies in the area.

From the outside in, we looked like a band of misfits: Marines, Georgians, dudes with beards, and intel cats from other services. But, we all wanted the same thing—to build the intelligence necessary to take the bad guys off the battlefield. With that first meeting, we'd set the wheels in motion, and, moving forward, our weekly intel synchronization meeting ("the synch") would be the primary venue for a variety of intel agencies on base to go "collection shopping." They'd tell us what they needed to know, and I'd incorporate those requirements into the next week's patrols and deliberate operations. In this fashion, one week's requirements would drive the next week's actions. And, each ensuing meeting would then begin with a wrap-up of the previous week's collections. Somehow, we'd figured out how to translate the whole "intel drives operations, and operations feed intel" saying into actual practice.

No question, the synch was an ugly baby. But, after that first meeting, Sleepy and I received one of the highest compliments of our deployment. As we were heading out, one of the bearded types who'd been at Bagram for a long time pulled us aside and said, "Fellas, I've sat in on a lot of different intel meetings, and this was absolutely the best." It was far from pretty, but we cut out all the fluff bullshit and got down to business quickly. *What do you need to know? Good, we'll take care of it.* Our synch ended up being an extremely effective venue to consolidate and incorporate patrol-related intel requests. Not bad for a shot in the dark.

# III-11

# COLONEL SULTAN AND AMINI

·············································

D URING THE PATROL turnover with TF Top Guns, we saw quite clearly the value of having Afghan National Army (ANA) soldiers with us outside the wire. And, we wanted to ensure the working relationship with the ANA unit on base who sent out those patrols didn't fade as TF Top Guns rotated home.

I mentioned it previously, but the whole portion of Bagram with the prison was run by the ANA by the time we arrived in country. Specifically, the 1st Military Police Guard Corps (1stMPGC) ran things over there. With that said, for years as security around Bagram was passed from unit to unit, no American forces coordinated patrols with the ANA, despite the fact that rockets are equal opportunity weapons, just as likely hitting the Afghan side of base as the NATO side. Seeing this reality as an opportunity, an enterprising company commander from TF Top Guns, Captain Kyle (his first name), reached out to the 1stMPGC and suggested conducting partnered patrols, and he ended up solidifying a relationship with one of the Afghan battalion commanders who offered to support him. If we were to be successful in our area of operations, we would need to continue this relationship, maintaining a strong bond with our ANA counterparts on base.

To fully understand this aspect of our deployment, you need

to understand two key personalities, without whom we would not have built the trust and rapport that we did with our ANA partner battalion. The first is the individual who initially bridged the gap between TF Top Guns and the 1stMPGC, the sine qua non of U.S.-ANA security patrol coordination on Bagram: Amini, a Canadian national serving as a contracted interpreter on base, and someone I consider a true friend.

Prior to describing Amini, I'll outline his significant value as an interpreter, though interpreter doesn't do him justice. He was more accurately a diplomat. As Captain Kyle explained things, "Amini knows more Afghan generals than most Afghan generals do." If I called Amini to set up a meeting with someone in the ANA or local government, I'd inevitably get a "I'll see what I can do," followed by a call back several minutes later with the confirmed meeting time and place. Characterized by his humility, dry sense of humor, and integrity, Amini could smile and charm his way to resolving the countless and inevitable problems we faced coordinating operations with the ANA. The trust and rapport he fostered between all parties serve as testaments to the good person he is.

As a young man fearing for his life, Amini was forced to flee post-revolution Afghanistan to Pakistan, ultimately making his way to Canada where he started a family, becoming a master chef in Italian cuisine along the way. The more time I spent with him, the more I realized that, rather than the Dos Equis guy, Amini truly was "the most interesting man in the world." But, I digress. Back to coordinating with the ANA.

In handing off responsibilities for ANA coordination, Captain Kyle drove me over to the ANA side of base for one of the weekly patrol coordination meetings held with him, the Czech company commander whose soldiers also conducted security patrols outside Bagram, and Colonel Sultan, the commander of the battalion with which the NATO units patrolled. In addition to

Amini, Colonel Sultan was that other individual integral to a successful relationship with the ANA.

Walking into his office in his battalion headquarters, I was struck by the outgoing and jovial nature of Colonel Sultan, a large and smiling ethnic Uzbek with hands the size of manhole covers. As I'd come to find out, Colonel Sultan had fought with General Dostum during the Afghan civil war, a man feared throughout the country for his battlefield prowess and ruthlessness. Though his gray hairs and protruding belly reflected his age, in my first meeting with Colonel Sultan, it was clear that he was a warrior, and certainly someone we wanted as an ally.

I spent that first meeting in observation mode, seeing how things worked and getting a sense of the dynamics, the intricacies of the quid pro quo nature of the Afghan-US relationship. We needed the ANA for security and legitimacy on patrol, and they needed us for logistical support. And, I also saw one of the more immediate benefits of working with Colonel Sultan. As part of our meeting, we enjoyed a delicious, home-cooked Uzbek meal of rice, lamb, flat bread, and local fruit—the perks of coordination.

With the times and link-up points for the following week's partnered patrols solidified by Colonel Sultan's signature on the translated version of the patrol schedule, our job was complete. For the next seven months, this Saturday meeting with Colonel Sultan and Amini would be an essential element of 51stGLIB operations.

# III-12

# THE GEAR SET NIGHTMARE

·····································

A S WE CONTINUED our transition with TF Top Guns, we gradually assumed more responsibility as they pulled back. Initially, each patrol had a handful of Georgians and Marines observing. Later, the Georgians and Marines were in the lead, with just one or two TF Top Guns Soldiers out with us to answer any questions about the Bagram area that popped up, and, by the end, we would patrol unaccompanied.

For the Marines and Georgians focused on outside-the-wire security and patrolling, this assumption of lead responsibility also coincided with the first week of patrolling solely with our armored vehicles (as opposed to riding along in the MRAPs that the Army cavalry troop we were replacing on patrol had been using). We'd soon realize that this new responsibility would bring to the forefront one of the most significant issues of our RIP—gear.

In addition to learning the daily tasks and operations of the disparate Army and Air Force units we were relieving, we also had to take custody of their gear inventories, consolidating them into a single account for the 51stGLIB (at least we'd be able to hand over this single account to the Georgian battalion that would relieve us, though). And, dealing with millions of dollars of gear, there are certain military procedures in place for accounting for everything.

Each gear account has a responsible officer (RO), the guy who signs his name on the dotted line. This is the guy who Uncle Sam comes to if anything goes missing, so it can be a stressful gig. In a turnover, the outgoing RO and the incoming RO need to jointly inventory all items, confirming serials numbers and functionality of every piece of gear on the account. Once everything has been jointly confirmed between these two individuals, both ROs sign a document confirming that every line item has been properly turned over.

Concurrently, the outgoing RO breathes a tremendous sigh of relief that he's made it through a deployment without being court martialed, and the income RO has a sphincter-tightening sensation that doesn't dissipate until the gear's no longer in his name.

Due to force movements into Bagram, our supply officer, Brendan, and his supply chiefs, who were flying separately with our enabler detachment from Camp Pendleton, didn't arrive until about three weeks after the rest of us. This gave these guys about two weeks to inventory, consolidate into a single account, and sign for a base's worth of weapons, computers, vehicles, and other equipment adding up to millions of dollars. The ultimate goal of these actions: get the gear into the hands of the guys who needed it the most, the Marines and Georgians who were taking over patrol responsibilities from TF Top Guns.

Naturally, this gear consolidation and accountability process was a total shitshow, and it became "let's get the guys patrolling what they need, we'll confirm the paperwork later, and hopefully the vehicle maintenance is good enough for them to get off base." The incredible work of Brendan, Derby, and the logistics and supply chiefs was the only way this could happen. Through a combination of A) understanding and supporting the priorities of our team and its support to the Georgians, B) drug deals with different maintenance and supply contractors on base, and C) give-a-fuck, these guys got us out the door on that first patrol where we took the lead from TF Top Guns.

Despite tons of maintenance issues with the gear we signed for, especially the readiness of our armored vehicles, we were able to just barely get enough MRAPs fully mission capable around 1am the morning of our first patrol in the lead. Our maintenance chief, a grumpy-as-fuck, 6'5" Lurch-looking staff sergeant, also happened to be an absolute wizard with getting vehicles ready to roll. Without his magic, there's no way we would've been able get enough Georgian and Marine vehicles out that first morning. It certainly wasn't pretty (or on time), but we limped out of the gate the next morning, finally in the lead.

# III-13

# "FUCK IT, WE'LL WALK"

·············································

A FTER GETTING THE bare minimum number of vehicles ready to head outside-the-wire the night before, we were ready Monday morning to push out our first two unaccompanied patrols, that is, no TF Top Guns ride-alongs. Now we'd operate as we would for the remainder of the deployment: Georgians, a Marine advisor team, and an interpreter.

Lieutenant Colonel Koba's guidance for the first, weekly patrol schedule: to meet "higher's intent" (TF Saber, the Army task force that replaced TF Top Guns manning the JDOC in the Pink Palace), we'd conduct two daily twenty-four-hour patrols, one to the northeast of our area of operations and one to the southwest. From a grunt's perspective, twenty-four-hour patrols are pretty much the worst. Shorter patrols are fine, because you don't need to sleep, and longer, multi-day operations aren't bad, because you get into a rhythm of movement, security, rest, repeat. But, there's no rest plan in a twenty-four-hour patrol; rather, it's just long enough to get you hallucinating towards the end. Bottom line, they're a terrible idea, but this policy remained in place following a large-volume rocket attack and knee-jerk reaction a couple months before we arrived. More on this later.

So, how'd that first patrol to head out Monday morning go? As I'm sure you can imagine, it was a complete dumpster fire. Things started fine during our pre-patrol procedures. While we would be refining how we did pre-mission briefs for the first couple months with our Georgian counterparts, for this first patrol, I confirmed the plan with the Georgian patrol leader and our Georgian interpreter then went back to conduct a final brief with the Marines on my advisor team, making sure everyone was on board with what we'd be doing.

Prior to any patrol departing friendly lines, you're required to do a "comm check" with your COC. This helps ensure that, if shit hits the fan and you need to request external support, you have the ability to talk to the COC. Apparently, in our late-night/early-morning push to get our vehicles ready, one of the radios had mistakenly been attached to the wrong antenna. Add a flat tire that would need to be replaced to the equation, and we missed our SP (scheduled start patrol time) by nearly four hours. Eventually, after fixing the screwed up Marine and Georgian vehicles (which we clearly hadn't gotten to the level of mission capability we'd thought last night), we "DFL'd" (departed friendly lines) - four Georgian vehicles and one of Marine advisors.

We'd missed our scheduled ANA link-up by hours, so we were rolling solo, which we would that whole first week as we got ourselves unfucked (this would be the first of many instances of leaning on Amini to patch things up with Colonel Sultan). And, our less than auspicious start would become even less so upon leaving.

The goal of that first patrol (and something we'd be striving towards our whole deployment) was confirming intel reports about key personalities in different villages in the northeast of our area of operations: the *maleks* (village elders) and *mullahs* (village religious leaders). Depending on where you were, one of these guys filled the roll of HMFIC in that village. So here's how things were supposed to work. We'd depart in our armored vehicles, establish security somewhere near a village, and patrol on foot through that village to do some "meet & greets." Once it got dark and people went inside, we'd transition from interacting with the locals to focusing on counter-rocket operations, trying to prevent the bad dudes from launching their 107mm rockets at the base.

The above was the plan, that is, until we had to call an audible. Heading out of the northeast side of the base, our planned route involved leaving down a long access road, making a right on a main road, then a quick left onto a secondary road to head towards some key villages in the area where that first patrol would focus. However, after making the right out of base, the Georgian vehicle in the lead blew right by our left turn, putting us on a route that would ultimately loop down to the southwest—not our focus.

As we still hadn't figured out the best way to communicate between the Marine vehicle and the Georgian ones (we'd crack that nut by keeping the Georgian interpreter in the Marine one with a radio to talk to the patrol leader), I told Sergeant Curtis to stop the vehicle. As we were the middle vehicle in our five-vehicle patrol, eventually the two Georgian ones ahead of us got the message, and turned around. With the patrol leader back, we established security, locked down the road, pulled out maps, and the interpreter, Georgian patrol leader, and I talked things over. I explained to them that, having missed our turn, we'd have to turn right 150 meters back up the road (it was close enough that I was also able to point to the turn, saying, "turn right there").

Confident that we were all on the same page, I got back in the vehicle, and the lead Georgian one took off...and turned left... back to base exactly the opposite of what we'd just discussed. Fuck this. Letting my emotions get the better of me, I once again stopped our vehicle in the middle of the road and grabbed the patrol leader and interpreter. My language was far more colorful and animated than this, but here's essentially what I told the interpreter to pass on: "Get everyone who's not a driver or machine gunner out of the vehicles. They're all walking. If you can't follow the route driving, we'll walk a foot patrol of the entire northeast area of operations until you know the area inside and out."

This little exchange was an example of the "shades of gray" inherent to combat advising. Technically, I couldn't order the Georgians to do shit. But, they knew I was fired up enough that it was probably just a good idea to do what I said. So, we spent the rest of the daylight hours on a mounted/dismounted integration patrol, walking along miles of routes in the area of operations with the vehicles providing overwatch security and the dismounted troops interacting with locals and familiarizing ourselves with the villages (what we should've been doing, anyway). Bottom line, we salvaged something from an otherwise awful first patrol.

I also had another first on this patrol: calling in a real-world "CASEVAC." The quotes are intentional because, after years of training and sending what seemed like thousands of practice CASEVAC reports so that it became muscle memory, I didn't imagine the first real one I reported would be like this. As night fell, we were in a vehicle patrol base when a Georgian came up to me panicking and holding his hand. When he pulled one hand away, blood was gushing out of his thumb. Apparently he'd shut his hand in the extremely heavy, armored door of his vehicle. Yep.

So, I called in a CASEVAC report, the Polish QRF linked up with us, and this guy went back to base to have his hand sewn up. Seems like the start of a joke: a Marine, a Pole, and a bleeding Georgian meet in a bar...

The next morning, after a night moving from one historic rocket launch site to another, we confirmed how awful twenty-four-hour patrols really are. After being awake and on edge for thirty-plus hours, guys were basically hallucinating (or passed out in the back of their vehicles). This just wouldn't work—I knew the Boss and Lt. Col. Koba would need to have some more conversations about how we were operating, as this wouldn't be sustainable (or effective) for a seven-month deployment.

# III-14

# INTERPRETER TELEPHONE

......................................................

I 'VE ALREADY WRITTEN about the role Georgian nepotism played in the selection of our interpreters, but here's how this policy of choosing connections over competence played out in Afghanistan.

Working daily with Davit spoiled me, but the interpreters in the COC (between the Georgian and Marine watch officers) and out on patrol left something to be desired. A handful of outstanding civilian interpreters contracted by the Georgian Ministry of Defense did, in fact, deploy with us, but they weren't allowed outside-the-wire, and there just weren't enough to go around inside-the-wire. And, for most of the MILTERPs, I can sum up performance with the following anecdote.

One day about a month into our time on Bagram, I needed one of the Georgian company commanders and his interpreter to pick me up at 12:00 p.m. to drive over and meet with Colonel Sultan on the ANA side of base. That morning, I looked the interpreter in the eye while he was standing next to the company commander, told him what time to pick me up, and had him restate what I said to confirm nothing had been lost in translation. At 12:05, with no sign of the Georgians, here's how my phone conversation with the MILTERP went:

*Me*: "Gio, where are you guys?"

*Gio*: "In the barracks." (the barracks are twenty minutes from where I needed to be picked up)

*Me*: "What time did I tell you to pick me up?"

*Gio*: "12:00."

*Me*: "What time is it right now?"

*Gio*: "12:05...oh fuck, I messed up, didn't I?"

Though certainly frustrating at the time, this example was a pretty laughable instance, but interpreter issues proved far more dangerous and troublesome on patrol. As we began patrolling, some friction developed between the Marine team leaders and the Georgian patrol leaders. The combination of our inability as advisors to legally task the Georgians and some initial patrolling insecurity on the part of the 51stGLIB patrol leaders, let to Georgian insistence that they lead all interactions with locals out on patrol. This practice led to what I not-so-affectionately refer to as "interpreter telephone."

On any given patrol, we'd meet the *malek* of a local town, and we'd want to ask some questions and start building relationships. With the Georgian patrol leader taking point, the process became very convoluted very quickly. The Georgian patrol leader would ask something to the Georgian MILTERP in Kartouli. The MILTERP would then pass along the inquiry to our Afghan terp in English. The Afghan terp would then address the *malek* in Dari or Pashto. By this point in time, the gist of the question had already been completely bastardized by a series of mistranslations.

Eventually, the Afghan *malek* would reply to the initial question and continue talking as the process reversed itself. So, by the time the Georgian patrol leader received the response to the initial (though mistranslated) question, the malek had already moved on to some other point. If you've ever seen the *Saturday Night Live* skit with Rob Morrow playing the guy who's always bringing up something two or three topics behind the conversation with Mike Myers and Beth Cahill, that was basically our life, only far less entertaining.

Clearly, the above status quo was wildly inefficient. In a best-case scenario, we would all just be fluent in Dari and Pashto, but that wasn't going to happen. The next best solution would be the Marines leading all interactions with locals, limiting the translation game to two, maybe three, languages. But, to get Georgian buy-in to this change, we would have to approach this recommendation delicately to avoid tweaking their pride the wrong way (which inevitably led to obstinate refusal to heed advice).

Eventually we implemented the *My Big Fat Greek Wedding* approach. That is, we convinced the Georgian patrol leaders that they decided that it'd be more efficient to have the Marine team leaders take point on talking with locals. And, in return, the Marine team leaders, prior to wrapping up a conversation with a local Afghan, would ensure that the Georgian patrol leader had nothing else to ask. While this wasn't a perfect solution, and we'd still refine things throughout the deployment, it made the interpreter telephone game far less ridiculous than it initially was.

# III-15

# FIRST CONTACT

........................

A S I STATED in the introduction, this is not a book about daily gunfights in the Korengal Valley or down in Sangin District. Relative to those dudes, our deployment and area of operations proved fairly docile. With that said, we were under no illusions about the fact that we were still in Afghanistan and, besides regular rocket attacks against base, face risks while outside-the-wire. Over the previous summer at Bagram, elements of TF Top Guns received multiple rocket-propelled grenade (RPG) and small arms attacks against patrols, found or hit numerous IEDs, and, the suicide vest attack that killed the four Czechs was never far from our minds.

A little over a week into taking the lead on patrols, we were still familiarizing ourselves with the local area. One of our "problem villages," a nice little vacation spot named Qaleh (*kaw-lee*) Nasro, lay to the southwest of base and adjacent to a field where more rockets had been launched over the past year than any other area around base. For the rest of our deployment, this village would be the target of countless patrols.

Following a dismounted patrol through Qaleh Nasro, Marines and Georgians were en route to a pre-designated vehicle link-up point where they'd meet up with the patrol's armored vehicles.

As our guys were patrolling along a *qalat* wall (ubiquitous mud brick barriers), a local who had been leaning against the wall a few hundred meters from the vehicles stepped out towards the patrol and exploded into a massive fireball. Immediate reaction from the Marines roughly twenty meters back from the explosion as they saw a couple Georgians engulfed in flames: "Holy shit! This is a MASCAS (mass casualty) situation!"

Though one of the suicide bomber's legs, his guts, and other unidentifiable body parts ended up all over the place, incredibly, no Marines or Georgians were seriously injured (one Georgian did take a piece of the bomber's bone as shrapnel through his arm, which became a point of pride for this particular soldier). Consequently, this attack would be a tremendous blessing in disguise for the Marines. No one was seriously hurt, but it still provided us serious ammunition to fight against the Georgians becoming complacent on patrols. The terrifying reality of this environment, as we'd see again shortly, was that any Tom, Dick, or Jane strolling along the street could be a walking bomb, and there wasn't a whole lot we could do about it.

On a lighter note, this incident also led to the establishment of a new moniker on the team. Staff Sergeant Johnny, who was the Marine team leader on patrol and who would spend a whole lot more time in Qaleh Nasro, became affectionately known as "Johnny Nasro." For sanity's sake, you have to find the humor in even the shittiest situations.

# III-16

# TOA AND ANDY DUFRESNE

·················································

THE QALEH NASRO attack was the last major event of our left seat/right seat period, that is, our supervised transition with TF Top Guns. With this turnover coming to end, we looked forward to the culminating event, the formal "transfer of authority," or TOA, on 1 November. Transition periods always suck, and we were just ready to get into our own rhythm. After a month and a half of unfucking gear, figuring out our mission, and operating with the necessarily imposed limitation of someone else being in charge, it felt good to finally be taking point.

In addition to the legal aspect of a TOA, with one unit officially assuming responsibility for a mission, many of these events involve some pomp and circumstance. On Bagram, ours took place on a cement pad/basketball court covered by a soft-skinned exterior known on base as the "Clam Shell," which was frequently used for events like this. (Sidenote: the Clam Shell also happened to be located adjacent to our command post and the area where we staged vehicles prior to and after patrol, which would lead to significant annoyance down the line).

In a remote outpost in the Helmond River Valley, this transfer of authority probably would've looked a bit different. On Bagram, it was replete with all the frills of a Stateside military ceremony.

With the all the national and unit flags unfurled—for both the incoming Georgians and outgoing Army unit—it had the look of a retirement ceremony back on Camp Pendleton (minus the Georgian flag, that is). It was a cool ceremony to watch, though. The TF Top Guns chaplain kicked things off with an invocation and was followed by COMBAF, the two-star general, who provided some opening remarks. Following the general, the TF Top Guns commander said some words, his unit's colors (unit flag) were removed and replaced by the 51stGLIB colors, and the ceremony concluded with words from Lt. Col. Koba.

Following the formal remarks, the ceremony turned to drinks (non-alcoholic) and hors d'oeuvres-type refreshments. The fact that I'm uncomfortable even writing the words "hors d'oeuvres" in a book about a combat zone goes to show how odd things were on Bagram—finger food, a military band, and socializing like a cocktail party at the Pentagon while dudes avoided IEDs and stopped rocket attacks a mile away.

Not too interested in "celebrating" in the Clam Shell, I cut out shortly after the conclusion of the formal TOA ceremonies. And, while it was refreshing finally having the mission, it would be another week or so before the training wheels truly came off. TF Top Guns owned part of the outside-the-wire mission that we'd be taking, and part of the inside-the-wire security mission we'd assume. However, they also ran the Pink Palace command post, the Joint Defense Operations Center, or JDOC (*jay-doc*). This last role, JDOC headquarters element, would've been a bridge too far for the Georgians due to both interpreter and manpower shortages. Consequently, another US Army headquarters, TF Saber, would assume JDOC responsibilities from TF Top Guns a week after our TOA.

In the meantime, after a ten-month deployment, TF Top Guns proved understandably cautious, not wanting to push the operational envelope too far. However, this significantly limited our ability to plan patrols and learn our way around the Bagram area of operations. The "party line" coming down from COMBAF was, if a rocket wasn't launched from there, you're not patrolling to that village. Clearly this didn't make sense, as the *people* who launch the rockets can come from anywhere, so learning the key players in an entire area is critical. Fortunately, the TF Saber commander and his operations officer were both on board with this reality, and they were willing to provide us the top cover we'd need to actually start patrolling to the areas we needed to go. So, yeah, I was ready for them to take the fight.

Back to the TOA ceremony. Rather than stick around the Clam Shell, Derby and I grabbed a couple of the non-alcoholic Czech beers those guys donated to the ceremony, a pack of cigarettes, and we sat outside. Smoking, bullshitting, and drinking an "ice cold beer," I felt a lot like Andy Dufresne in *Shawshank Redemption*, sitting on top of the prison roof without a care in the world, if only for a moment.

# III-17

# FROM TERRAIN DENIAL TO COMMON SENSE

..............................................

I N OUR PURSUIT of a more effective way to conduct counter-rocket patrols, we'd cleared two hurdles. The Georgians were now on board with intel-driven operations, and we'd established our weekly intel synch to actually drive those operations. Now, we needed to get our higher headquarters' approval to shift from the status quo.

As we arrived in September and started taking over the mission in the October/November timeframe, our patrol flexibility was severely limited. I outlined it above, but we weren't receiving approval to patrol through a large number of villages around Bagram, as rockets hadn't been launched directly from those villages. To understand the situation in which we found ourselves, you had to look back to the previous summer. After a significant attack against Bagram, with over fifteen rockets launched at the base on one day, COMBAF's staff kicked down a knee-jerk reaction to TF Top Guns in the JDOC.

Moving forward, as the JDOC coordinated the daily patrol schedule, they were directed to provide a 24/7 presence in a handful of open fields where rockets had been launched. No room for flexibility in actually targeting the insurgent networks that facilitated this attack—just go to those fields and stay there.

Clearly, the above policy wouldn't stop rocket attacks. As friendly patrols hunkered down in a couple fields, insurgents just began launching rockets from other areas. And, in addition to this terrain-denial mission being ineffective, it was dangerous. When you set a pattern of sending patrols to the same place every day, you become an easy target. This had to change.

We knew how the 107mm rockets were flowing into our area of operations. As Bagram was located in a massive bowl, there were only a few routes in an out of the area. But, we were regularly denied permission to patrol to the villages along these routes, despite the fact that we knew locals living there helped facilitate the inflow of rockets. In our higher headquarters' justification for disapproving regular patrol plan submissions to these facilitation villages, we consistently saw: "Disapproved—no rockets have ever been fired from these villages." Well no shit. A shark eats with its mouth, not its tail, but the tail certainly helps get that mouth where it needs to be.

Here's the closest domestic parallel to our situation: picture a handful of guys selling drugs on a couple street corners in a city. With terrain-denial patrolling, police would park out on these street corners to ensure drug dealers no longer sold there, despite knowing that the drugs are being prepared elsewhere in the city. In this example, the police would be addressing the symptoms, drug sales (i.e. rocket attacks), instead of the root causes, drug labs throughout the city (i.e. the free flow of rockets into our area of operations).

Fortunately, we were at a good time to push for a change in the patrol requirements imposed on us. TF Saber would relieve TF Top Guns after our own TOA, and a new two-star general and his staff were replacing COMBAF. This combination of events—a series of TOAs and our ongoing frustration about the limitations imposed on our patrol objectives—led to a proposal, but not without me receiving a little mentoring first.

The Boss's "hooch" (a shipping container converted into a living space) was located right next to our command post, and it served as my primary place to go vent. As an impetuous and cynical captain, I often found myself in there bitching about one thing or another—the Georgians, our higher headquarters, the situation in general, etc. After dealing with the frustration of our most recent patrol being disapproved for targeting a village "not on the approved list," I found myself complaining to the Boss about our patrol restrictions, to which he replied something like this: "If you don't like it, then do something about it. Put together a formal proposal to change the patrol objectives, and we'll brief it to higher."

Basically, the Boss told me to quit being such a whiny bitch and take action if I wanted to make a change (pretty good life advice), and this served as the kick in the ass I needed to remove myself from this rabbit hole of frustration. And, as with pretty much all of his advice, the Boss's suggestion was spot-on. The military runs on Microsoft PowerPoint, so I put together a slide deck proposal to change our patrol objectives. While maintaining an element of terrain denial, this proposal would significantly broaden our ability to A) conduct patrols and operations driven by intelligence, and B) avoid setting patterns.

After routing my proposal through TF Saber and a follow-up call seeking some clarification from Saber's operations officer, we got the green light. Six months later, rocket attacks against Bagram Airfield had been reduced by over fifty percent.

# III-18

# THE MARINE CORPS' BIRTHDAY

·················································

W HILE NOT CRITICAL to my overall narrative, I wanted to include a quick blurb further illustrating the uniquely joint (fellow US services) and combined (other partner nation militaries) dynamic of our mission.

For Marines, celebrating the Marine Corps' Birthday every November 10th serves as a highlight to the year. Stateside, there's usually a fair amount of booze involved in this celebration, something not typically included (or allowed) in a combat zone. However, regardless of where Marines find themselves, you can guarantee that they're going to take a moment to recite and reflect on General John A. Lejeune's first birthday message, written and read back in 1921. It begins:

> On November 10, 1775, a Corps of Marines was created by a resolution of the Continental Congress. Since that date many thousand men have borne the name Marine. In memory of them it is fitting that we who are Marines should commemorate the birthday of our Corps by calling to mind the glories of its long and illustrious history...

Despite being in Afghanistan, we couldn't pass up the opportunity to celebrate the birthday and read General Lejeune's words.

Unofficially, our celebrations began the night of the 9th as midnight rolled into November 10th. At that time, we had two patrols outside-the-wire, and the Marines in both patrols had direct radio communications with both the Marines in the Georgian COC and the ones serving as liaisons right in TF Saber's JDOC, a predominantly Army command center. Like clockwork, midnight hit and, for the next ten minutes, the only traffic on the radio consisted of Marines wishing each other "happy birthday," much to the consternation of all involved not wearing a Marine uniform. But, it certainly put a smile on my face as I wrapped up a twelve- hour patrol.

The next night, we insisted on a formal ceremony, cake and all. If the other services and contractors on Bagram could have "Combat Salsa" nights, we sure as shit were going to get together for a little cake on November 10th. Sending out invites to everyone we worked with, the GLT ended up hosting a Marine Corps Birthday that included Marine, Georgian, US Army, Aussie, Czech, and Jordanian personnel—truly a joint/coalition event, and a brief moment of festivity and fun in the midst of seven months of continuous stress. Our celebration, though certainly different than my previous Birthday Balls (the formal, Stateside celebration), made us all appreciate the Marines who came before us much more.

# III-19

# LITTLE KIDS ARE LITTLE KIDS

···········································

O N PATROL, TALKING with village elders and, really, any adults in the Bagram area, you got the sense that, at best, locals withheld a significant portion of the truth, and, at worst, they actively lied to you. We saw a good example of this conducting an initial patrol in Aroki, a village northeast of base.

As we patrolled through the village, noting key infrastructure and introducing ourselves to people, we saw multiple wells in town, the sort that U.S. funds have been used to build during our time in Afghanistan. However, while having chai with the village's *malek*, he indignantly claimed that, while the surrounding villages had received Coalition aid, Aroki had not (despite the clear evidence to the contrary, and the fact that the previous unit had already told us about the wells they'd built specifically for this *malek*).

It's difficult to fault these village elders for coloring the truth. From the Afghan revolution in 1978 through the Soviet occupation to the civil war and the emergence of the Taliban and finally the U.S.-led occupation, these people have known nothing but war, and changing regimes, their whole lives. If elders are still alive, it's because they've learned to survive, which is part playing into the hands of the biggest guy on the block (the U.S. at the time), and part hedging one's bet with any other significant power brokers in the area (the Taliban and local criminal groups during our time). With that said, dealing with any of the local elders, you expected duplicity and just chalked up the bullshit and lies to "it is what it is."

However, for all the frustrations of never getting a straight answer from adults, dealing with the little kids around Bagram was always refreshing—a glimpse of humanity, of little kids being little kids, before their environment hardened them. While we experienced countless examples, one of my favorite interactions with the kids around Bagram came one afternoon early on in our time in-country.

On patrol in a local village, I was holding security during a stop, and a little kid approached and pitched me that ubiquitous pitch of Afghan children: "pen *baksheesh?*" (will you give me a pen as a gift?), a request for handouts we'd be getting on a daily basis for seven months. Smiling and not trying to part with my pen, I put my fist out for the kid to give me a "bump," which he did with all his might, winding up and punching my gloved hand. Reaction: immediate sobbing. So, I took hold of his hand, looked it over, and saw that it was fine. After seeing that everything was okay, the kid's crocodile tears disappeared, he looked at me with a grin, and, in near perfect English, asked, "Chocolate?" Still makes me smile thinking about it now.

# III-20

# COGNITIVE DISSONANCE
·············································

I N AN OVERALL strange deployment, two particular cultural situations blew my mind. Neither of these stories are essential to any overall narrative, but I figured I'd write about them anyway. The first involved a morning spent over at Colonel Sultan's office, and the second an afternoon at a Bagram local's compound outside-the-wire.

I've sung Davit's praises throughout this book, but it's hard to put into words just how unique a guy he really was. Sitting in Colonel Sultan's office one Saturday morning, after we'd finished our weekly patrol coordination, I saw just one more example of how fortunate I was to be working with Davit and a mish-mash of cultural experiences slamming into each other.

Though he speaks a little broken English, Colonel Sultan conducts his meetings in Dari, his native tongue. This particular Saturday, Amini couldn't join for one reason or another, so, following our weekly meeting, I found myself hanging out in Colonel Sultan's office with him and Davit. As we hung out, smoked cigarettes, and vodka was consumed (emphasis on the passive voice, as it took a lot of discipline to say "no thanks" on my part), I was blown away by the overall situation. While I observed, Davit and Colonel Sultan chatted away in Dari, the Afghan equivalent of

C-SPAN played on the television, with Parliamentarians yelling at each other in the background, and we filled ashtrays with the butts of local cigarettes. An Afghan, a Georgian, and a U.S. Marine spending a day in the office...

The second odd cultural experience also involved the coincidence of shared language. Out on patrol one day, Jag, a Georgian patrol leader, met a local Afghan who spoke Russian. Jag, growing up in post-Soviet Georgia, also spoke fluent Russian, so the two struck up a conversation, with the local saying he'd like to meet to discuss some concerns in the future. Back at base that day, Jag and Bane (who'd been on the same patrol), stopped by to talk with me, explaining what had happened and asking that I send Jag's platoon back to the same village and join the patrol (Jag knew I spoke very broken Russian and wanted me along for the follow-up to help assess this guy's intentions). Easy.

The following week, we headed out on patrol, knowing that we'd conduct some dismounted operations in this guy's village, which we could use as an excuse to drop by his compound (as a rule of thumb, it's good to avoid the appearance of going directly to a local's place, even if that compound is, in fact, the objective of your patrol). After the platoon established security, Jag, Bane, and I headed into the compound, where we spent the next hour talking in Russian about local security concerns, eating fresh eggs from the chickens running around the compound's courtyard, and drinking chai. From an intelligence perspective, we didn't gain anything of tremendous value. But, from a wow-is- this-really-happening perspective, this proved another bizarre interaction: a Georgian, an Afghan, and a couple of Marines hanging out and shooting the shit—in Russian!

# III-21

# HMMWVs AND THE MORPHINE DRIP OF AID

·············································

F ROM OUR TIME training in California to Georgia to the
first couple months in Afghanistan, I'd been able to dual-hat
as both an infantry advisor team leader, responsible for a small
team of infantry and fire support advisors partnering with the
Georgians out on patrol, and as our broader advisor team's operations officer, responsible for planning and coordinating all outside-the-wire operations. Within about two weeks of our TOA, it
became clear that I couldn't sustain both the regular pace of patrols
and all the bullshit associated with playing marionette behind the
scenes, pulling the strings and planning the battalion's operations.

The above reality, combined with the Boss walking into the
office to find me asleep at my desk in filthy cammies after an
overnight patrol, led to me transitioning to full-time operations
officer, handing my infantry advisor team over to one of our
staff NCOs, Claymore Bravo. With more time now to look at the
bigger picture, coordinating our actions with Colonel Sultan's
Afghan soldiers and keeping them out patrolling with us became
a huge part of my weekly "battle rhythm," with HMMWV maintenance always at the forefront of our interactions.

I've yet to mention, but the HMMWVs Colonel Sultan's soldiers used to patrol with us were the result of some prior drug deal in which old U.S. HMMWVs were passed over to the ANA as we acquired the updated MRAP armored vehicles. In theory, the Afghan Ministry of Defense had the logistical ability to provide its various units the repair parts necessary to keep its vehicles out patrolling. In reality, it took some serious creativity and cannibalizing of other vehicles to keep enough HMMWVs on the road to patrol. During our time in country, President Ghani had centralized all Ministry of Defense logistics support to a few key hubs in an attempt to cut down on theft and corruption. Though a noble pursuit, the effect was an extremely lengthy (and at times, seemingly nonexistent) process for getting repair parts for everything from vehicles to machine guns out to the guys on the ground.

The above put us into a tough spot, and it represents the paradox of being an officer with both A) a vested interest in an improving security situation in Afghanistan, and B) Marines outside-the-wire on a daily basis. With respect to the former, the long-term, sustainable solution to the HMMWV problem would be forcing Colonel Sultan to wait on the tortuous and unreliable Afghan National Army supply system, thus ensuring an "Afghan solution." However, the cost of this approach, and the nature of this paradox, would be my Marines out on patrol without ANA partners, as they would not join us without a minimum of two armored HMMWVs per patrol.

So, I had two options. *Option 1*: Stop conducting partnered patrols with Colonel Sultan's forces due to a shortage of functioning HMMWVs and wait for the Afghan supply system to work itself out. *Option 2*: Say fuck it and fix the HMMWVs, because I care more about the short-term well-being of my Marines than a long-term Afghan solution. Naturally, I chose Option 2, and you can bet your ass that every week our maintenance chief joined me on the Afghan side of base and worked absolute miracles to keep Colonel Sultan's HMMWVs running. Enter the morphine drip of aid: As small-unit leaders, our primary concern was bringing our dudes home alive, not a grand solution to the "Afghan problem." Consequently, as we worked short-term solutions to systemic problems, these band-aid approaches disincentivized any major overhaul of the logistics nightmare facing the Afghan Ministry of Defense.

Ultimately, I valued the safety and lives of our Marines and Georgians more than some abstract notion of fixing a broken system. You cannot ask the guys on the ground, the ones who put their lives on the line day-in and day-out, to make sacrifices for the "greater good" when the system has failed. What's the resolution? Fucked if I know, but we kept fixing HMMWVs, and we kept the ANA patrolling with us.

# III-22

# SCHOOL AND IEDS

......................................

P ART OF MY transition from team leader to full time operations officer involved handing off relationships I'd built with
locals in our area of operations prior to officially turning over my
team to Claymore Bravo. When you go to the same villages a
few times to drink chai and eat raisins with the same village
elders, you establish some rapport (notice I'm not naïve enough
to suggest loyalty or camaraderie here). Bajawri, located a few
kilometers northeast of base, proved to be one of these villages.

The focus of a fair amount of threat reporting and the source of
more than a few rocket attacks, we knew we'd need to spend a lot
of time in Bajawri. Over the past couple months in Bagram, we'd
built some relationships with the village *malek, mullah,* and other
elders, and we'd spent some time discussing the village's need
for a new school, a common theme throughout the area.

There are a couple of rules of thumb when dealing with the ubiquitous requests for Coalition money and aid. First, never promise
something you can't deliver. And second, if you can make something happen, ensure you under-promise and over-deliver. In the
case of Bajawri, we didn't have the juice to build a school, but the
base had received a couple full-size shipping containers of school

supplies (notebooks, pens and pencils, backpacks for young children, et cetera). So, we looked at this situation as a win-win-win:

*Win 1*: Opportunity to transfer relationships with Bajawri elders to Claymore Bravo.

*Win 2*: Continue to build the legitimacy of the ANA, who'd accompany us on the mission, and the Georgians, whose civil-military affairs officer, Major Zaza, would be the 51stGLIB face of the school supply delivery.

*Win 3*: Actually help some local kids with school supplies, which are drastically lacking in Afghanistan.

The morning of the delivery, our patrol linked up with the ANA outside of Bagram, coiled up our vehicles near Bajawri, and transferred the bags of school supplies from our vehicles to the ANA HMMWVs, which would be small enough to drive through the narrow alleys into the village center. With the HMMWVs in the lead, we dismounted and patrolled on foot into Bajawri, meeting the *malek, mullah*, and a few other village elders in the village's main square.

With perimeter security established around our meeting, we began our ceremony in the traditional Afghan way—sitting in a circle, drinking chai, eating local raisins, and making small talk. And, we couldn't have asked for a more beautiful day—nothing but clear, blue skies.

After the requisite banter, the *malek* said a few words of thanks and organized the village children. In previous supply drops, units had run into the issue of *maleks* and *mullahs* hoarding donated supplies in order to increase their own wealth and influence ("wasta"), so it was a good sign that we'd be giving the school supplies directly to individual kids.

With huge smiles on their faces, about twenty kids from the village all received backpacks stuffed with school supplies. (Sidebar: interesting how priorities in life are so relative. As a seven-to ten-year-old kid, I definitely wouldn't have given a shit about receiving more school supplies. This actually would've been a bit of a downer, as summer was likely wrapping up—makes me feel like quite the bratty little bastard looking back on things.)

After handing out all the school stuff, we said our goodbyes and began our foot patrol to link-up with the vehicles. Adhering to that fundamental tenet of patrolling—never leave the way you came in—the vehicles had moved to a new position, and we headed that way. As we exited the windy allies of Bajawri proper, the ANA HMMWVs parted ways with us, and we were off to finish the rest of the patrol.

As we patrolled down a dirt road with *qalat* walls on either side, the Marines and Georgians were strung out roughly 100 meters from tip to end, keeping some distance between each guy. It happened quickly. I was in the middle of the patrol when a motorcycle flew by me, and, about twenty meters in front of me, a massive fireball erupted, sending a blast wave, dirt, and debris back through the patrol. My first thought was *Oh fuck, someone stepped on an IED!* I didn't even have the time to process that the motorcycle itself was the IED, with a suicide bomber triggering the explosion.

Two Georgians were down hard, and our JTAC (fire support lead), who'd been the man ahead of me, was scraped up pretty good. "Corpsman up!" Man, if you ever want to meet an impressive group of people, spend some time with Navy docs serving in Marine units. Before I'd even yelled for him, Doc S, who'd been at the end of the patrol, was sprinting to the blast scene to assess the two Georgians. Reaching them, he treated one directly and oversaw a Georgian medic treating the other. Fast forward, and after these two came out of surgery back on base, the surgeon said unequivocally, were it not for Doc S's actions, the Georgian he'd treated would be dead.

I've tried to state it pretty clearly, but this story is definitely not a "heroics of battle" book—certainly no *Lone Survivor* situation here. With that said, as soon as that IED went off, training kicked in, and our hundreds of reps conducting "immediate action drills" paid off. Like clockwork, the following occurred: 1) I established security with the dismounts; 2) the Marines and Georgians in the vehicles drove them from the coil spot to a field immediately adjacent to the blast site; 3) our JTAC, despite shrapnel and blast wounds, began coordinating air support to prevent any follow-on attacks (after I'd helped him with the obligatory "dude check my balls; are they still there?"); and 4) Claymore Bravo began relaying casualty information I yelled to him back to our COC so that a MEDEVAC helicopter could be launched.

Walking the perimeter to ensure the Georgians had all security sectors covered, I came around the corner of a *qalat* wall and, turning, saw a kid on a bicycle riding towards us about twenty-five meters away. I raised my weapon, clicked off safe, and yelled, "Get the fuck back!" While he may not have understood English, he certainly understood my tone, and he immediately turned around. Watching a couple of friends get blown up does funny things to you. While in retrospect that kid likely wasn't a threat, had he not stopped, I wouldn't have hesitated to shoot him in the chest. Fortunately, he did stop.

As I watched the kid pedal away, I finally had time to pause and assess the situation more fully. At the blast site I saw the charred remnants of a motorcycle chassis, a destroyed *qalat* wall, and the bombers guts strewn all over the path. His head made it about seventy-five meters out into the field to our north, where we had to pick it up to get a proper picture of his face for intel purposes—not something people should have to do, hold a head in one hand as you snap a photo of it with the other.

When the MEDEVAC bird landed, we loaded the two Georgians on and sent our JTAC along with them (though not life threatening, he definitely needed his wounds addressed). The QRF eventually arrived to relieve us at the blast site and complete the full exploitation (intel gathering) of the area. One of the evac'd Georgians was the platoon leader, so the unit was definitely not in the right state of mind to continue patrolling.

Back on base a couple hours after the initial attack, the adrenaline finally faded, and the shakes started. Sitting back and smoking more than a few cigarettes outside our COC, I thought about a few things:

1. How thoroughly had the suicide bomber been checked by the Georgian at the rear of the patrol, and would a more thorough check have even made a difference with the IED built into the chassis of the bike?

2. Did the ANA know the attack was going to happen, and that's why they peeled away so quickly after we left Bajawri? (cynical view, yes; other view, no, as Afghan security forces have received the brunt of Taliban attacks over the years; conclusion—don't know).

3. The worst question, the one that never goes away: What could I have done differently?

The internal wound caused by this last question would be ripped open a half year after we left Afghanistan.

# III-23

# REFLECTIONS ON "ESCALATION OF FORCE"

·············································

A S I THOUGHT more about the previous story, and specifically the part about almost shooting a kid for riding his
bike towards us, it made me realize I should probably talk a little
more about "escalation of force," or EOF. Looking for a suitable
definition of EOF (besides the you'll-know-it-when-you-see-it"
cop out a la pornography), I stumbled upon an article by an
Army officer, Lieutenant Randall Bagwell, from a 2008 Department of the Army Pamphlet title *The Army Lawyer*. I'm a big
fan of not reinventing the wheel, and this guy definitely explains
it better than I could.

> The traditional role of escalation of force (EOF) is to
> help with the proportional application of force in self-
> defense situations. The basic idea is simple—to increase
> the magnitude of force applied to an identified threat
> until the threat is deterred or, if necessary, eliminated.[1]

---

[1] Randall Bagwell, "The Threat Assessment Process (TAP): The Evolution of Escalation of
Force," *The Army Lawyer*, April 2008, 5.

I think Bagwell's definition is sound, but it rests upon one huge assumption - that you can actually identify a known threat, something absolutely not taken for granted in a counterinsurgency. In the Afghan (or Iraqi, Somali, or insert other insurgencies here) environment, the enemy lacks a uniform and blends in with the population, making positive identification a pipe dream until rounds are already down range.

Addressing this inconsistency between his definition and the struggles of positive identification, Bagwell continues:

> How then did EOF find its way on to the counterinsurgency battlefields of Iraq and Afghanistan? In these conflicts, the issue has not been the excessive use of force against low-level threats, but rather the identification of who to use force against in the first place.[2]

Basically, we establish EOF procedures to avoid "bad kills," that is, shooting an innocent civilian due to a mistaken threat, a significant challenge following a few suicide attacks, when anyone around you can be classified a threat.

So how does EOF actually play itself out? What are junior soldiers and Marines doing out on the battlefield? While the mnemonic devices vary, a common one in the Marines is "shout, show, shoot." As a potential threat approaches (e.g. a motorcycle along a road, a civilian approaching a foot patrol, a car driving up to a checkpoint, etc.), you provide 1) an audible warning by yelling or using a bullhorn ("shout"), 2) a visual warning with a flare if you have enough time, or raising your weapon if time and space are limited ("show"), and 3), you engage with your weapon

[2]Ibid, 5.

("shoot"). No warning shots—if you're pulling the trigger, it's because someone needs to go down.

It's pretty easy to write a paragraph describing escalation of force. But, it's one of the hardest things in combat to actually do, to have the discipline and confidence to identify a potential threat and trust in your EOF procedures, knowing that failure to execute them properly entails a lose-lose situation. Shoot too early, you kill a civilian. Fail to shoot, you and your buddies get blown up.

These EOF challenges beg the question: Why are we here? Is what we're doing in Afghanistan worth the lose-lose situations into which we put these young men? When we put America's youth in a position where they need to make a choice between potentially shooting an innocent civilian or getting blown up, there better be some pretty good justification.

I can already hear the typical counter-arguments to my line of reasoning: "A well- trained Marine doesn't have to worry about EOF problems," or "Bad kills are a product of bad leadership," blah, blah, blah. Bullshit.

At the end of the day, we need to ask: Do we as a society want our warriors put in a situation where they may need to live with the moral, psychological, and legal effects of killing a civilian for the rest of their lives? Or, on the flip side, not doing anything and watching their buddies die as a result? Maybe the answer is yes, but it's a discussion worth having.

Being "patriotic" doesn't mean blindly supporting America's use of military force—it means having the courage to question whether what we're doing is right. Anything short of that frank conversation does a tremendous disservice to the warfighters putting their lives on the line day-in and day-out, only to have their decisions picked apart on CNN by the same people who voted to send them overseas in the first place.

Okay, I'll get off my soapbox now.

# III-24

# THANKSGIVING PRIORITIES AND COMBAT SALSA

······················································

I KNEW THANKSGIVING would be different in Afghanistan—
no drunken Buffalo Turkey Trot here. Instead, I'd be leading
the Georgians on a night infiltration to an overwatch position just
outside of one of the higher threat villages in our area of operations.
The plan would have one platoon infiltrate ("infil") to high ground,
and another platoon conduct a patrol at dawn through that village—
far more appealing task when you have friendly machine gunners
covering you. Despite turning over my daily patrol responsibilities,
the Boss still let me take lead on the larger operations, which helped
me maintain my sanity, and the Georgians listened to me more
outside the wire due to my relationship with Major Nik.

In addition to this Thanksgiving operation being more complex
than our daily patrols due to the coordination required between
multiple units, briefing it also led to another entertaining (now,
not then) language barrier story. Prior to briefing the plan, Davit
had translated copies of it and passed them out to the Georgian
patrol leaders, and I'd given the Marine leads their English-language versions. So, when I started talking through things over a
map, everyone already had a few hours to familiarize themselves

with the written version, which led me to kick things off with the following conversation:

*Me*: "Everyone's familiarized themselves with the plan, yeah?"
*GEO PLs*: Nod heads and say, "*Qui, qui*" (yes, yes).
*Me*: "Okay, we'll cover phase 1, infil, first [...] And the vehicles will stop here, where we'll establish security, dismount, and begin our infil to our overwatch position."
*GEO PL* (who would be with me at the overwatch position via a terp): "Whoa! Stop! We're walking?"

Clearly, the Georgians hadn't read the plan. *Another* gray hair.

Despite the cultural frustrations, this story outlines where the Marine and Georgian priorities rested on Thanksgiving: prepping for patrol, patrolling, or sleeping/recovering post-patrol. There was a different mindset throughout base, where the majority of civilian contractors and service members didn't leave the wire, which is fine, that is, until it's not. Despite coming to terms with the realities of our "country club deployment," sometimes things were just too much, and Thanksgiving happened to be one of them. Really, three things occurred in close proximity that came close to putting me over the edge.

First, the chow hall shut down early so people could decorate it for the holiday. No issues here—until shutting it down early meant one of our Marine patrol teams wouldn't get to eat prior to a twelve-hour patrol. Fortunately I heard about this second hand, as I don't think I could've controlled my temper with that one. Second, as one of our teams was prepping for patrol, a soldier walked by and asked what they were doing. When one of our Marines explained that they were heading out with the Georgians, the soldier responded incredulously, "There're still guys patrolling here?" That about sums up the give-a-fuck for our mission. And, lastly, as I went through final checks with my guys before our night infil, music blared from the Clam Shell next door. The reason? "Combat Salsa Night." Nice.

As we were rolling out, hundreds of people on base were salsa-ing away the night, not a care in the world. I'm all for finding ways to stay entertained overseas, but this was a tough pill to swallow. Apparently priorities and experiences will vary.

# III-25

# ROCK CITY

·····················

I MENTIONED IT above, but the target village of our Thanks-giving op was a nice little spot in the western reaches of our area named Khwajakhel, built on the slopes leading up to the Hindu Kush. With the geography of the "Bagram Bowl," there were only a few routes in and out of the area, and, by extension, a few routes for weapons to flow. Khwajakhel happened to be one of those places—located just a couple kilometers off Afghanistan's "Ring Road" and along a small path through the mountains to our west. Bottom line, we knew it was a key node for weapons facilitation in Bagram. And, due to its location on the outskirts of our area of operations, friendly forces had for the most part ignored the place, something we'd need to change if we wanted to disrupt the flow of rockets being lobbed onto base.

After catching a quick nap, we rolled out little after midnight, winding our armored vehicles through and around dark villages to the western reaches of the Bagram Bowl. The whole intent of an infiltration ("infil") is for people to not know you're in an area, which is pretty difficult with massive vehicles rolling around on an otherwise quiet night—driving right up to Khwajakhel's doorstep was out of the question. Instead, the vehicles established security about six kilometers southeast of the village, and all the dismounts began a foot movement to the high ground above Khwajakhel to the west.

At risk of appearing more "cool, bearded guy" than we really were, there was very little high-speed and sexy about this infil. If you've seen any movies with Navy SEALs and other special forces types operating with their night-vision goggles (NVGs), picture the exact opposite of how they worked, and you've got us. As I navigated the movement into our overwatch spot, I looked back at the line of Georgians strung out 100 meters or so behind us, and it looked (and sounded) like a conga line of infrared light (visible through our NVGs), with each of the Georgians decked out with an infrared glow stick—not visible to the naked eye, but it looked like a rave with your NVGs down.

Despite the very non-tactical nature of our movement (and a lot of bitching from the Georgians about how far the movement was), somehow or another, we made it undetected to our overwatch position before sunrise. Just to the west of the village, with a clear vantage down the only road leading up from the Ring Road, we posted up in an abandoned *qalat* complex. And, as the sun came up, we ensured the villagers knew we were there. I'll tell you what, a five-hour foot patrol in sub-freezing temperature is absolutely worth it when you see the look in a local villagers face first thing in the morning that just says, "Holy shit, there are a bunch of soldiers outside of my house, and I have no idea how they got there."

By revealing ourselves in the morning, we ensured that, fairly quickly, everyone in Khwajakhel would know we were there. With friendly rifles and machine guns clearly holding the high-ground, we could prevent any local fighters from trying to ambush the platoon rolling into the village first thing that morning. So, without incident, the second platoon departed base and drove their vehicles to the doorstep of Khwajakhel, dismounted, and began their foot patrol through the village to confirm key infrastructure and personalities.

A couple of hours later, as the dismounted patrol through the village was supposed to be wrapping up, we heard a sharp crack from inside the narrow lanes of Khwajakhel. Immediately after, I heard broken radio traffic from a Marine with the dismounted platoon that sounded something like this: "Dozens of kids... rocks... flash bang." It didn't take a detective to figure out that the adults in the village didn't want us there, and they'd rallied the village children to begin throwing rocks at the patrol (which led to a "flash bang" grenade being thrown to back these kids away).

A few minutes later, I watched the Marines and Georgians spill out of Khwajakhel's dark, windy lanes into the open fields where their vehicles were linking up with them, chased by a mob of at least a hundred kids, all throwing rocks towards the patrol, with our guys keeping them at bay shooting paintball non-lethal rounds. Using kids was a pretty good tactic by the locals, as we obviously couldn't shoot them, but the rocks still forced us out. From our overwatch spot, had these been adults with AK-47s shooting at our guys, we'd have opened up with machine guns (known as a "support-by-*fire* position). Improvising, we instead opened up with all the signal flares we had, knowing they would scatter the kids without hurting them (jokingly dubbed a "support-by-*flare* position").

While the flares bought us a little time from the tiny hellions, there were too many of them, and too few flares, to hold them off for long. As we all loaded into vehicles to depart and travel down a couple kilometers of road out of Khwajakhel, we faced a 500 meter linear "rock ambush" with kids popping up all over the place to hurl rocks at our vehicles. Fortunately, our turret gunners avoided any serious injury from the hurled projectiles.

Back on base and able to think a little more clearly, we knew we'd stumbled into a real shithole of bad guys in Khwajakhel, henceforth known as "Rock City." On the surface it was just little kids being little kids—throwing rocks at the outsiders. But, piecing together our experiences that morning with threat reporting we'd

received, we knew there were some bad guys in that village that
didn't want us poking around, something that would be validated
a couple weeks later with the last friendly casualties of the ISAF
mission. For the rest of our time in Afghanistan, Khwajakhel
would be a key player in our narrative.

# III-26

# MARRIAGE COUNSELORS AND PUTTING OUT FIRES

......................................................

A S WE CONTINUED to operate with a hodgepodge of na-
tionalities, another role for the Marine advisors out on
patrol gradually emerged: marriage counselor. Frequently frustrated with each other, the Georgians would call the Afghan soldiers "Taliban," and the Afghans would call the Georgians "Russians," each slur infuriating the respective group.

As advisors, we tried to live by a "golden rule" of sorts. If you
treat people you're working with like your brothers, they'll fight
for you. Conversely, if you treat people like shit, why would
they be motivated to have your back in a tight spot? Furthermore,
the threat of "green-on-blue" attacks, where Afghan forces turn
their weapons on Coalition Forces, was never far from our minds.
Bottom line, it was good for everyone to make sure a solid working relationship existed between the Georgians and Afghans.
And, from a practical perspective, we already had our hands full
on patrol providing general security and tactical guidance to both
the Georgians and Afghans. The last thing we needed was to
also have to continuously monitor the growing tension between
these two groups.

Things came to a head a couple months after we'd officially taken the mission. Following a particularly contentious patrol of bickering, the Afghan patrol leader returned to base thoroughly offended by the way he'd been treated, which led Colonel Sultan to threaten stopping partnered patrols all together.

I've said it frequently, but having the ANA on patrol with us, especially during the day, was absolutely critical to our success. They provided increased security, cultural understanding, and legitimacy with the local population. Plus, in theory, the more proficient they became, the less work and risk we'd need to undertake securing the Bagram area (this was the long-term strategic goal, helping establish an Afghan force capable of conducting unilateral security operations). So, losing Colonel Sultan's soldiers as partners would have been catastrophic on multiple levels, and this issue required immediate action.

To address the issue, we needed the guys at the top to sit in a room together and hash things out, so I arranged a meeting between Colonel Sultan, Lt. Col. Koba, the Boss, and Amini. Everyone met over on the ANA side of base, had a huge Afghan lunch, and Colonel Sultan and Lt. Col. Koba bonded over the shared experience of fighting the Russians. Far beyond my expectations, an extremely solid relationship between the Afghan and Georgian commanders was born from this meeting. And, that evening, Lt. Col. Koba delivered some fire and brimstone "guidance" to his platoon leaders to treat the ANA as their own brothers. Moving forward, there was a tangible change on patrol as the Georgians embraced the ANA as integral members of the team. Crisis averted.

# III-27

# "CELEBRATING" PEARL HARBOR REMEMBRANCE DAY

....................................................

W HEN YOU'RE IN Afghanistan on 7 December, I suppose it's only natural to "celebrate" Pearl Harbor with a rocket attack against base. Shortly after sunset, the fireworks show that is the counter-rocket, artillery, and mortar (C-RAM) ripped into action, firing thousands of projectiles into the night sky to deflect the incoming rocket. Inside the COC, we tracked the response of the Georgian internal-QRF tasked with responding to rocket attacks, learning that the round had impacted near a laundry facility on the far side of base. Initial reports: multiple casualties.

Over the next hour, we monitored the situation and confirmed our team's accountability as the base hospital dealt with the mass-casualty incident (MASCAS)—with Navy corpsmen and medics from all over the base supplementing hospital personnel to assist with trauma care. And, as we gained a clearer picture of what happened, we learned that two of our Marines posted at the command post on that side of base had been first responders to the impact site. Late that night, once things had quieted down, these two Marine NCOs came over to my office to provide a full account of what happened.

As he headed to grab chow, Sgt M. heard the "incoming" alert of an impending rocket attack, and he heard/felt the impact around the corner. Running from the chow hall to the laundry facility, he saw that the entire roof had collapsed, sending debris and a cloud of dirt all over the place. After calling Sgt F. back at the area command post to report the location and request QRF assistance, he ran into the collapsed building, tearing through debris and pulling casualties out from the wreckage.

Doing what Marine NCOs do, Sgt M. took control of the situation. He established a casualty collection point and coordinated the response and casualty evacuation procedures until base emergency teams could arrive. It's funny, but when shit hits the fan, rank and seniority become irrelevant in an initiative vacuum. Instead, people look to whomever's willing to step up to the plate and take charge. Sergeants M. and F. filled this role at the impact site. While on scene, these two Marines provided critical, combat life-saving techniques to three casualties, at one point using a "beanie" to hold a man's organs in over a gaping abdominal wound.

Unfortunately, two Afghan contractors died in the attack, but these Marines' actions and courage in "running to the sound of gunfire" saved the lives of several others. Listening to them recount the events in my office that night, I had to fight back tears of pride—one of those odd combinations of exhaustion and emotion that just hit me. Don't get me wrong, I'll bitch about the bureaucratic bullshit of the Marine Corps seven days a week and twice on Sunday, but this is what makes it all worth it. These NCOs weren't trained special operators (or medics for that matter)— one was a comm Marine and the other a vehicle mechanic. But, they took charge in a shitty situation and made things happen, doing what hard-nosed Marines do, regardless of job title.

# III-28

# THE TORTURE REPORT

........................................

O N 9 DECEMBER 2014, the Senate Select Committee on
    Intelligence released the redacted version of its report cov-
ering the CIA's "Detention and Interrogation Program," a study
known widely as the "Torture Report." Looking to the past as
precedent, widespread riots were expected throughout Afghanistan
following the report's release. In 2011, a Koran burning ceremony
in Florida sparked mass riots throughout the country. In 2012,
after word got out that Korans had been burned in the detention
center on Bagram (Taliban detainees had been using the religious
texts to write messages to each other), more rioting kicked off
throughout the country, with Afghan Members of Parliament calling on locals to "wage jihad" against Americans.

These events led to hundreds of Afghans and at least four
Americans dying. And, this chaos framed the expected response
to the Torture Response, with mass rioting around U.S. bases
anticipated throughout the country. In an attempt to avoid inciting
further rioting and not put American and Coalition forces un-
necessarily at risk, our patrols were cancelled for a day-and-a-
half following the report's release. If Afghans were going to riot,
why add fuel to the fire with U.S. troops rolling through Afghan
streets? Or so the logic went. I'm not sure whether cancelling

patrols was an order from the two-star on Bagram, COMBAF, or the four-star in charge of the entire Afghan mission, COMISAF. Regardless, TF Saber relayed to us that we'd be standing down patrols and restricted to base.

In retrospect, it's easy to find fault with the decision to cancel patrols after what happened the following day. But, with the above history of riots in mind, it's hard to argue with the decision's rationale.

# III-29

# RCP

........

A FTER CANCELLING PATROLS for a day-and-a-half following the release of the "Torture Report," we had units
back out on Friday 12 December. It turned into a pretty tough
night. In addition to the standard Georgian/Marine and Czech
security patrols around Bagram, our Route Clearance Platoon
(RCP) partners were conducting an IED clearance mission down
Highway 1 towards Kabul and back. RCP was a U.S. Army unit
we worked with closely, as we relied heavily upon them to help
us stay ahead in the cat and mouse game of roadside counter-
IED operations in our area.

Things started off as a pretty standard Friday night. After the
Boss and I wrapped up the nightly Georgian staff meeting, I
grabbed some chow and headed back to the office to work—the
most productive time of day tended to be around 8:00 p.m. As
the COC night shift takes over, things usually quiet down for a
while, allowing me to focus on planning future patrol schedules
and deliberate ops. Sitting at my desk, I heard an explosion from
outside- the-wire. Usually a bad thing.

By the time I walked down the hall to our COC, one of the big
screens on the wall was already piping in black-and-white footage
from a drone overhead of what looked like a massive crater. Ori-

enting myself, it became clear that an entire section of the road had collapsed, and a mangled armored vehicle lay on its side next to the crater. My immediate reaction was that no one could have survived an IED that big.

Within about thirty minutes, Lt. Col. Koba, the TF Saber commander, an explosive ordnance disposal (EOD) team, the "wrecker" tow vehicle, and two Georgian patrols were heading out to the blast site to provide support and security. As these units prepared to depart friendly lines, we watched the silent hulks of two Blackhawk helicopters as they appeared in the display of the drone footage. After circling the blast site several times looking for a place to set down in the midst of the *qalat* walls and grape rows, the two CASEVAC birds landed directly on the road. Monitoring the chat traffic with reports from the scene, we learned that, of all the casualties from the destroyed vehicle, two soldiers were killed immediately.

Shortly before dawn Saturday morning, the wrecker crew and patrols returned from the blast site, with the destroyed vehicle in tow. Though wounded, the soldiers from the vehicle not killed in the initial attack all survived, which, seeing that vehicle in person, was difficult to believe. Our wrecker team didn't return to base with an armored vehicle. They returned to base with a charred metal skeleton.

After conducting their post-blast analysis, the EOD techs estimated that the IED, planted in a culvert under the road, consisted of over 200 pounds of high explosive. As I said in the previous vignette, I understand the rationale for holding back patrols for a day-and-a-half—historical precedent from previous riots throughout Afghanistan created cause for concern. But, the correlation between not patrolling for an extended period of time and then hitting the largest IED we'd seen in our area of operations immediately after this gap would significantly shape my outlook moving forward.

I am absolutely not saying that by not patrolling, we caused these two soldiers to be killed. At the end of the day, the scumbags who planted and detonated the IED were the ones who killed them. But, to ignore the correlation would be naïve and dangerous.

Dragging 200 pounds of high explosive under a main road in our heavily trafficked area of operations would certainly be possible, but significantly more difficult, had we been patrolling rather than restricted to base. Unfortunately, we can't know for certain if friendly patrols may have prevented that emplacement, but I certainly didn't want to have to wonder about that again, whether our inaction contributed to guys getting killed.

# III-30

# BARYALI

·················

A COUPLE DAYS after the 12 December attack, I experienced a few firsts. I attended the memorial ceremony honoring the two RCP soldiers who had been killed, and I stood at attention during the ramp ceremony as their flag-draped coffins were loaded onto a transport plane to be brought back to grieving loved ones in America. These two ceremonies represent the love and devotion service members have for each other, honoring our brothers and sisters who have made the ultimate sacrifice. But, for obvious reasons, I hope I never need to attend such sobering experiences again.

My other first focused outward. For the first time in my life, I could put a face and name to someone I truly wanted to kill, and not in an abstract, watching-al-Qaeda-on-TV sense. With the post-blast materials EOD gathered from the IED attack site, the military forensics lab discovered human DNA. After a couple of days, DNA analysis confirmed the attacker, a local scumbag I'll call "Baryali." Turns out, he'd been a detainee on Bagram several years prior as a low-level terrorist, so his picture and DNA remained in the database.

When I looked at the picture of Baryali dug out of the detention center records, it was the first time in my life I could look at a picture and feel a visceral hatred driving me to want to kill someone. This is a strange sensation. Seeing the results of terrorist attacks on TV, or reading about a school shooting, I've often been overcome with anger and hatred towards the perpetrators. But, these experiences had always been abstract and detached from the day-to-day realities of my own life. With Baryali's face printed and hanging in my office, this changed. I was now driven by a desire to kill someone that would significantly influence operations for the rest of our time in Afghanistan.

# III-31

# "OPERATION CHRISTMAS OFFENSIVE"

·············································

O N DEPLOYMENT, EITHER in a combat zone or just some-where around the world, boredom and routine inevitably lead to Marines devising seemingly silly ways to entertain themselves. For me, I did this through picking different names for our deliberate operations. In a given week, we sent out multiple, daily security patrols. For these, our weekly intel sync drove certain objectives, I'd assess and prioritize these objectives, and Davit would translate them into Georgian so we were all on the same page.

For the higher risk objectives, and in line with the "marionette" approach, I'd plan a deliberate operation that employed more Georgians and Marines, going into far deeper levels of detail and coordination, for three reasons:

1. This level of detailed planning helped minimize room for misunderstanding between Marines and Georgians conducting the mission (as long at Davit translated it). All key players were briefed and understood the full plan, not just a specific patrol objective.

2. For better or worse, planning a deliberate, "named operation" increased the likelihood of "higher" providing us supporting assets, aka cool toys, to employ (Army Apache and Kiowa helicopters, Air Force F-16s, Predators, EOD teams, etc).

3. As part of the "long look," I could use these deliberate operations to incrementally increase the tactical complexity of missions
the Georgian/Marine team could successfully execute.

The above reasons, combined with our intel that Baryali lived
in a village just west of Highway 1 called Nurjan Kala, made
planning a deliberate op to track him down necessary. Nurjan Kala
abutted Khwajakhel, ol' Rock City, and was also a known hub for
the facilitation of weapons into the Bagram area. And, as we were
getting close to the holidays, why wouldn't we name our op into
Nurjan Kala "Operation Christmas Offensive"?

To be clear, jokes about being "team guys [*cough...*] Georgian
Liaison" aside, we were under no illusions of grandeur that we
were some direct action, special forces unit conducting high-level
capture/kill missions. If you watched us operating at night, you'd
know in a second we were far from this "tier 1" status. *But*, what
we could do and had done regularly was gather intelligence on
our patrols that could be handed off to the guys in beards who did
conduct those types of missions. Basically, we understood where
our cog fit in the greater machine, and we were itching to do our
part to find Baryali.

Within the above context, we planned a two-platoon operation
into Nurjan Kala, with a particular focus on where we believed
Baryali's father lived, to show photos of the asshole to locals.
Once again, not really some high-speed op out of a movie, but, we
had realistic expectations of 1) getting some more information
about the guy, and 2) hopefully spooking him into doing something
stupid that would bring him out into the open.

# III-32

# INTO NURJAN KALA/SHAWSHANK PRISON

...............................................................

O N CHRISTMAS EVE, the night before our Nurjan Kala op, one of the Marine vehicles in a patrol hit an IED—no casualties fortunately, but another reminder of the threat. With this attack fresh in our minds, we conducted our final preparation before dawn Christmas morning. Having transitioned from dual-hatting to full-time operations officer, for deliberate operations like this one, I'd link up with one of the platoons executing, let the Marine team leader coordinate with his Georgian counterpart, and focus on A) coordinating actions between the multiple pla-toons, and B) talking back to the COC to ensure external support, as required.

"Christmas Offensive" plan: I'd go to Baryali's father's house with one platoon, while the other platoon would go directly to a couple other houses in the village with reported connections to the guy. The rationale for this distributed approach was that, with multiple units operating in sync with each other throughout the village, guys trying to shoot us (or, the greater threat, send a suicide attacker) would struggle to pin down and isolate one friendly ele-ment. And, to reiterate, we weren't conducting "hard hits" at these houses involving dynamic breaches, full house clearances et cetera. Quite the opposite, Coalition Forces weren't even allowed into Afghan compounds without an explicit invitation (plenty more on that later). Rather, we fully recognized the limits of both our training and rules of engagement, and we looked at these home visits as attempts to get some information that could be acted on later by "stirring the hornet's nest."

With final coordination complete, the two platoons' vehicles departed base together, linked up with our ANA partners, and split up at a designated release point outside. While the other platoon inserted directly to their objective compounds in their vehicles, the unit I accompanied took a different approach. Due to the terrain and Nurjan Kala's narrow dirt roads and *qalat* walls, we established security with our vehicles about three kilometers from Baryali's father's house and conducted a foot patrol into the village from another direction than the other platoon.

For deliberate ops like this one, there was significant benefit to having a couple extra Marines out on patrol (in this case, our intel chief and I). Bane, the team leader, could focus on security with the Georgians and ANA soldiers, while we could focus on talking with and questioning locals while flashing pictures of Baryali, knowing that the other dudes had our backs. As alluded to in the title, I felt like we'd entered Shawshank Prison, where everyone was innocent (just fucked by their lawyers...). Despite our knowledge that this village was an absolute hub for weapons facilitation, all the villagers loved flashing smiles and giving us, "there are no bad people in this village" lines.

Eventually, we isolated one younger guy who was clearly afraid to talk with us, but it was obvious the photo of Baryali sparked a reaction with him. When pushed, he eventually spoke in an odd allegory: "In the jungle, there are good animals, and there are bad animals. This village is like the jungle." We couldn't get anything more concrete from him, so I decided to play along with the jungle allegory and take a page out of Wyatt Earp's *Tombstone* playbook: "Do you see that base over there? (pointing to Bagram in the distant low ground off to our east). That's where the biggest and baddest animals in the jungle live—the beasts with the green eyes (night-vision goggles) who come at night and take people away. And when you see Baryali, let him know that these green-eyed beasts will ride in on their pale horses (Blackhawk helicopters), and hell's coming with them." Sleepy Bravo, our intel chief, had to walk away he was laughing so hard.

Was anything I said true? No, probably not. But, talking with dozens of locals, sometimes you need to say some ridiculous things to keep yourself entertained, throw some shit against a wall to see if it sticks. With nothing else to gain, we patrolled out to a different link-up point with the vehicles, coordinated with the other platoon, and pushed back to base.

Two days later, we received an intel report that Baryali had fled the area after hearing of Coalition forces looking for him in his village. Would he be back? Absolutely. Was this result as good as killing him? Certainly not. But, in our world, we looked for small victories. And, for the time being, we'd removed a scumbag from the battlefield, if only temporarily.

# III-33

# SKYPE DATE WITH A PRESIDENT

·················································

S IMILAR TO THANKSGIVING and Christmas, New Years
in Afghanistan would certainly be different, especially when
you throw the Georgians into the mix. To celebrate New Year's
Eve, the 51stGLIB wanted to have a formal ceremony, the highlight of which would be a Skype session with the President of
Georgia, with him projected on a big screen addressing the soldiers of the problem.

Neat idea. The problem: how, in Afghanistan, do you set up a
Skype connection reliable enough to talk to a head of state in another country? But, Lt. Col. Koba said it was going to happen, so
this pretty quickly became SloMo's and SloMo Bravo's (communications officer and chief) problem. The solution: FITFO. The
Boss—the Godfather—had a leadership habit that, at times, proved
extremely frustrating, but in the long run made us all better Marines
and, by extension, made our team a much stronger unit. When one
of the guys on the team faced a challenge or difficult task to figure
out, the Boss generally knew the solution. But, he also truly grasped
the basic leadership tenet that, doing something himself, we would
learn nothing. On the other hand, letting us work some FITFO operations made us all far more proficient problem solvers.

So, back to the Skype date with the president. SloMo Bravo, through hard work, more than a little frustration, and drug deals, eventually tracked down a communications unit that possessed a "portable internet" capability, essentially letting us set up an extremely strong, standalone network in the Clam Shell. Crisis averted, and it turned out to be a pretty unique way to spend a New Year's Eve. All the battalion's soldiers not on post or patrol filled up chairs in the Clam Shell and sang the Georgian national anthem with the president presiding over the ceremony on the big screen. Following the anthem, the president spent several minutes addressing the battalion with words of support and confidence before signing off. To wrap things up, everyone there had a bunch of snacks and desserts brought over from the chow hall.

Definitely a first (and likely last) for me—a sober New Year's Eve spent with a president and a bunch of Georgians. And, while alcohol is forbidden in combat zones for U.S. troops, judging by the number of sunglasses and slow gaits the next day, the Georgians had enjoyed some drinks. I'm still convinced that they'd gradually accrued enough grapes from the chow hall over the past few months to make their own wine in the barracks. Hey, good on them.

# PART IV

# THE MINISTRY OF TRUTH
## (Afghanistan, Resolute Support)

*January-March 2015*

# IV-1

# THE WAR'S OVER! (TRANSITION TO RESOLUTE SUPPORT)

......................................................

O N 1 JANUARY 2015, "Combat operations in Afghanistan ended." More specifically, the NATO International Security Assistance Force (ISAF) mission ended, and the NATO Resolute Support (RS) one began. As part of this transition, the Regional Commands that divided Afghanistan (RC East, RC South, etc.) became Train, Advise, & Assist Commands (TAAC East, TAAC South, etc.). But, besides the appellation sleight of hand, nothing had changed about the daily realities of our patrols.

Sure, the Afghan government, NATO, and other troop-contributing countries agreed that the time had come to end "combat operations," but it takes some seriously naïve perspectives (or willful disbelief) to think slapping a new name on a shit sandwich would change the consistency of that meal. There's an aphorism in the military that the enemy gets a vote— something the decision to declare "mission accomplished" completely ignored.

Rather, 1 January 2015 represented an arbitrary date that one side of the equation unilaterally deemed a politically expedient milestone for wrapping things up. Now, don't get me wrong, I'm certainly not saying we should be in Afghanistan forever. I'm just pointing out that it's a little ridiculous to simply declare victory by completely ignoring what's actually happening in the country.

According to NATO's press release, the ISAF mission was completed 31 December 2014.[3] But what does "completed" mean? Due to our limited ability to offensively target the enemy in our area of operations (due to rules of engagement limitations), a recurring, macabre joke of ours to this point had been that we were the bait, guys thrown out into the wilderness to wait and get ambushed—only then could we respond with deadly force. On 29 December, this idea was reaffirmed when Czechs on a night patrol took contact—an RPG. Fortunately, no one was injured. And, on the positive side, the Czech forces killed the guy who took the RPG shot, and we watched a couple Apaches kill the other two.

Frankly, this was pretty good for morale: finally killed a few guys after months of IEDs, rocket attacks, and suicide bombers. But, this incident, two nights before "mission accomplished," confirmed the absurdity of this situation. Nothing had changed in the enemy's eyes. But, as we would soon see, things certainly changed for us. While the tongue-in-cheek joke of us as bait before the RS mission was just that, a joke, we would very quickly discover that this joke would become our reality in the world of Resolute Support restrictions.

---

[3] "Resolute Support Mission in Afghanistan," North Atlantic Treaty Organization, 18 July 2018, https://www.nato.int/cps/en/natohq/topics_113694.htm.

# IV-2

# DOUBLETHINK AND NEWSPEAK: THE NEW MINISTRY OF TRUTH

••••••••••••••••••••••••••••••••••••••••••••••••••••••••••••

I WILL BE the first to admit: I'm not a smart man, and I have very few original ideas. My "perceptive insight" comes not from a profound grasp of reality, but by drawing analogies between the words of much smarter people than I and the life I live. One such person is George Orwell, as his dystopian novel *1984* resonated significantly with me during this transition into Resolute Support and "the end of combat operations."

Frankly, I couldn't help but draw parallels between the new rhetoric and restrictions imposed on us by the top headquarters in Afghanistan—COMRS (Commander, Resolute Support—same four-star general and staff that made up COMISAF, but with a new name), Orwell's "Ministry of Truth," and the author's complementary concepts of "doublethink" and "newspeak." Here are some quotes from the classic novel that set the stage for the analogous situation we now faced:

1."If you want to keep a secret, you must also hide it from yourself."

2."Doublethink means the power of holding two contradictory beliefs in one's mind simultaneously, and accepting both of them."

3. "The Ministry of Peace concerns itself with war, the Ministry of Truth with lies, the Ministry of Love with torture and the Ministry of Plenty with starvation. These contradictions are not accidental, nor do they result from ordinary hypocrisy: they are deliberate exercises in doublethink"

So how does this happen, this deliberate exercise in doublethink? By implementing newspeak: "Don't you see that the whole aim of newspeak is to narrow the range of thought?" This newspeak, an entirely foreign vocabulary that COMRS imposed on us, encouraged the internal contradiction that was our own version of doublethink. That is, despite the fact that nothing changed from 31 December 2014 to 1 January 2015 (beyond some externally imposed political timeline), we awoke to a whole new reality of Resolute Support and the end of combat operations. Essentially, doublethink was the strategic goal, and newspeak became our means of accomplishing it.

We wanted to believe our own lies, and here are just a few of the rhetorical absurdities we were forced to adopt that accompanied this desire:

1. "Counter-indirect fire (C-IDF) patrols" would now be called "indirect fire-defense (IDF-D) patrols."

2. "Enemies of Afghanistan" or "insurgents" would now be referred to as "force protection threats (FPTs)."

3. And, most ridiculously, all of our CONOPs for missions now had to explicitly state that the U.S. role in that particular mission was "supporting Afghan forces." This despite the fact that the reality on the ground certainly had not changed, and the Afghan forces were absolutely not in the lead on operations.

In this distorted environment, it was only natural to revisit a joke from early on in our time in Afghanistan and assign the COMRS headquarters a new moniker: Ministry of Truth.

# IV-3

# "INQUIRIES INTO EDIFICES OF CONCERN"

..................................................

A S THE PREVIOUS vignette illustrated, our *newspeak* facilitated the overarching strategy of *doublethink* in this new world
of Resolute Support. By calling the situation something different
than it actually was, the security realities on the ground would
change (or so the theory seemed to go). Unfortunately for the guys
out patrolling, this new Ministry of Truth did not stop at merely declaring a new vocabulary—new restrictions were imposed as well.

By the end of the ISAF mission, rules of engagement already
proved fairly restrictive. I've mentioned it, but Coalition Forces
were not allowed to enter Afghan compounds without the explicit
approval of the owner. This prevented us from conducting a unilateral "cordon and search," where a suspect building is surrounded
by friendly forces and searched for weapons and other contraband.
Rather, we partnered with ANA soldiers to conduct "investigations
of compounds of interest," essentially meeting the same goal, but
with an Afghan search party - pretty good system, as it still allowed
us to partially disrupt the free flow of weapons in our area.

I discovered very quickly into 2015 and the Resolute Support
mission that these types of operations were no longer going to

fly. My first "investigation of a compound of interest" plan I submitted for approval came back denied with a, "Whoa! You can't do that! It's a cordon and search." *Ok, I'll play your game.*

My revised plan called for "street-level engagements in vicinity of buildings" (semantic absurdity for "okay, we'll just go talk to people near target compounds and, coincidentally, our partnered ANA will knock on those doors"). In gallows humor typical of the military, Derby, our logistics officer, had a pretty good idea: "If we can't do 'investigations of compounds of interest,' how about 'inquiries into edifices of concern'?".

Dripping with sarcasm, Derby's comment struck the heart of the matter. These new restrictions rounded out the environment of *doublethink*. For us, the threat outside-the-wire hadn't changed. Consequently, we couldn't in good conscience stop our attempts to disrupt "force protection threats" shooting rockets at Bagram and blowing us up with IEDs. We know bad guys live in specific compounds, but we're told we can't do anything about it, all while bearing the brunt of these same assholes' IED and rocket attacks?

Here's my problem: If COMRS truly wanted to embrace the doublethink of Resolute Support, actively ignoring the realities on the ground, that's fine. But, this new approach should have entailed a complete cessation of Coalition patrolling—either gives us the tools to conduct the mission, or don't send us out in harm's way.

# IV-4

# MY VENN DIAGRAM OF FRUSTRATION

························································

A FEW WEEKS after the Resolute Support mission began, I developed an analogy for my sources of stress, which became my "Venn diagram of frustration." I remembered this diagram from my elementary and middle school days, the charts of overlapping circles that helped one visualize where different topics overlapped, and where they differed.

I had three circles in my Venn diagram, each of which moved and overlapped a little more or a little less depending on the day. And, though each of these circles represented a stress-inducing entity, the overlap of two or three of them truly caused my frustration.

*Circle 1, the Taliban*: This almost goes without saying. These guys wanted us dead, so it's understandable to say they'd cause some levels of stress.

*Circle 2, the Georgians*: If you've done any time as a combat advisor, this one's self- evident, too. Between the language, culture, and training barriers - all wrapped up in a warzone - it's to be expected that these guys would put some gray hairs on my head (actually, the entire sides of my head when all was said and done).

*Circle 3, the COMRS Headquarters*: This was the circle that really fucked with my dope. I anticipated the first two circles heading into this deployment, but I didn't expect the Coalition headquarters in Afghanistan would induce as much personal stress and frustration as the Georgians and Taliban.

In our first deliberate operation of the RS regime (a very tongue-in-cheek "Operation War's Over"), we planned on bringing explosive ordnance disposal (EOD) teams and military working dogs into Nurjan Kala and Khwajakhel. Despite reports of IED cache sites at several compounds in this village, to align with COMRS's policy of *newspeak*, we had to phrase the operation in terms of "street-level engagements" (SLEs) for our plan to be approved. Now, those SLEs just so happened to be planned to occur right next to the suspected cache sites, but we were still particularly hamstrung. Rather than actually searching these suspected cache sites, we would be restricted to walking the mud-wall perimeters with our explosive-sniffing dogs, hoping for them to catch a scent.

It would have been far easier to be apathetic were it not for the fact that Route Clearance Platoon, the Czechs, and the Georgian/Marine team still patrolled these areas regularly. So, to revisit my Venn diagram of frustration: The Taliban ("force protection threats") naturally induced stress, as they were trying to kill us. Unfortunately, the COMRS headquarters provided about equal overlap by sending us outside-the-wire without the ability to properly target these guys trying to kill us.

# IV-5

# SMALL COMFORTS
······································

O PERATION WAR'S OVER": Unfortunately, there were
no IED cache finds, though it was a hail mary thinking the
dogs would pick up the scent of home-made explosive from the
outside of mud-walled compounds anyway. But, we had some
positive takeaways, regardless.

*Tactical proficiency*: This op continued the theme of gradually
increasing the tactical complexity of things we were able to do.
In addition to incorporating two, mutually-supporting Georgian
platoons, we also tied in two ANA patrol elements into, getting
those guys used to conducting missions beyond your run-of-the-
mill security patrol.

*Reach*: By regularly pushing west of Highway 1, an area largely
ignored by previous units, we established a presence of both Coalition Forces and Afghan soldiers in an area known for weapons facilitation. And, in doing so, we continued to disrupt, if only in our
own limited way, the freedom of movement of Baryali and his
crew (still no word of him returning to the Bagram area).

*Assets*: This was the first time we incorporated military working dogs into our operations. And, while the dogs didn't pick up
any scents along these compound walls, there are tremendous
benefits to having them along. Personally, it's comforting being

able to send a dog out through a field to sniff for emplaced IEDs ahead of your patrol. These incredibly talented animals and their handlers are something else to watch in action the way they work together to systematically sweep an area for explosives. And, there's a psychological advantage of rolling through these villages with massive German shepherds, as this significantly messed with the locals—one more way to keep people on their toes and, ideally, make them think twice about emplacing IEDs or launching rockets.

And, having the ANA along with us on this operation brought one other small comfort. I've said it before, but, due to the rock-throwing ambushes we faced there, the Khwajakhel and Nurjan Kala villages not-so-affectionately became known as "Rock City. As we began our foot movement out of the area this time, the rock throwing began in earnest. Little kids would run in and out of the qalat wall complexes, lobbing rocks at our patrol.

I'm sure that, reading this, some people will say, "well, it's just little kids throwing rocks - no big deal." Yeah, but getting hit in the face with a rock fucking sucks, regardless who throws it. And, as a combined patrol, our Afghan National Army counterparts faced the same frustrations (though we at least had helmets on that protected most of our heads).

With the rock throwing increasing significantly as we entered the fields on the outskirts of the villages, the ANA patrol leader with us decided to take action. We continued on our way, while he grabbed one of his soldiers and snuck off along the outside of a qalat wall. Right as a kid jumped out to hurl a rock our way, the patrol leader yoked him up, threw him to the ground, tied up his hands, and blindfolded him. Naturally, all the other kids immediately beat feet out of there when this happened.

A huge grin on his face, the ANA patrol leader dragged the blindfolded kid along, stumbling behind him, back to the rest of our group. The kid—probably twelve or thirteen—was crying and shaking uncontrollably by this time. For the next two kilometers or so, blindfolded and crying for the duration, the ANA patrol leader led this kid back to our vehicle link-up point. When we finally arrived, the PL unbound the kid, gave him a stern talking to, and cut him loose to run back to his village.

Once again, I'm sure plenty of people will read this story and judge us for the small comforts and smiles this incident provided. But, it was pretty damned good for our morale to see one of these little punks get his comeuppance. Does this make me a bad person? Maybe, but it was refreshing to see, and something that definitely would have gotten the Marines onto CNN for the wrong reasons had we been the ones to yoke up one of these kids.

# IV-6

# THE CRIMINAL JUSTICE SYSTEM'S REVOLVING DOOR

·······················································

D ESPITE MY FRUSTRATIONS with the Ministry of Truth's restrictions on our operations, we all took solace in the role special operations forces (SOF) played. In the world of Resolute Support, U.S. and other Coalition SOF partners continued to facilitate Afghan SOF rolling up scumbags in raids throughout our area of operations. Unfortunately, though, the pleasure of reading about these raids always proved short-lived.

Corruption is rampant in Afghanistan, a persistent characteristic of doing business there. And, the country's criminal justice system was no exception, with corruption winding its way through all facets of the judicial process, leading to a phenomenon we dubbed the "revolving door." Here's how it worked:

1. Afghan SOF, supported by U.S. or Coalition forces, rolls up a dude.

2. The bad guy ends up in an Afghan detention center pending trial.

3. A local Afghan Member of Parliament (MP) receives a bribe.

4. The guy who was just detained is back on the street a couple of weeks after being rolled up—in and out, hence, the revolving door.

I cannot speak for all of Afghanistan, but the MP representing Parwan Province, where we were, proved particularly resourceful in making this happen.

Every time we watched the revolving door in action, our morale sunk a little lower. To us, the Afghan justice system became the punchline of a joke, a couple-of-week-long government food and shelter program—more summer camp than criminal justice system.

## IV-7

# A GLIMMER OF HOPE

·····································

IF IT'S NOT already readily apparent in my tone, I'd become quite cynical a few weeks into the Resolute Support mission. Between the new restrictions on operations and the imposition of the Ministry of Truth's newspeak, things just seemed to get more ridiculous every day. But, a glimmer of hope shone through when word trickled down to us that COMRS had lifted the restrictions on "investigations of compounds of interest (COIs)."

We still couldn't conduct a full-blown cordon and search, but this new development was a step in the right direction. The U.S. powers that be in Afghanistan recognized that the guys out on security patrols needed to be able to, at a minimum, poke around at the compounds of guys planting IEDs and shooting rockets at base, even if we couldn't enter these compounds ourselves (only Afghan police could do that—a challenge I'll discuss in detail later).

As this restriction on patrols targeting COIs was rescinded a few weeks after it was implemented, it appeared my pervasive, RS-related cynicism may have been misplaced, and that the knee-jerk reaction of "ending combat" may be a temporary one. We knew Baryali would return, and we knew we'd need to be able to continue disrupting bad guy freedom of movement in his village west of Highway 1 to prevent another IED attack along that route. This renewed operational freedom gave us some hope that, if we still had to conduct security operations, we may at least be given some of the tools to conduct them successfully.

# IV-8

# HOPE DASHED

..........................

T URNS OUT IT was naive of me to become too optimistic about the above loosening of restrictions—brought back to the reality of the new Ministry of Truth shortly after getting word that "investigations of COIs" were once again acceptable.

Here's the situation. We took a significant number of rockets from the northeast of Bagram. Out to our east, there was a long, well-maintained route following the Panjshir River into the Bagram Bowl from Tagab District, a cesspool of Taliban fighters and weapons facilitation. This route entered the southeast portion of the Bowl, wound up to our northeast before looping back towards the southwest and Bagram.

Every few days, guys would hop on their dirt bikes, cruise up this high-speed corridor from Tagab with a 107mm rocket in their saddlebag, find an open field, lean the rocket against a dirt mound with a timer, and trust some "Kentucky windage" with a shot at Bagram. By the time the rocket actually launched, they'd be well out of the area, sheltered in one of the villages heading back towards Tagab.

As we couldn't actively target these guys in Tagab, and patrolling historic launch sites only proved a temporary deterrent, we were always on the lookout for ways to "get ahead of the bang." That is, how could we stop Taliban fighters from Tagab freely moving into our neighborhood and firing rockets?

After being in the area for a while, Bane came up with a pretty solid plan. In the northeast of the Bowl, the dominant terrain feature was a massive crag jutting up from the Panjshir River. Pockmarked from years of mining, it provided a dominating view of the historic launch sites northeast of Bagram, the places where the rockets from Tagab were staged. And, from the peak, you could see our entire area of operations, with a clear line of sight down the ten miles or so of small villages along the river down to the Tagab pass.

Recognizing the advantage this peak's view provided, Bane proposed "Operation Olympic Mons"—sending a large dismounted patrol to the top of the peak during the day, then discreetly leaving a "stay-behind" element in a hide to observe the historic launch sites that night. Shot in the dark? Maybe, but at least it was a plan to do something proactive, vice just waiting for the next rocket to hit.

To really solidify the plan, we needed one thing—snipers. If we saw a guy setting up a rocket, we'd need a way to engage (read, "shoot") him. Unfortunately, our advisor team lacked a Marine Corps Scout Sniper capability, so we'd need to get creative. One day a couple of weeks after Bane initially proposed this operation, a solution coincidentally walked into my office. In pretty small world fashion, a high school football buddy of mine happened to be serving on Bagram as an Army Special Forces officer and liaison with the COMBAF staff. After he heard my name mentioned in a brief, he swung by and said hello.

In a ridiculous stroke of good luck, my buddy happened to know about a Special Forces sniper team with some time on their hands. Apparently these guys weren't being employed at all, so they jumped at the opportunity to support "Olympic Mons." Perfect. We just needed to route our plan up to COMBAF for the green light.

A week later our request came back—denied. Apparently we wouldn't be allowed sniper support due to these marksmen being an "offensive capability." No shit! So are rockets! Political decisions and the "end of combat operations" fallacy were once again placed ahead of the realities on the ground.

# IV-9

## THE MINISTRY OF TRUTH AT WORK

······················································

HERE'S ANOTHER ANECDOTE to further demonstrate the new, Resolute Support atmosphere. A few weeks into January 2015 and the RS mission, Route Clearance Platoon hit another IED (fortunately no casualties). We had clear intelligence linking the bomber, at least temporarily, to two compounds along the route where the IED had been emplaced. And, post-blast forensics gave us DNA evidence from the actual explosive device. With intelligence as clear as this, we naturally sought permission to A) search the compounds, and B) gather DNA samples from the potential "force protection threats" there, aiming to identify the IED "emplacer."

As discussed, in the RS world, we could not search the compounds ourselves, and nor could our Afghan National Army partners. Furthermore, all operations needed to be framed as "Afghan led," so, to actually get into those compounds, we would need to coordinate with the Afghan National Directorate of Security (NDS), roughly analogous to our FBI. These NDS agents were authorized by Afghan law to enter and search compounds. Recognizing these limitations, we developed and coordinated a plan with both NDS and ANA. The former would send agents to search the compounds, and the latter would provide an outer cordon of security with the Georgian/Marine team.

This seemed like a straightforward plan, and one that shouldn't receive tremendous scrutiny from our own headquarters, especially following an IED attack. Naïve again—nothing was simple in the RS world.

In this new, Ministry of Truth atmosphere, no one wanted to be the first unit to take a casualty after the "end of combat operations." Once again, this is fine, but we shouldn't be operating at all if people prove too risk adverse to provide the forces outside-the-wire the tools they need to defend themselves.

To actually receive approval for this operation, one deemed "high risk" like a cordon and search (albeit one where we solely serve as the cordon), a general officer needed to sign off on it. So, the week prior to our planned op, I found myself, as the ground force commander for the mission, sitting in the office of TF Saber's commander. As I sat and listened to the teleconference, the commander briefed COMBAF, the two-star general in charge of Bagram, our plan for approval. Fortunately, the general signed off, and my narrow perspective started expanding. On the one hand, politically, no one wanted to deal with the ramifications of the first RS casualty. On the other hand, this general was willing to go out on a limb for us to make this operation happen.

As an angry, cynical captain focused on executing local security operations, it was very easy to motherfuck "higher," blaming the layers of command above us for the Ministry of Truth-like atmosphere and restrictions of Resolute Support. But, sitting in on this brief to a general one step removed from the four-star in charge of all forces in Afghanistan, I had an epiphany of sorts. The military commanders wanted to do what they could, but that was only so much within a broader system of arbitrary deadlines imposed on ending combat operations (and staff not questioning this system, but more on that later).

# IV-10

# SHAKEN CONFIDENCE

·············································

W ITH THE CORDON and search approved, we conducted
our final coordination with the NDS agents who'd actually search the compound, Colonel Sultan and his soldiers, and
the Georgians. And—one positive to Resolute Support designating this a higher risk mission—we had Apache attack helicopters
assigned to support us. In addition to the warm-and-fuzzy feeling
you get from having a couple flying tanks overhead, the pilots
also provide real-time insight into what's actually going on inside
the towering compound walls ubiquitous in our neighborhood.

The morning of the op, we linked up with our ANA partners and
the NDS agents outside Bagram, rehashed the plan one final time,
and pushed to our objective area—a couple of compounds southeast
of us in the Panjshir Valley with a ridgeline rising up to their west.
At our rally point, half of the Georgian and Marine dismounts left
the vehicles and established an over-watch position on the ridgeline,
while the ANA in their HMMWVs and the other Georgian and Marine dismounts formed the actual cordon around the two compounds.

With the two compounds isolated (that is, no one in, and no one
out), we gave NDS the thumbs up to search the first compound.
Here's where the friction began. Through the interpreter, the NDS
agents told us they weren't going into the compound. *Excuse me?*

*Then why the fuck are you here?* As we would come to learn working with these NDS guys, this was par for the course— agree on something then completely change the plan (or, in this case, flat out refuse to support).

Eventually, after using a combination of groveling, raising my voice, shaming, and colorful language (which I'm fairly certain the Afghan interpreter sanitized), the agents capitulated. Clearly not happy, they agreed to go into the first compound, send the men outside for DNA samples, and search the area for explosives and/or IED-making materials. A few minutes later, a dozen men, from the disgruntled patriarch to young teenagers, came outside, and we collected DNA swabs from all of them.

Concurrently, the Apache pilots overhead gave us real-time updates of what was happening inside the compound walls. Apparently, the NDS agents never left the immediate courtyard inside the compound doors, clearly not searching much of anything. When they came out thirty minutes or so later (after they'd had chai and some smokes, per the pilots), the NDS agents told us they would not search the second compound. At that point in time, we may as well have thrown out our DNA swabs. Even if the bomb maker or "emplacer," whoever left his DNA on the IED, was in one of the compounds, he certainly wasn't one of the dozen men who volunteered to come outside.

Significantly frustrated, and with any confidence I had in the NDS shattered, we broke down our over-watch position and cordon and returned to base. It's hard to work up enthusiasm to conduct operations when the local security forces we're supposed to be supporting in their quest for national stability didn't give a fuck.

# IV-11

# GOOD NEWS STORYBOARDS

·················································

A LREADY FRUSTRATED FOLLOWING our cordon and search abortion with NDS, I just had to laugh when I found out about the newest addition to our newspeak lexicon: "good news storyboards." In new guidance from Resolute Support Headquarters, we would now be required to submit a weekly, PowerPoint one-slider outlining some positive interaction with Afghan National Security Forces (ANSF). The military lives and breathes PowerPoint, and the storyboard is an extention of that reality—anything significant that happens receives a slide with some images and the "5 Ws" of the event.

Typically, we develop these products following some enemy interaction—IED strike, rocket attack, etc. So, what's a "good news storyboard?" Here's the exchange I had with an assistant operations officer from our immediate higher headquarters, with whom I generally had a pretty positive relationship, despite the fact that they often served as the bearer of bad news.

*TF Saber*: "Hey, man, I need you to build a weekly storyboard featuring some sort of positive interaction with ANSF."

*Me*: "So, do you want a weekly SITREP (situation report) on our work with the Afghans?"

*TF Saber:* "No…RS is just looking for, well, positives…"

*Me:* "What if there haven't been any positives in a given week?"

*TF Saber:* "Read between the lines. We need storyboards."

*Reading between the lines—RS is going to get these storyboards one way or the other, reality be damned, so just do us all a favor and put together some good news slides. Okay, roger that, I'll play the game. I'll give you flowery language, pretty pictures, and a rainbow-lensed look at a pile of dog shit all day long.*

From an information operations perspective, I get this desire to promote the ANSF's growth. In theory, successful Afghan security operations meant we could leave the country, and these positive stories could help boost confidence and morale. But at what cost? Are we willing to divorce realities on the ground (e.g. NDS agents walking away from a cordon and search) from the narrative we want to push? And, the timing couldn't have been worse. Just after the storyboard directive made its way to us, an Afghan soldier killed three U.S. contractors at Kabul International Airport in a "green-on-blue" attack. *And you want us writing about the "good news?"*

# IV-12

# TACTICAL WELLS VERSUS THE MoT'S DITCH

······················································

I 'M GOING ON a bit of a tangent here, but it's a relevant one, as it provides further depth to the absurd Ministry of Truth environment. In the States, the Commander's Emergency Relief Program, or CERP (pronounced "serp"), has received a fair amount of negative press. Specifically, the Special Inspector General for Afghanistan Reconstruction (SIGAR) has published some scathing reports about rampant fraud, waste, and general ineffectiveness of the program. On Bagram, we found ourselves right in the thick of things.

CERP began in Afghanistan and Iraq as a means for commanders to quickly access funds to aid in the rebuilding of those countries. It's a noble goal, and the program accomplishes the three-fold goal of: 1) rebuilding war-torn infrastructure; 2) infusing money into the local economy; and, 3) providing U.S. commanders non-lethal leverage to influence key local players (I don't think this last item is an officially sanctioned goal of CERP, but it's a nice by-product).

As CERP is tied to US funds, it requires US forces to actually use the program's funds on the ground. Consequently, the Georgians would need us to officially sponsor projects they sought to complete in the Bagram area, leading to our intimate involvement.

Broadly speaking, two differing philosophies exist for CERP projects, one at our level, and one at the Ministry of Truth level. The former entailed small-scale, "bulk-fund projects" of $5,000 or less, to include things like building wells and repairing damaged drainage culverts. Altruistically, these projects helped local communities and the economy by hiring local contractors. Realistically, by focusing on these smaller projects, we could quickly gain influence with key leaders and access to intelligence collection in otherwise hostile villages. The saying in Afghanistan goes, you can't buy loyalty, but you can rent it. So, for us, CERP provided tangible, tactical advantages while still helping out some local Afghans.

On the other hand, the Ministry of Truth, in this case personified by US Forces-Afghanistan (USFOR-A), took things to a whole other level, and not a good one. As a cynical observer, I viewed the situation as follows. USFOR-A had some engineers on staff, so, to justify the self-licking ice cream cone that was its Resolute Support existence, decided to build a large-scale drainage project in the village of Yozbashi, just outside the Bagram perimeter.

Noble thought, right? But, one of the key CERP lessons learned by units that operate outside-the-wire is that, like democracy, infrastructure projects cannot be imposed on people, rather, they should be requested and facilitated. Ignoring this CERP tenet, the Yozbashi project was planned and implemented without villager request or input. And the cherry on top? USFOR-A planned the whole project around a ditch that would have to be dug right through the middle of the village. Why? Because, rather than actually go to the site to survey the ground, they planned the project off of outdated imagery that didn't show multiple new compounds built in the village.

The end result of this planned-in-a-vacuum-without-local-input exercise was about what you'd expect: villagers threatening to kill the contractors (hired from outside the village—another cardinal sin of CERP) if they returned to work, and a partially dug ditch with $850,000 of contractor funds dumped into it. So, yeah, this doesn't necessarily fit the narrative arc of my story, but it provides further context to my Venn diagram of frustration and the craziness that was the new Ministry of Truth.

# IV-13

# A CLEARER PICTURE EMERGES

......................................................

R OUGHLY A MONTH into Resolute Support, we continued to be frustrated by a seemingly arbitrary mission approval process – some operations and patrol objectives approved one week, then denied the next. This frustration ultimately led to a member of the COMBAF staff coming over to the Pink Palace, the TF Saber headquarters, to brief us on the whole mission approval process. One step removed from COMRS, the four-star staff running the show in Afghanistan, hearing a guy from the COMBAF Operations Section explain things from his perspective would be a good opportunity to pull the curtain back.

Going into this meeting, I knew that, though frustrating, getting some inside baseball would help give me the tools to accomplish our mission within the current, "higher-imposed limitations." And, my major initial takeaway was a positive one: These guys (the COMBAF staff) wanted to support us, but they were receiving tremendous pressure from the COMRS staff that significantly limited our tactical flexibility (and efficiency). I've said it a few times already, but, in this new environment, commanders sought to avoid the political ramifications of having to report the first RS casualties, now that "combat was over."

How did this risk aversion manifest itself procedurally? First, every security patrol we sent outside-the-wire required a detailed concept of operations (CONOP) to be submitted to and approved by COMBAF. While somewhat micromanaging having a two-star general reviewing squad- and platoon-sized security patrols, this oversight was understandable, as COMBAF was ultimately responsible for the security of his own air base. Second, and most absurdly, every CONOP we submitted that included any ANSF element (which, as explained, made up the bulk of our daily patrols), needed to be submitted all the way up to the COMRS, four-star staff for approval ninety-six hours out, a timeline that would factor significantly into an adult temper tantrum I'd throw in the next few weeks.

This four-star review of security patrols made Commander, Resolute Support history's highest-ranking platoon commander (which is not a complimentary moniker). On the one hand, I get it. These commanders, COMRS and COMBAF, owned the risk of any operations by their subordinate units, and they faced significant pressure themselves about an RS casualty. On the other hand, and related to the ANSF aspect, the naïve (and downright deceptive) mandated framing of these combined operations truly drove parallels with Orwell's Ministry of Truth.

As stated, all of our patrols now needed to be framed in terms of "U.S./Georgian support to ANSF in the lead." To this point, I'd treated this as semantics—smoke and mirrors means of appeasing the political requirements of putting the Afghans in the lead. However, the fact that we needed to write our CONOPs employing this newspeak was insane, as it was simply a lie; the Afghans were neither proficient enough nor suitably manned and equipped to defend our base. But, COMRS put blinders on to that reality on the ground, insisting that, regardless of what we were actually doing, all they wanted to hear was the double-think version of reality that the Afghans, post-31 December 2014, were now ready to maintain their country's security. Ultimately, this was a very tangible manifestation of a political agenda (that is, arbitrarily ending combat operations in Afghanistan) trumping the security realities on the ground.

The 51stGLIB command post on Bagram Airfield, Parwan Province, Afghanistan. The portraits are part of a memorial wall commemorating the Georgian soldiers killed in Afghanistan while supporting the International Security Assistance Force (ISAF) mission there.

The author on Bagram Airfield with the two men most responsible for the 51stGLIB's successful deployment: Captain Davit (L), the Georgian interpreter from the battalion's operations department, and Amini, the Dari linguist who knew more Afghan generals than most Afghan generals did.

The author with Amini (*L*) and Colonel Sultan (*C*), the commander of the Afghan National Army *kandak* (battalion) that conducted partnered patrols with the 51st GLIB and a critical supporter of the Georgian/Marine mission at Bagram.

True international cooperation: The author sharing a delicious Afghan meal hosted by Colonel Sultan with Afghan, Georgian, Czech, and US Army soldiers.

Author (*C*), team, and Afghan linguist (*2nd from right*) prior to a partnered patrol with a 51stGLIB platoon and a team of ANA soldiers from Colonel Sultan's *kandak*.

The Godsons recovery vehicle ("wrecker") operator giving a class on HMMWV maintenance to Colonel Sultan's mechanics. Keeping these Afghan vehicles running was a full-time battle, but it kept the Marines and Georgians safe by ensuring the ANA could conduct partnered patrols.

Author and Georgian patrol leader with the village elders from Bajawri, a village several miles from Bagram Airfield. A red flower is a generous gift from the local boy in the ball cap.

Author and Major Zaza on a patrol to deliver school supplies to the children of Bajawri village. This photo was taken approximately an hour prior to a suicide bomber attacking the patrol. Showing incredible courage and composure, the US Navy Corpsman ("Doc") on patrol that day saved Major Zaza's life by stabilizing his wounds to the point that he could be removed from the battlefield on a MEDEVAC helicopter and reach a surgeon.

A Georgian medic on patrol overlooking the floodplains of the Panjshir River with the Hindu Kush mountains in the background.

Afghan linguist on a patrol supported by US Army military working dogs, some of the most incredibly proficient and loyal animals in the world.

Author and an Afghan linguist discussing local affairs on patrol with village elders outside of Bagram.

An Afghan boy and his dog during a patrol outside of Bagram. These high, mudbrick walls, windy alleys, and entryways were ubiquitous in the villages surrounding the airfield.

New Year's Eve in the "Clam Shell" on Bagram Airfield, shortly after being addressed via Skype by the Georgian President—a unique experience: (L to R) SloMo, Georgian soldier, Bane, Georgian soldier, and the author.

The author (L), Amini (C), and Georgian, Afghan, and Czech partners organizing relief supplies for Afghan villagers trapped by massive avalanches in the Hindu Kush mountains.

# IV-14

# A CYNICAL CAPTAIN'S
# ANGRY E-MAIL

··············································

T HIS VIGNETTE REPRESENTS the high-water mark of
my frustration with the Ministry of Truth, and it must be
framed within the context of the 12 December IED that killed
two soldiers. Specifically, prior to the 12 December attack, we'd
ceased patrols for a day and a half to mitigate concerns of violence
following the release of the CIA "Torture Report." Could Baryali
and his "force protection threat" accomplices have dragged a 200
pound IED under a culvert on Highway 1 had we been patrolling?
Maybe, maybe not, but it certainly would've been more difficult.

These thoughts were on my mind when I received an e-mail
that two of our partnered patrols had been disapproved by COM-
BAF without even getting pushed to COMRS. In accordance with
the new, ninety-six-hour submission requirements outlined above,
I'd forwarded the CONOPs for approval the day before, so we
were now at seventy-two hours from scheduled execution when I
got word of the disapproved ops. One patrol had been planned
for Dih Khwaja, a village to our east and a known facilitation
node along the main route from Tagab District, the shithole that
had nearly completely fallen to the Taliban at that time. Due to

the fact that a rocket had never been launched from Dih Khwaja, we couldn't go there. Next, a patrol to Sayghani, a village about three kilometers to our east, was denied, because no rockets had been launched *directly from the village* (dozens just happened to have been launched from the fields surrounding it, which I'm sure was pure coincidence...).

While I was annoyed with these disapprovals, I'd play the game and figure out where we could get the green light to patrol, so I called my counterpart up at TF Saber:

*TF Saber*: "Dude, I know you're going to be pissed, but the patrols are completely cancelled."

*Me*: "What?"

*TF Saber*: "Yeah, Division (COMBAF) is saying that, because we're inside our ninety-six-hour approval window, you can't submit any other patrols to replace the ones that weren't approved."

*Me*: "So, because of some bullshit timeline, we're just not going to send out any security patrols that day?"

*TF Saber*: "Yeah, man—sorry."

I spent the next twenty minutes sitting in front of my computer, paralyzed by rage. How could anyone in their right minds actually think it was acceptable to cancel two security patrols tasked with protecting a base of over 10,000 personnel? Furthermore, had they forgotten about the two Route Clearance Platoon soldiers killed by Baryali after our last patrol hiatus? So, in today's military, what was my natural recourse here? Send an angry e- mail, of course.

In my e-mail, I laid out exactly what had happened and the tactical rationale for sending patrols to Dih Khwaja and Sayghani, which was fine. The content became problematic with the e-mail's conclusion: "When we take a rocket tomorrow from the North East Battle Area, or a CF patrol hits an IED in vicinity of Sayghani, it will be the result of COMBAF concerning itself more with the political ramifications of doing the right thing than actually keeping Coalition Forces safe." Oh, and I CC'd every relevant person I could think of short of the two-star general himself: COMBAF chief of staff and operations officer (both colonels), the COMBAF command sergeant major, the TF Solid commanding officer and operations officer (TF Solid was in the midst of relieving TF Saber as our higher headquarters), the TF Saber commanding officer and operations officer, the Boss, and basically anyone else whose name I thought of that auto-completed in my Microsoft Outlook. Childish and certainly unprofessional, but yeah—shot, over.

Sending this e-mail provided me enough immediate catharsis that I stopped physically shaking with rage enough to storm over to the Boss's office.

"Sir," I said, "I just wanted to give you a heads up that I CC'd you on a very unprofessional e-mail, but it needed to be sent."

After reading the e-mail, the Boss said, "Well, we'll see what happens."

Back in my office, I received a phone call from the TF Solid operations officer (who I'd put in a difficult position, as he'd just taken over responsibilities when I sent out this e-mail).

"Your e-mail ruffled some feathers up at Division (COMBAF)," he told me. (This was a polite way of saying I'd pissed off a lot of people.)

"Yes sir, that was the intent," I said. "This is so fucked up. How can anyone think it's a good idea to cancel patrols meant to protect a base of over 10,000 people that regularly gets rocketed?"

He agreed, and at the same time, the Boss received a call from the TF Saber commanding officer (CO), with whom he'd established a very good working relationship and friendship over the past five months or so of working together. And, as this happened to be the day of TF Saber's formal transfer of authority (TOA) to TF Solid, I did feel bad about putting a shit sandwich on the CO's desk his last day in charge.

*TF Saber CO (extremely heated)*: "That was a real bonehead stunt Captain Naylon pulled!"

*The Boss*: "I know, but he was right."

*TF Saber CO (wind out of his sales)*: "I know, damn it, but couldn't he have been a little more professional about it?"

With a lot of people pissed off at me, we headed to the formal TOA ceremony, where the COMBAF commanding general (CG) would preside over TF Solid's official relief of TF Saber. Following the ceremony, I watched the CG (one of whose staff members had clearly shown him my e-mail), absolutely lay into the Boss, with the general "knife handing" him as the Boss stood there at parade rest, receiving the full force of the CG's wrath. To put this in context, a sight like this is something you'd expect to see between a Marine corporal and a newly minted private, but between a two-star general and a lieutenant colonel, not so much.

There were two major takeaways from this heated exchange. First, though I already knew this, the Boss's interaction with the CG reaffirmed that there was no one I'd rather work for; there aren't many people willing to take a thrashing from a general and not throw his fucked-up operations officer under the bus. Rather, the Boss took his lashing and calmly said, "Sir, he's right," to which the CG responded, "But it wasn't my intent to cancel patrols!"

This final comment by the CG led to the second major takeaway. These cancelled patrols were not a product of the general disapproving them (he actually knew nothing about it prior to my e-mail); they were a product of a staff so enmeshed in the Ministry of Truth system that they refused to let common sense trump the system and its associated timelines. Specifically, the

COMBAF staff made a decision in accordance with risk aversion and an unwillingness to bring the hard choice before the commander, who ultimately held the responsibility for making that hard choice. I was starting to see that, despite the COMBAF command post serving as the visual embodiment of my frustration, the Ministry of Truth existed as a mindset permeating the system as a whole, an unwillingness to put security decisions ahead of political ramifications throughout the entire country.

# IV-15

# TAIL BETWEEN MY LEGS

·············································

M AJOR ANTHONY (FIRST NAME), the outgoing TF Saber operations officer and someone I respected tremendously, provided me some serious mentoring late that afternoon. Sanctimonious and tunnel-visioned, I refused to see any negatives to my "blast e-mail." The black and white of it was clear: "Higher" was fucked up, and I was in the right, which made it a very difficult pill to swallow when Major Anthony explained to me how selfish my actions were.

I, full of self-righteousness, responded, "Selfish? How the fuck can my actions have been selfish? I was watching out for the safety of the dudes out patrolling every day and the people they protect on this base!"

Well, as he had a way of doing, Major Anthony very calmly spoke reason to me. Was I right to be upset? Absolutely. Was the way I handled things the best approach for the Georgian/Marine team? Absolutely not. While my soapbox e-mail rant proved personally satisfying, it set back our team. Our ability to operate independently (even within the current RS restrictions) depended on the trust higher headquarters (that is, COMBAF) had in our judgment and abilities. By sending out such an unprofessional e-mail, I undermined our credibility in the minds of both the COM-

BAF CG and the incoming TF Solid CO. As Major Anthony made clear (and against all odds thinking back to our training struggles in Georgia and Germany), the 51stGLIB with its Marine advisors had become the "go-to" force in our area of operations, selected over American, Czech, and Afghan units when a deliberate operation needed to happen. This e-mail shook the confidence that led to our current "go-to" status.

So, as he did so aptly and frequently, Major Anthony once more helped me see things his way; that, no matter how right I thought I was, I handled things poorly, selfishly hurting our team. As we wrapped up our conversation, I felt like a scolded dog with his tail between his legs, disappointed in myself for my emotions getting the better of my reason.

This talk led to a couple of things. First, I immediately got back on my computer and sent a "reply-all" e-mail to everyone on my previous note, apologizing for my unprofessionalism and requesting that my selfishness not reflect upon the 51stGLIB and its Marine advisors. Second, the Boss and I set up a "come-to-Jesus" discussion with the two of us and the new TF Solid CO so we could all get on the same page, as we'd be working together closely for another few months.

# IV-16

# "WHAT INTERESTS MY BOSS, FASCINATES ME"

·······················································

AFTER DROPPING A shit sandwich on the incoming TF Solid CO's desk the day of his transfer of authority with my e-mail stunt, the Boss and I headed up to his office to talk about the path ahead. I've said it before, but a good working relationship between the GLT Marines and the task force higher headquarters was critical to playing the "mommy/daddy" game of influencing the Georgians.

In a nutshell, the Marines can't task the 51stGLIB, but the Army task force can. Conversely, the Marines have rapport established with the Georgians and understand their culture, while our higher headquarters does not. So, if the Marines and task force, in this case TF Solid, can't work together, employment of the Georgian forces becomes not only inefficient, but a tremendous pain in the ass for all involved.

With TF Saber, the Marines had an outstanding working relationship. If we needed the Georgians to do something, a backchannel discussion with TF Saber followed by a formal tasking from this headquarters got the job done. Convoluted and ridiculous? Sure, but it's part of the marionette approach inherent to successful advising. Heading up to meet the TF Solid CO, we knew we'd need to establish a solid relationship to ensure this above system continued working.

The meeting went fine, I guess. Up in the task force office in the Pink Palace, the Boss and I made some small talk and discussed in vague generalities the importance of close cooperation—no issues there. But, I essentially checked out of the conversation after a figurative slap in the face by an extremely "careerist" approach (a derogatory term implying the needs of an individual career take priority to the needs of the mission).

A dry erase board in the office had a list of about a half dozen "Fascinating Items." According to the TF Solid CO, "What interests my boss, fascinates me." Talk about an absolutely ridiculous notion. Now, I'm certainly not saying that you don't need to execute the tasks and intent of your boss, especially in the military, but his whims shouldn't be your driving force. This probably comes back to me being a naïve and cynical captain, but what accomplishes the mission should fascinate us!

I was becoming more bitter daily, and here was another very tangible example of how the Ministry of Truth existed as mindset throughout the entire broken system of Coalition Forces in Afghanistan. But fuck it, we'll cooperate to graduate, and, if it keeps us moving forward, we'll play this game.

# IV-17

# THE FRUSTRATION OF DIFFERENT PRIORITIES

·············································

H ERE'S ANOTHER BIT of a non-sequitur, but it ties into my growing frustration of being focused on accomplishing a mission while so many others focused on, well, not that. The day following our meeting with the TF Solid CO, I angrily scribbled the below note to myself. Rereading these comments years after I wrote them, my blood still boils:

> *I fucking hate this place more and more every day—cannot wait to leave. Some douchebag sergeant major gave one of our Marines shit today about wearing FROGs in the chow hall, despite the fact that he's a wrecker operator on-call 24/7. I'm going to leave here with PTSD, and it's not going to have anything to do with combat, just my frustration with the system.*
> *Fuck this.*

I'll translate a few things from the above to better put my rage into context. First, "FROGs"—Flame Resistant Organizational Gear—are combat utilities that won't melt to a Marine's skin like our normal camouflage ones would. So, in the world of ever-present IED threats, FROGs are required outside-the-wire to help mitigate burn wounds. Second, a "wrecker" is, in essence, an armored, heavy-duty tow truck used to recover vehicles in combat. If one of our MRAPs hit an IED, the wrecker operator is the Marine who drives out with the QRF to tow that vehicle back to base.

Having outlined these terms, I'll talk through my anger at this incident. While we were on Bagram, our Marine wrecker operator was the only one on base. And, as you can't predict when someone will hit an IED, and there were nearly always troops outside-the-wire, this Marine was on-call to respond at a moment's notice around-the-clock. As such, he always wore his FROGs, because it wouldn't make a hell of a lot of sense to have to delay a wrecker response for something as trivial as going back to his room to change.

On the other hand, I recognize my words seem pretty sanctimonious, and I understand the sergeant major's perspective on the perceived discipline and hygiene concerns of wearing combat utilities in the chow hall. In isolation, I'd have just chalked this up to "sergeant major doing sergeant major things." But, this anecdote served as one more element reinforcing my growing notion of a whole system focused on everything except keeping the base and the Marines, Georgians, Czechs, and US Army soldiers who were defending it safe.

# IV-18

# "CALL ME MAYBE"

········································

AS I SLOWLY lost my mind with frustration, moments of
humor helped me cling to sanity. And, sometimes these moments of humor just found us. A month or so before our replacements arrived, I was out patrolling with Claymore's team and a
platoon of Georgians in Sayad, a village a few kilometers northeast
of base. Despite moving to full-time operations officer, I tried to
get outside-the-wire a couple of times a week to keep my finger
on the pulse on our area and, more importantly, the dynamics between the Marines, Georgians, and Colonel Sultan's soldiers.

As we moved through this village, I found myself holding security across an alleyway from one of the ANA soldiers accompanying us. At first, I could have sworn I was hearing things, but
I looked over at this guy and yep, there he was, busting out the
following lyrics: "Hey I just met you, and this is crazy, but here's
my number, so call me maybe!" Holy shit, is this guy really
singing Carly Rae Jepsen right now? Naturally, I started laughing.

He then looked at me, smiled, and immediately transitioned
into the following, modified version of "Bad Boys": "Taliban,
Taliban, what you gonna do, what you gonna do when they come
for you? Taliban, Taliban." While the slant rhyme was a bit of a
stretch, the rhythm was spot-on.

Immediately after wrapping up his tune, this Afghan soldier let out a crazy sounding laugh that led me, of all things, to think of a quote from Stephen the Irishman in *Braveheart*: "The Lord tells me he can get me out of this mess, but he's pretty sure you're fucked!" So, as my stream of consciousness led to this image of a kilted Irishman holding security in a mud-brick village in Afghanistan, I laughed even harder at the absurdity of the situation.

Regardless of the fact that we were in Sayad, a village with recent reporting of a suicide vest threat, looking for an explosives cache, humor found us. This served as a key theme throughout the deployment: with all the daily frustration, if we couldn't find reasons to laugh, we all would have lost our minds.

# IV-19

# MARINES CAN DO SOME STUFF, TOO

......................................

F ROM GETTING YELLED at for wearing the wrong uniform in the chow hall to sending out wildly unprofessional
e-mails to the general's staff, I often felt like COMBAF viewed
the Marines as the red-headed step children of Bagram. This
changed in February-March 2015. I wrote about it previously,
but the Army task force we relieved, TF Top Guns, was the first
unit to reach out and begin partnered security operations with
the Afghan soldiers on Bagram, building that relationship with
Colonel Sultan's unit. Prior to this relationship, no regular coordination, and certainly no US training, existed with Afghan units
outside-the- wire in the Bagram area.

This lack of coordination seemed particularly astonishing in
2014, thirteen years after we initially entered Afghanistan. For
years, US forces had partnered with local Afghan security forces
as "best practice" throughout the rest of the country, for all the
reasons I've outlined: legitimacy provided by ANSF presence,
Afghan understanding of local cultural dynamics, and, ultimately,
helping train Afghans to take the fight themselves.

Why hadn't this lesson been learned in the Bagram area of operations, the area surrounding the largest Coalition Force base in

the country? I don't think it was laziness so much as lack of institutional knowledge. The defense of Bagram had always been a pick-up game until the Georgian/Marine team assumed the mission, a hodgepodge of Army and Air Force units with no sense of continuity. In this environment of ad hoc base security assignments, little motivation existed for long-term capacity building of the ANSF units outside-the-wire. Rather, far more emphasis was placed on the Bagram detention facility within the base.

Recognizing this gap, this lack of formal training of our Afghan partners, we took TF Top Guns initial coordination a step further. While enthusiastic, Colonel Sultan's soldiers were trained as military police, not infantrymen. To both develop small-unit infantry skills and continue strengthening our relationship, we began a small-unit infantry skills training program. Every week, a handful of GLT Marines would head to the Afghan side of base to train the junior officers in different infantry skills, skills we'd then employ and reinforce during the following week's patrols.

About this same time, the COMBAF CG began pressuring his staff to do something about the fact that no formal plan existed for transitioning security responsibilities over to the Afghans, despite the fact that, in this *doublethink* world, "combat was over for US forces." Enter the Marines and our training program. We became the COMBAF staff's "main effort" in their knee-jerk response to accomplishing the CG's intent. Overnight, we went from red-headed step children to the major show in town, as we were the only forces with A) actual outside-the-wire knowledge of our area of operations, and B) any semblance of a formalized training plan in place with the Afghans.

Our weekly training became the central pillar of COMBAF's "Unified Parwan Security Plan" (UPS-P), referring to the Afghan province where Bagram was located. Bottom line, UPS-P was a fancy way of saying, "Fuck, the war's supposed to be over. How can we make it look like we're actually doing something to transition security responsibility to the Afghans?"

While I absolutely supported this new focus on training the Afghans to assume a larger security role, I questioned the sincerity of implementation. Up at the COMBAF headquarters, I was brought into a meeting on UPS-P, where I once again "ruffled some feathers."

Staff members began talking about an ad hoc, send-a-few-staff-members-over-to- the-Afghan-side-of-base-for-a-few-hours-a-week type program to "train the ANA in staff functions." Bullshit. If I'd learned anything about advising over the past ten months, it was that it can't be an afterthought. Any influence we had with the Georgians and Colonel Sultan's soldiers was a result of hours and hours of time spent building rapport, training, and operating together, "shoulder to shoulder." This is how trust is built.

Recognizing this reality, I asked the question no one wanted to hear: "Why are we doing this? To train Colonel Sultan's *kandak* to standard, or to check a necessary box to cover our exfil from the country?" No clear answer. If we wanted to accomplish the former, it would take tremendous effort and dedication. If we were okay with the latter, let's at least call a spade a spade.

# IV-20

# INCONVENIENCING A GENERAL AND PUTTING OUT FIRES

........................................................

A S FRUSTRATED AS I remained with the whole Ministry of Truth system, I took a significant measure of pride in the work we were doing with our ANA counterparts. Ideally, our efforts would play a small role in getting the Afghan National Security Forces as a whole to a level of independent operations. And, the massive amount of time we poured into planning and executing this training plan made the following situation particularly tough to swallow.

A couple months before our redeployment, one of our ANA-partnered patrols temporarily stopped traffic to dismount from vehicles. This is a standard practice—blocking traffic both ways—with vehicle- and motorcycle-borne IEDs a real threat. Getting out of vehicles leaves troops particularly vulnerable. And, understanding that this security practice can piss off locals trying to get from point A to point B, we'd put the ANA HMMWVs with Afghan soldiers at the two blocking positions. That way, there was an Afghan face (plus language ability) at the points of friction, letting Afghans interact with fellow Afghans.

Unfortunately, on this particular patrol, one of the local Afghans inconvenienced by our temporary traffic stop happened to be an

ANA general stationed on Bagram on his way into base. Irate at our patrol for having the audacity to stop traffic, the general got out of his car, berated the ANA soldiers with us, and ordered them to immediately return to base, which they of course did.

Back in the COC, I received a report from our patrol about what happened just as Amini called. As my go-between with Colonel Sultan, Amini had just hung up the phone with him.

Apparently, the irate general had ordered Colonel Sultan to cancel all patrols with the Georgians for the rest of the day, and there was nothing the colonel could do about it. It's truly refreshing seeing a senior ANA leader buying into assuming responsibility for his country's own security (yes, that's dripping with sarcasm).

I'm sure I sound like a broken record by now, but having the Afghans on patrol with us hugely increased our legitimacy and safety, so this cancellation was a huge deal—another fire to put out. Fortunately, it happened to be a Saturday, so we had our weekly sync meeting with Colonel Sultan already scheduled for early afternoon. After working our standard, weekly patrol coordination, Amini and I headed over to this general's office on the ANA side of base.

Amini, as I've said, knew more Afghan generals than most Afghan generals did—one of the reasons he was absolutely integral to our success—so he already knew this guy. When we got to the general's office, I introduced myself, apologized profusely for any inconvenience our patrol caused, and then Amini went to work. He spent several minutes stroking the general's ego, and all I needed to do was stand there deferentially with an apologetic look on my face. After a few minutes of back-and-forth I didn't understand, Amini smiled and said, "Everything's okay, sir." So, I smiled, said thank you, and crossed my chest with my right hand in Afghan style to the general—another fire put out.

Do I like groveling? Absolutely not. But the ends certainly justified the means here, as our dudes on the next patrol were now heading out with ANA support.

# IV-21

# TRUST BUILT

.......................

F IVE MONTHS INTO our time in Afghanistan, plus the previous one in Germany and three in Georgia, and we'd now
spent nine months partnered with the 51stGLIB. Undoubtedly,
Georgian-induced friction still represented a full circle in my
Venn diagram of frustration, and the Marines patrolling every
day still complained incessantly about Georgian tactics and absurdity on patrol. But, three things converged to make me realize
how tight of a team we'd become.

First, every night, the Georgian battalion staff and company
commanders met for an 1800 staff meeting to share information,
address any major issues, and frequently, get yelled at by the
battalion commander. Emphasizing the intractable nature of our
team, Lt. Col. Koba insisted that the Boss and I be present as the
Marine representatives at each of these meetings, always wrapping things up by giving us an opportunity to address the group.
While this was always a painful hour, as I depended on piecemeal
translation by the battalion commander's interpreter to follow
things, our presence helped keep us and, by extension, the entire
GLT informed, and demonstrated how much Lt. Col. Koba had
grown to trust and value our input and opinions.

Second, as we approached the arrival of the replacement Georgian battalion, the 43rdGLIB, a video teleconference was scheduled between Lt. Col. Koba and his staff and the key players in the next battalion. This absolutely qualified as a Georgian-to-Georgian event, an opportunity to answer questions and outline expectations prior to arrival in-country.

Regardless, Lt. Col. Koba insisted the Boss, our senior enlisted adviser, and I all sit in on this conference, explaining that he would not think to brief the incoming battalion staff without us present.

The last event that confirmed the level of trust built between the Georgians and Marines occurred out on patrol. As combat *advisors*, we had no tasking authority over the Georgians—we couldn't tell them what to do. Rather, we needed to rely on established trust and rapport to influence them. Early in the Afghan deployment, this led to significant friction between the Marine team leaders and Georgian platoon leaders out on patrol, with the Georgians often refusing to listen to Marine advice.

In the spring, we were out on an operation I'd planned in an area that had been the source of numerous rocket attacks. Generally, if I planned an op, Davit would translate the order, and I'd brief it with him to the Marines and Georgians executing. And, though not technically in charge of any Georgians, I would join these larger-scale operations to provide guidance to the Georgians and top-cover to the Marine team leaders.

On this particular op, as soon as we arrived at our vehicle dismount point, the Georgian patrol leader approached me and, in broken English, said, "We follow you, *commandi*." Previously, it took some mental jujitsu and Jedi mind tricks to get the Georgians to follow a plan once we began executing. Now, despite not officially being in charge, the Georgian patrol leader ceded command to me, demonstrating a level of trust that practically floored me.

Plenty of friction continued between Marines and Georgians, but, in the realm of the relative, things had become pretty good. Significant trust, starting from the top and permeating through the ranks, had been built between the GLT/51stGLIB team.

# IV-22

# THE CACHE CLEARANCE JOKE

······················································

D ESPITE POSITIVE STRIDES on the Georgian front, the Ministry of Truth was still firing on all cylinders. In particular, we had solid intel about an explosives cache located in vicinity of the area where Route Clearance Platoon had hit its last IED, near the compound from the failed cordon and search. Apparently, local "force protection threats" (still Taliban...) were temporarily storing explosives outside of a compound as they brought them into the Bagram area from the east, something we wanted to disrupt.

For higher headquarters approval, we were on a weekly planning cycle. Every Friday I submitted A) an overview of the next week's patrols, and B) the more in-depth plans for whatever larger scale, deliberate operations we'd be conducting. With respect to the latter, every week for a month - this explosives cache kept popping up in threat reporting—I'd submit a plan for approval to go clear it. The new TF Solid operations officer was absolutely on board with this, so we'd talk about the plan each week. We were tasked to secure the base, so it'd be stupid not to try to get IED materials off the battlefield when given the chance.

You can probably guess, but each week we submitted this cache clearance plan up to COMBAF it was denied. Rationale - the village and an explosives cache were not direct threats to the base. Yep, that's technically accurate. But, this distorted justification for disapproving our op sure as shit ignores the direct threat these explosives pose to the guys outside-the-wire everyday protecting the base.

After a few weeks of our op being disapproved, it became a joke between me and the TF Solid operations officer. I'd submit the plan Friday, and by Monday I'd receive a call telling me, "Yep, you know the deal...no cache clearance this week." By the final week, I'd stopped even accounting for the cache clearance in our projected patrol schedule, instead just submitting the plan knowing it would be disapproved. But, on the plus side, there seemed to be some lingering, positive effects from my unprofessional e-mail. Now, when ops were disapproved, the COMBAF staff figured out a system for us to submit replacement patrols in lieu of the denied one, despite being inside the COMRS ninety-six-hour window— far better than simply not sending patrols at all. Positive strides, I suppose.

# IV-23

# NAÏVE ALTRUISM AND HELPING THE LOCALS

······················································

R ECOGNIZING MY GENERAL cynicism regarding the Ministry of Truth, a sense of altruism—certainly naïve—served as an element of my personal justification for our presence in Afghanistan. Can the things we do somehow help the lives of individual Afghans? I wrote about this in the context of using CERP funds to build wells, providing fresh water to local villages. But, this idea of helping locals truly came to the forefront in late February 2015 with the catastrophic avalanches in the upper Panjshir Valley.

In the rugged Hindu Kush, most mountain valleys have single, dirt roads for villagers to access the outside world, and this is certainly the case in the upper Panjshir. When these heavy snows hit, massive avalanches not only cut off access to the area, but they also destroyed entire villages, basically wiping them off the map. Looking at the aerial reconnaissance photos, it was hard to imagine how anyone up there could have survived.

While this area was outside of the Bagram Bowl, and definitely outside of our area of operations, our Czech partners found a way to support. Captain Josef, the Czech civil- military coordination officer, organized dozens of pallets of relief supplies (donated blankets, jackets, portable stoves, etc.). And, he'd built a relationship with the ANA battalion commander responsible for security in the far north of the Bagram area, the man whose forces would be able to respond to the avalanche victims.

How do I fit into this situation? As the Georgians manned the entry-control points on Bagram, I served as the English-speaking point of contact for any movement of humanitarian assistance goods in and out of base for the Czechs. So, while we didn't contribute directly to helping the avalanche victims, we spent an afternoon loading ANA trucks with supplies so those guys could provide some relief. Did we help? I think so. Does this justify all the other Ministry of Truth bullshit we dealt with on a daily basis? I don't know, but we played the mind tricks we needed to in order to justify our own daily existence.

# IV-24

# THE GEAR SET BAND-AID AND MORE MORPHINE

.................................................................

I INITIALLY FRAMED THE ANA's "morphine drip of aid" in terms of keeping HMMWVs up and running—it didn't resolve Afghan supply chain issues, but it helped keep our dudes safe. This notion of a drug dependence morphed and grew with the advent of COMBAF's UPS-P, that is, the plan to train the ANA around Bagram Airfield to take over the base security mission. And, on a side note, defense of the airfield wasn't just a selfish American desire to protect their own—rockets were equal-opportunity killers, and Afghans on base were being killed by them, too.

Back to morphine. As discussed, Colonel Sultan's battalion was a military police unit, not infantry. Consequently, in addition to not receiving standard infantry training, these guys were not equipped with an ANA infantry battalion's worth of gear (weapons, vehicles, communications equipment, counter-IED gear, etc.). This was a tough situation, because when these guys were out on patrol, they certainly fulfilled an infantry role.

Naturally, COMBAF's solution to the gear problem involved throwing a band-aid on the situation and calling it good. That band-aid—requesting a full infantry battalion's worth of gear for

Colonel Sultan. On face value, this seemed like a great idea: *These guys need some gear, so let's get them some more gear.*

I viewed this proposal cynically for two reasons. First, this battalion couldn't maintain the ten HMMWVs we already provided without regular maintenance trips over to their motor pool by our mechanics, so how would they maintain a whole battalion's worth of gear? Second, even if the battalion gained the know-how and skills to maintain all this new gear, I've already covered the endemic supply chain issues within the broader ANA—the ability (or lack thereof) to logistically support units crippled the government's fighting potential. You can't fight if you can't get parts, fuel, bullets, and other war-fighting necessities.

So, what did these realities mean? The gear set we were looking to provide would shortly become a really expensive junkyard. As one piece of gear would break, the needed part would never arrive to fix it, leading to a deteriorating cycle of cannibalized gear. Parts from one item would be pulled to fix another until there was nothing left. Now, I get this is a cynical perspective, but I was in a very cynical frame of mine by this point in time. And, like the ad hoc attempt to spend a couple hours a week training Colonel Sultan's staff with a hodgepodge of random folks, this gear band-aid was just that—a quick, superficial fix to a systemic problem that would fall apart with our withdrawal.

With that said, who am I to criticize the status quo? I've fully conceded that I'm a part of the problem, focusing on the short-term fixes to keep Colonel Sultan's guys out patrolling with us, which leads to the crux of the whole issue. We needed the ANA on patrol with us to A) keep us safe, and B) gradually phase security responsibility to them. And, to keep them on patrol, they would need to develop the organic systems to acquire and maintain gear. However, experience demonstrated that cutting them off of our morphine drip, forcing them to acquire and maintain their own gear and supply chains, led to significantly deteriorated fighting ability.

What's the problem here? We have to choose between short-term benefits (ANA on patrol with us) and long-term gains (forcing the Afghans to supply themselves and figure out ANA-wide logistics). Sitting in a coffee shop writing about this years later, it seems like a pretty easy solution. Just cut the ANA off and force them to figure it out—much easier to say when you're not sending guys out into harm's way on a daily basis who depend on the support of Afghan forces.

To go Greek for a moment, we found ourselves between a rock and a hard place. Look long term, and we sacrifice the security of our dudes outside-the-wire. Look short term, and we sacrifice true capacity-building within the Afghan National Security Forces. For better or worse, I'll pick the latter option seven days a week and twice on Sunday.

# IV-25

# SHAKE HANDS WITH THE ENEMY

·········································································

TOWARDS THE END of our deployment, the revolving
door of the Afghan criminal justice system had become affectionately known as the "catch and release program." A guy
would get rolled up and thrown in jail, and within two weeks a
corrupt Member of Parliament (MP) had paid for his release.
Now, he's back on the streets and, as he was already arrested,
cannot be rolled up again until a new target package had been
built, essentially "re-setting" his insurgent status.

As you can imagine, this situation proved extremely frustrating
to us, seeing assholes thrown in jail for planting IEDs, then back
out a few weeks later. Cynically, we viewed prison a lot like an
Afghan summer camp—place for insurgents to get some hot
meals and a few weeks rest. For our first few months in-country,
this situation was an abstract frustration for us, knowing it was
happening but not facing any ramifications directly. This changed
after the first of the year, as ISAF rolled into Resolute Support.

Qaleh Nasro was one of our "problem villages." In addition to
taking countless rockets from the fields surrounding it, this was
the place where we were hit by the first suicide bomber of our
deployment. While we suspected several key families in the village of insurgent activity, one family in particular stood above

the rest. The patriarch of the family owned a sprawling compound on the main drag passing by the village. Though the father did a good job, at least visibly, of keeping his hands clean, one of his grown sons eventually got rolled up. An Afghan special operations unit received actionable intelligence from the US that connected this son, Mohammad, to rocket attacks.

Good stuff, right? Another guy shooting rockets and suspected of planting IEDs was taken off the streets. Within three weeks, Mohammad's father, a wealthy resident of the Qaleh Nasro area, leveraged his influence with the area's MP to kick-start the catch and release program, and Mohammad was back home.

A few weeks later, one of our mounted patrols hit an IED a half-mile down the road from Mohammad's house. Fortunately, no one was seriously injured, but the dudes in the Marine vehicle certainly had their bells rung. While we lacked conclusive evidence linking Mohammad to this bombing, plenty of "chatter" in the area indicated he was responsible. So, it was a big deal the following week when we sent one of our patrols to the area near the father's compound, and the dismounts met Mohammad outside— not trying to avoid us at all and flaunting an untouchable status.

This interaction led to an excited call from the patrol back to our COC and on to TF Solid's JDOC: "We've found Mohammad!" The patrol stated that they were in a position to detain this guy in connection to the IED, they just needed a green light. Pushing the request up to COMBAF's command center, TF Solid eventually received the following word: "He's been released and no longer on the target list—let him go."

What did we do? Confirmed biometric data (retinas and fingerprints), shook the asshole's hand, and carried on with the day. While I'm certainly for the rule of law and due process, this was just one more example to us that we were nothing more than bait to the Ministry of Truth.

# IV-26

# PRIDE AND AN INTERNAL STRUGGLE WITH REALITY

·················································

O NE OF THE last operations we ran with the Georgians prior to our replacements arriving became a culmination of sorts. Recognizing that, with the fighting season starting to kick off, more and more fighters were heading into the village of Khwajakhel west of Highway 1, we needed to get in there and disrupt some things. To do this, we planned an op with a level of tactical complexity I never would've imagined suggesting six months prior when I kicked the Georgians out of their vehicles and made them walk through our area of operations.

The plan incorporated Marines, Georgians, ANA, and a US Army intelligence team, with the objective being to get that intel team into Khwajakhel to build our understanding of insurgent activity and weapons facilitation in the area. And, the incredible thing? We actually executed the op as I planned and briefed it. The Georgian/Marine team with Army intel in our vehicles linked up with our ANA partners outside of Bagram at 0200. From there, we blacked out our vehicles, moved to a vehicle dismount point roughly five kilometers from the objective village, and conducted a dismounted night infil into Khwajakhel. As the sun came up, we were on the streets of the village, with Marines and Georgians locking down all avenues of approach so the Army intel team could safely and freely conduct street-level engagements throughout the village. Concurrently, our vehicle-mounted element established blocking positions to prevent ingress/egress along the single road from Highway 1 up into the village. Objective complete, we safely patrolled to a new link-up point with the vehicles and returned to base.

I cannot emphasize enough how immensely proud I was of how far we'd come. Upon arriving at Bagram, we'd been the red-headed step children of the task force. Our higher headquarters initially thought all Marines were "shoot first, ask questions later cowboys," and that the Georgians would be uncontrollable, tactically inept foreigners. By the time we were preparing to leave, the Georgian/Marine team had become the force of choice in the area for the most high-risk, mission-critical conventional operations to protect the largest base in Afghanistan.

With all that said, and despite my pride, I still faced a significant internal struggle—why the fuck were we here, and what did our actions matter? This feeling was exacerbated by an incident the week following the above op.

One of our patrols was near a village north of Khwajakhel, but still in the "wild west" stretch west of Highway 1. Our guys received some inaccurate AK-47 fire from the village and moved in to cordon off the area, asking some locals about the shooter. Our ANA partners talked with a few villagers, but, with no concrete information about a shooter, the patrol departed. The next day, the Army intel folks received word from a source in the area—one of the locals our patrol talked to had his throat slit and was dumped in the street, apparently as a warning to other villagers not to talk to ANSF or Coalition Forces.

This killing was a particularly tough pill to swallow. Six months into the deployment, what had we actually accomplished? Sure,

I was extremely proud of the Georgians' tactical development, but in the big picture, what the fuck did that matter? Afghans were going to keep killing other Afghans, regardless of our presence. I get this is some fatalistic cynicism, but that's where we were.

# IV-27

# LETTING ONE GO

··································

M OST OF THIS section has been focused on the higher headquarters circle of my Venn diagram of frustration, but Baryali still loomed large in the Taliban, correction, "force protection threat," circle. To us, he remained the asshole we most wanted dead. The last solid word we'd received was that he'd fled the area following "Operation Christmas Offensive," spooked by us showing his picture and asking questions about him around his village. Towards the end of our deployment, we began to hear rumors that he was back in the area—no solid intel, just unsubstantiated reports.

Following Baryali's IED attack on Highway 1 that had killed the two Route Clearance Platoon soldiers, we'd focused our attention on his father's house in Khwajakhel, where the attackers had all lived. However, we also knew Baryali's mother lived a few miles away from there, closer to base on the east side of Highway 1. Lacking any solid intel, we would periodically send a dismounted patrol by his house. On one of these "drive-bys," Bane saw a military age male on top of Baryali's mom's house. Coordinating with the Georgian platoon leader, Bane completely cordoned off the house before this guy could bolt. We had him.

Next, due to our rules of engagement, and the fact that neither we nor the ANA could enter the house, we spent two hours convincing NDS to enter the house. Eventually, two NDS agents entered, spending three minutes inside before coming back outside to say that no one but the mother was home, despite real-time reporting from Apache pilots overhead that multiple males were inside the compound walls.

This proved to be our ultimate frustration, and it was symbolic of the broader failures in Afghanistan. In the neat, closed-loop narrative of a novel or film, Baryali would have stormed out of his house, AK-47 blazing, and been gunned down by Georgian, Marine, and Afghan bullets, a fitting end to Scumbag #1. But, we weren't living in that neat loop. Rather, I fully recognize my own cowardice in this situation. Back in the COC, I could've ordered them to clear the compound and accepted the repercussions myself, but I didn't. I suppose I'd become just another cog in the wheel of the Ministry of Truth.

Bane's patrol departed, and that was that. Who knows, maybe it wasn't Baryali inside, but I'll never know for sure. Months later, I'd carry significant guilt for a Georgian on the next rotation dying in an attack. While I have no idea who was responsible, I'll always wonder if we could've done more.

# IV-28

# LUNCH WITH THE "MINISTER OF TRUTH"

......................................................

I N A FITTING end, I had a unique opportunity towards the end of deployment. After mother-fucking the system and the limitations imposed by it over the past six months, I finally had a chance to sit down with the Minister of Truth himself. The COMRS CG, the four-star general in charge of Resolute Support and all Coalition Forces in Afghanistan, would be on Bagram.

The Boss called me one Thursday afternoon. TF Solid received word that the COMRS CG would be on base and wanted to have lunch with a group of company grade officers, and he explicitly requested a Marine from the GLT join. So, I got tapped to represent our team, with explicit instructions from the TF Solid CO to "be good" (he still had my e-mail fresh in his mind).

About eight of us, captains from different commands around base, posted up in a side room in one of the chow halls, waiting for the COMRS and COMBAF CGs to arrive. Ironically, this would be the first time seeing the COMBAF CG face-to-face since blast e-mailing his staff (minus watching him tear into the Boss at the TF Saber–TF Solid TOA ceremony). Apparently, I'd become a "legend" at their HQ—a lot of pent-up frustration existed throughout the base, and people approved of any raging against the sources of that frustration.

Eventually, the generals arrived and standard military etiquette ensued; that is, announcing "attention on deck," standing at attention until the generals took their seats, and conducting formal introductions. Once that was out of the way, COMRS CG provided a brief introduction to why he was doing this—not to deliver a prepared speech, but to field our questions and understand the captain-level perspective in Afghanistan.

What struck me the most, after listening to some of his responses, was the CG's personal level of frustration. Writing this now, I understand how ridiculous it sounds, but I'd worked myself up into such a state of disdain for the entire Ministry of Truth in Afghanistan that I saw every commander and staff above us as part of this system. I naively projected my frustration on their intentions, that is, assuming that all these staffs above us existed solely to create red tape.

Sitting with the highest-ranking US military member in Afghanistan, the one serving as the liaison between the Pentagon, the rest of the DC Beltway, and this war, it became clear that his frustration probably surpassed my own. He very clearly insinuated that his hands were tied by Stateside entities. Political decisions have real-world consequences for guys on the ground. Talks of caps on troop levels, ROE, and "direct combat operations" actually impact the safety and security of service members. These aren't just abstract phrases and concepts.

In accordance with the "dead white guy" philosophy of war, armed force is an extension of policy. If policy objectives don't drive the military action, or, in our case, if military action cannot accomplish the policy objectives (limited military presence somehow enabling stability across a "country" that's never truly existed), something's fucked up. This isn't to say that military use necessarily needs to be restricted to total war. But, if ambiguously defined national policy objectives cannot be achieved by the use of military force, the guys on the ground carrying out that military force should not be subjected to the risk inherent to combat.

Sitting in the little side room across from the COMRS CG, my naïveté hit me like a brick wall. The commanders in Afghanistan were trying to do the best with the shit situation they'd inherited. Due to my limited perspective, COMBAF initially represented my vision of the Ministry of Truth. I cynically saw lieutenants checking IDs at the COMBAF HQ and lieutenant colonels putting out name tags as waste and inefficiency, while we struggled to get another corpsman assigned to support combat patrols. In reality, this was just another example of all the units in-country doing what they could with what they had.

As I finally saw, the Ministry of Truth wasn't one person or one command. It was the whole system, from the forces in Afghanistan to the political figures playing puppet master within the Beltway. I quoted Orwell previously, stating that, "The Ministry of Truth concerns itself with lies…" To update this definition, our new Ministry of Truth did not represent a conspiracy-esque entity designed to intentionally manipulate the truth and mislead the public. Rather, the Ministry of Truth existed as a broader system of a whole lot of people churning ahead with their daily tasks, refusing to acknowledge that in doing so, we were all misleading ourselves into seeing some possible positive outcome arise from our activities.

Where did this leave us? Personally, my initial inclinations of fatalism solidified. We could focus on bringing our guys home alive, and hopefully helping some locals in the process, but that was about it.

# PART V

# THE WRAP-UP
## (Afghanistan, Resolute Support)

*March - April 2015*

# V-1

## DAVIT & AMINI

...........................

A S OUR REPLACEMENTS' arrival approached, a couple of events served as bookends of sorts to the deployment, or at least transitions to the next phase. I've said it before, but I'll reiterate here anyway. Any success the Georgian/Marine team had was the result of two individuals, our interpreters—Davit and Amini.

Davit served as the critical link between the 51stGLIB, the Marines, and our US Army higher headquarters. In addition to a level of English proficiency far superior to the other military linguists, he had a work ethic and critical thinking ability that just got things done.

Without Davit, the operations we planned would not have A) been translated and disseminated to the Georgians, and B) been so strongly advocated for in the Georgian camp. He truly was the lynchpin that enabled my marionette approach to advising. So, with the massive amount of pressure on his shoulders and work on his plate for our entire deployment, it amazed me when, the week before our replacements arrived, Davit volunteered to extend for another deployment. He would remain as the critical link in the chain for the incoming Georgian/Marine team. His selflessness and dedication amaze me to this day.

The next interpreter event towards the end of our deployment involved Amini, our Dari-language interpreter. About the same time Davit decided to stick around for Round Two, Amini headed back to his family in Canada for a month of well-deserved leave. As Davit represented our *sin qua non* in working with the Georgians, Amini filled the same role with the Afghans. Yes, we had other hard-working, proficient Afghan linguists, but no one could do what Amini could. In addition to having a digital rolodex of what seemed like every general in Afghanistan, his sense of humor and sincerity allowed him to work well with anyone. And, his relationships and dedication to helping us got us out of hot water with our Afghan counterparts multiple times.

Losing Amini for a month before we took off forced me to reflect on just how lucky I was to work with him over the course of the deployment. At our final Saturday meeting with the ANA before introducing our replacements, Colonel Sultan told me, "You're not allowed to go home." This bond, both professional and personal, that we established over the last half year working together, would not have been built without Amini.

As the end of deployment approached, I realized just how lucky I'd been to work with both Davit and Amini, and to call them my friends.

# V-2

# THE REPLACEMENTS ARRIVE

......................................................

IF AMINI HEADING home on leave and Davit signing on for the next deployment hinted at a transition, the arrival of the Marines replacing us solidified the end of one phase of our deployment and the beginning of another. At the end of March 2015, the Marines from the GLT replacing us arrived with the first flight of Georgians out of Tbilisi. Our partner battalion, the 51stGLIB, would be replaced by the 43rdGLIB.

In another transition, because the "war was over," the new Marine team would be part of Georgia Deployment Program–*Resolute Support, Rotation 1*, vice our designation as Georgia Deployment Program–*International Security Assistance Force, Rotation 14*. This was nothing more than *newspeak* sleight of hand—same mission, different name.

Cynicism aside, it was certainly a watershed moment for our whole team having these guys arrive. To accommodate the new GLT, we moved out of our billeting and into some transient "cans" (shipping containers converted into rooms—actually really nice digs), and we helped all the new Marines move into their permanent rooms. After loading their gear onto flatbeds at the airfield's arrival terminal, we dropped their stuff off in the rooms and walked down for some MIDRATs (midnight rations) at the chow hall.

As expected, there was plenty of "butt sniffing" between our guys and the new Marines as they felt each other out, but it was clear from the onset that our transition with these guys would go far more smoothly than our initial one. Rather than cobbling together a mission and gear set from disparate units and services, we'd have a one-to-one transition with these guys—Georgians replaced Georgians, and Marines replaced Marines.

For me, I was just glad to finally meet my replacement, Dylan, face-to-face. We'd had several secure VTCs with the new GLT's leadership, answering questions about the area, the mission, etc. But, sitting in the chow hall slamming a midnight sandwich, we could finally drop formal pretenses and just shoot the shit. We had a lot of work left to ensure a successful transition, but actually having our replacements here was a good start.

# V-3

# RSO&I

..........

W ITH THE FIRST flight of new arrivals, both Marine and Georgian, in Bagram—and four more flights inbound over a week and a half stretch—we needed to begin the required training for guys entering a combat zone. Reception, Staging, Onward Movement, and Integration (RSO&I) is meant to hit all the pre-requisites for going outside-the-wire—rules of engagement, counter-IED training, and BZO'ing, or calibrating, rifle optics (helps ensure that what you aim at, you hit).

Due to the shortage of Georgian interpreters and the multiple units we relieved, the RSO&I we received entering Afghanistan felt like nothing more than an administrative check-in-the-box, something to brief as complete, but not an actual attempt to prepare us for combat operations. We had to make this process better. So, I coordinated with Major Nik to put together a thorough RSO&I package for each wave of arrivals, something that would, ideally, set them up for success. We established a two-day, three-station rotation plan for each wave of new arrivals:

*Station 1*: An Army JAG on base would brief rules of engagement (ROE), and I would brief the Tactical Driving Directive (an ROE supplement designed to minimize the likelihood of civilian casualties while driving massive armored vehicles). Seven

months in and a "bad kill" remained a major concern of mine—
I sought here to help these new GLT members get their Georgian
counterparts on board with what's allowed and what's not.

*Station 2*: To help the 43rdGLIB BZO their rifle optics, we
would organize the administrative requirements for the rifle
range, and our 51stGLIB counterparts would actually run the
firing line—critical roles due to the language differences.

*Station 3*: For the final station, we received some outstanding
support from our Army EOD partners, the guys we'd worked
with the entire deployment. Instead of presenting some bullshit
PowerPoint slides and calling it good, this EOD team put together
an incredible counter-IED package—formal classes, IED component demonstrations, counter-IED equipment instruction, and
lane training actually applying the skills and lessons learned in
these classes.

There were a lot of moving pieces, balancing each of the above
stations and their required logistical support with the five flights
of new arrivals inbound every couple days. And, per usual, we
fucked things up pretty good initially due to a lack of Georgian/Ma-
rine face-to-face coordination. So, after that first round of putting
out fires, we implemented a daily RSO&I sync— logistics and
operations Marines and Georgians sitting around the table to make
sure everyone was on the same page for the following day's events
and support requirements.

Reflecting on the RSO&I, it still seemed unbelievable to me
how far we'd come. After creating our mission from scratch—and
building all associated products and procedures through a trial and
error series of fuck-ups—we'd learned far more than I realized.
This knowledge finally dawned on me as Sleepy, our intel officer,
and I gave the new group of Marines an O&I (Operations and Intelligence) brief about our mission and the area of operations.
Every slide, every comment, was another potential tangent of
knowledge and experience we acquired here. During the daily

grind of operations, you don't realize it, but we'd learned more than I ever would've expected since arriving in September 2014.

It was a huge weight off my shoulders once RSO&I was complete, as each wave of newly arrived troops transitioned into learning their specific missions. And, wrapping up this initial training allowed me to focus on what I needed to do, that is, turning over my responsibilities as operations officer to Dylan.

# V-4

# THE AFGHAN HAND-OFF

······································

T URNING OVER OUR relationship with the ANA would be one of my first, and most significant, responsibilities with my counterpart. The training, partnered ops, and the regular HMMWV maintenance—these were all elements of the complex relationship with Colonel Sultan and his soldiers. And, at the foundation of it all was trust and rapport—without these elements, partnered operations didn't exist.

I'd already brought Dylan over on a couple Saturday sync meetings with Colonel Sultan, which gave him some insight into the procedures for scheduling and approving partnered patrols. So, for the formal relationship hand-off, we could focus on the small- unit training we'd worked so hard to develop. By this point, we were a month into our training program for the junior officers of Colonel Sultan's battalion, with two months remaining in this initial package. By using this training as a vehicle for formally transferring our relationship to the new Marines, we would A) help the new guys continue to build rapport with our ANA counterparts, and B) continue to develop the skills of the Afghan soldiers who watch our backs on patrol.

As I should have expected, this handover became a tremendous dog and pony show, with tons of US, Georgian, and Afghan "brass," to say nothing of the US public affairs officers and US media, present to watch the Marines train Afghan small-unit leaders in patrol skills. Specifically, the incoming and outgoing Marines conducted the training together with the ANA junior officers, demonstrating and leading practical application in "buddy rushing," a critical small-unit infantry skill.

As senior officer after senior officer rotated through interviews, praising the strong relationships developed through this training and our partnered ops, I just smiled. The real praise belonged to the junior officer and staff NCO Marines and Afghans who made this training possible, the ones who actually sweat and bled together on patrol. But, I guess it's another fact of life that the ones truly deserving credit are never the ones being interviewed.

With patrol planning and training turned over, the last major ANA-related responsibility would be HMMWV maintenance. Eventually, the morphine drip of support to the Afghans would have to be cut off to build the ANA's ability to support itself, but we sure as shit weren't going to be the unit to do it. We'd do whatever we had to do to keep Colonel Sultan's soldiers patrolling with us, and the new GLT felt the same way. So, I brought Dylan, the logistics officer, and the maintenance chief over to meet Colonel Sultan at his battalion motor pool. We talked through the details of moving vehicles back and forth between the ANA and US sides of base, and basically just gave the guys more of a chance to get to know each other.

As we left, Colonel Sultan looked at Dylan and said, "You have a lot of work to do to replace Captain Naylon." I feel like a douchebag even writing about this compliment, but, I'm not going to lie, I'm extremely proud of the work we'd done with these guys, and the personal relationship I'd developed with Colonel Sultan. I'll always have great memories of the time following our formal Saturday patrol syncs—sitting in his office, chain-smoking cigarettes, drinking chai, and just getting to know each other.

# V-5

# PASSING THE "SYNC"

······································

T HE PIECEMEAL COMPOSITING of multiple tasks in and around Bagram Airfield into a single mission had given our deployment a pick-up game feel. And, we attempted to impose some semblance of order onto an otherwise ad hoc set of actions, particularly in the initial stages of "unfucking ourselves."

This ad hoc nature proved particularly prevalent in our initial patrol objectives, the terrain-denial mission of "go out and stay in this area 24/7." Not only was this ineffective in preventing rocket attacks (the Taliban just moved to another place), but it created unnecessary risk by forcing us to set clear and predictable patterns. Transitioning from this terrain-denial approach to actual intelligence-driven patrols and operations remained one of the most significant accomplishments of our deployment.

These intelligence-driven patrols were facilitated by our weekly operations- intelligence sync meeting, and, in retrospect, it seems crazy that this didn't exist before we arrived (anyone with a lick of counter-insurgency experience, or a shred of common sense for that matter, will look at the below and say, "no shit, man").

*Me to Sleepy*: "Hey, why don't we use intelligence and intelligence gaps to set our patrol priorities and deliberate operations?"

*Sleepy*: "Yeah, that makes sense—I'll reach out to the intel folks from the different agencies around base, set up a meeting, and we'll see who shows up."

That was at the beginning of our deployment. And, this initial conversation set the stage for our weekly sync, which, over the course of the past half year, provided us both current intelligence and intelligence requests from multiple agencies on base, driving our operations and fostering an increased understanding of our area as a whole. We became the eyes and ears of every organization on base that wasn't outside-the-wire on a daily basis. As a result, passing these sync responsibilities to our Marine and Georgian replacements, more than the rest of the transition to that point, felt like a true culminating point to the deployment. Furthermore, seeing these replacements buy into this system we'd established and refined gave us the feeling of some lasting legacy, despite all of our other failures.

Nothing we did was perfect. Quite the contrary, most of our actions were pretty amateurish as we scrambled to keep our heads above water, and this sync process was certainly not perfect either. But, by the time we left, successful rocket attacks on base had been reduced by fifty percent—certainly a small victory. I'll be the first to recognize that correlation does not equal causation—plenty of other factors went into this reduction—but, leaving Afghanistan and struggling to grab onto something positive, we could at least look to those numbers.

# V-6

# TRANSFER OF AUTHORITY

·················································

A FTER A FEW weeks, all tasks and other mission requirements had been turned over to the new Georgian/Marine
team. Making it formal would be the last thing we needed to do,
that is, having our transfer of authority (TOA) ceremony. Fittingly, our TOA would be held in the "Clam Shell," that gathering
place of such frustration to us as we prepared for and wound
down from patrols immediately next to it, with sounds of dance
("combat salsa"), roller derbies, and comedy shows juxtaposed
against the frustrations of another shitty patrol.

The morning of the TOA, I received the highest compliment of
the deployment. I bumped into one of the captains from the COM-
BAF staff whom I'd worked with on a variety of things, said goodbye, and, as I was walking away he said, "Thanks for keeping it
real, man." This comment wasn't aimed at me. Rather, the way I in-
terpreted it, it was aimed at all the Godsons Marines. Did we make
plenty of fucked up decisions and mess plenty of things up? You
bet. But, vainly and in retrospect, I like to think we spent seven
months in Afghanistan focusing on what mattered—the mission.

The TOA ceremony itself went well. The COMBAF CG, the
Georgian Chief of Defense, Lt. Col. Koba, and the incoming Georgian battalion commander all spoke—basically all the pomp and

circumstance of a ceremony held on a base that might as well be back in the States. But, it still felt nice formally passing the torch. I'd be lying if, inside, I didn't appreciate the recognition, too.

We were certainly no closer to ending the war or solving Afghanistan's problems than when we arrived, but human nature being what it is, it still felt good to see a number of people from across the base come out to our ceremony—a testament to the relationships we'd established.

# V-7

# SAYING GOODBYE TO THE 51ST

·······················································

D ESPITE ALL OF the frustrations with the 51stGLIB, largely resulting from the post-Soviet, centralized-control mindset of the Georgian military, you couldn't ask for a better group of guys. I've said it frequently since finishing our tour with them, but the Georgian military is one of the most frustrating institutions in the world, while the individual Georgian soldiers are some of the most loyal and hospitable people I've ever met. In that vein, it was tough leaving Davit, especially knowing he'd be sticking around for another seven months of this bullshit. We said goodbyes and hugged it out. I hope we'll cross paths somewhere down the line.

The Marines all left together on one flight – heading to Kuwait for a couple-day layover then home – while the Georgians would fly straight back to Tbilisi. Lt. Col. Koba and Levan, his interpreter, came out to say goodbye to all the Marines as we waited to board our plane. Lt. Col. Koba was genuinely happy, because he recognized that the Marines' and Georgians' success was inextricably linked. As we left, I took a picture with him and Levan, and he had the largest smile I'd seen on his face for the past eleven months. The relief of getting out of this place with, despite some close calls, no Marines or Georgians killed was tangible in the air.

Despite my disagreements with some of his decisions regarding his battalion's employment, we couldn't have asked for a better commander as a partner. More than I realized at the time, Lt. Col. Koba intimately perceived the capabilities and limitations of his battalion. The decisions he made, such as not wanting to send his guys out on multi-day patrols without vehicle support, were not due to a lack of aggression or tactical prowess (as I, the naïve and arrogant captain with a fraction of his experience, thought at the time).

Rather, his actions were indicative of his recognition of just how far he could push his men, the hallmark of a true leader. I'll miss him, too.

# V-8

# REFLECTIONS

··························

O N 16 APRIL 2015, we caught our plane out of Bagram, a C-17 to Kuwait to wait for transport back to California. Finally leaving allowed for some reflection on the past seven months. Despite having officially turned over the week prior, it was impossible to shed the feeling of stress while still in Afghanistan—always something more to do, some task to accomplish. For seven months, we lived in a state of constant stress, regardless of the "country club" nature of our deployment.

Our deployment certainly came nowhere close to the intensity of firefights and ubiquitous IEDs faced by forces throughout the country during the war in Afghanistan. But, that doesn't change the stress. Every day walking across open areas on base, every patrol outside the wire, and every deliberate operation, we make decisions that could get our guys killed, and for what? With the Ministry of Truth blindly churning ahead in an unwinnable war, how do we rationalize these risks? What's the "greater good"? I suppose we all do our own Jedi mind tricks to justify the stress we live with, the risks we take, but I ultimately settled on two goals to justify our daily existence: *Goal 1*: Bring the dudes on our left and right home alive. *Goal 2*: Make the lives of the local Afghans we deal with just a little better.

How else can you deal with the constant stress of knowing that your decisions could potentially get people—your friends and fellow Marines—killed? How else can you not lose your mind blaming a government that put you in an unwinnable situation while restricting your ability to defend yourself?

Sitting on a plane leaving Afghan airspace, all these cares fell to the wayside as the stress seemed to melt off my shoulders…if only temporarily.

# EPILOGUE

······················

*May- December 2015*

B ACK IN THE States, the Godsons had another couple of weeks together on Camp Pendleton—mandatory transition training to help us "re-acclimate" to life outside of a combat zone. While many of the required classes and lectures seemed like quickly pieced together checks-in-the-box, this proved to be valuable decompression time, time to come into work, bullshit with the guys, and keep an eye on each other before we all went to the winds. That's the odd thing about deploying as a group of combat advisors, it's not a bunch of Marines and sailors from the same unit who return and remain together; when GDP-ISAF ROTO 14 broke up, we all went back to our own units, our own separate Marine Corps lives.

In the above context, I spent a couple more months with my old battalion out in Camp Pendleton, doing random jobs and check-out procedures, before transferring cross-country to Virginia for my next set of orders. During this time at home, while you're back but still haven't completely shed the constant stress of seven months overseas, your link to the past (or at least mine) proved to be compulsive Google searches of "Georgians Marines Bagram," or any permutation of the sort, constantly seeking information about what we've left behind, still feeling that sense of ownership for the mission. These searches eventually delivered the news I dreaded.

In September 2015, a month before the 43rdGLIB's (the Georgian battalion that relieved us) redeployment, one of its soldiers was killed in an ambush on patrol outside the base. In December 2015, six US Airmen died in a motorcycle-borne IED suicide attack in the village of Bajawri—same style attack, same village as the attack on our patrol thirteen months prior that sent Major Zaza to Germany as a casualty.

This one hit home. I don't know whether it was the fact that I'd had a few drinks when I found out, or that it was just so similar, but the guilt almost became overwhelming. *What could we have done differently? Could we have done more to track down the guys responsible for the attack on us? Could we have done a more thorough job passing on our lessons learned to other units on Bagram? Would any of that have helped prevent this?*

After a sober look at the situation over the next few days, and following some much-needed heart-to-hearts with guys from the Godsons, I realized that none of it would've mattered. Perhaps this is just a mental trick necessary for self-preservation, but it eventually dawned on me that as long as we remain in Afghanistan, we're going to continue to die there, regardless of what we do.

So what? I don't know whether we should be in Afghanistan or not. By killing terrorists there, do we keep them from planning attacks here? I don't know. While the fatalist in me sees our continued occupation as simply fuel to an unstoppable tidal wave of Islamic radicalism, logically suggesting we may as well leave, the optimist says maybe we are having an effect. Ultimately, the debate about whether we should or shouldn't be there is irrelevant to me. We are there. And, as we remain in Afghanistan, not providing our warfighters the tools they truly need to protect themselves and the bases to which they're assigned, we as a society continue to sanction a tremendous crime against these servicemen.

It may be politically convenient to try to have our cake and eat it too, that is to say, stay in Afghanistan but not engage in "combat operations," but this is nothing more than the smoke and mirrors propagated by the Ministry of Truth, our modern *newspeak* and *doublethink.*

With that said, I hope my criticism of the war in Afghanistan in no way diminishes the sacrifices of the servicemen who fought and died there. Those who made the ultimate sacrifice did so for their brothers- and sisters-in-arms and to better the lives of the Afghan people; they fought the good fight, and no one can take that away from them. Rather, I intend to speak out against a government that betrayed these individuals by putting them in impossible situations for the wrong reasons with no clearly defined (or obtainable) political objectives while restricting their military means to defend themselves. And, as US bases (or whatever the *newspeak* term of the hour for a military base becomes) proliferate in conflict zones around the world, will we continue to commit this crime? Will we continue to send America's youth into harm's way without, at a minimum, a frank and public conversation about what our political objectives are and whether or not our military means can achieve those objectives?

Lacking this conversation, the Ministry of Truth will surely continue to churn, sending servicemen abroad while restricting their ability to defend themselves.

# AKNOWLEDGMENTS

····································

I FIRST NEED to thank Harley Patrick and the rest of the Hellgate Press team. Without their professional support and encouragement, this book would never have become reality.

Next, to John T. Lescroart, an author and my cousin—thank you for all of the advice, and for showing me that writing for a couple hours before work every day can eventually lead to a completed manuscript.

Related to the above, to my wife, Jenna—thank you for putting up with years of early mornings and loud coffee grinders. I couldn't have finished this without your support. But, more importantly, thank you for the love and patience you've always shown, regardless of the anger and frustration I've dealt with at times.

Lastly, to the Godsons—there's no other group of warfighters I'd rather have had on my left and right. Thank you. Without your support, humor, and countless cigarettes, I would have left all of my sanity in Afghanistan. I held multiple titles throughout my time in the Marine Corps, but being Anvil Actual was the greatest honor. *Semper Fidelis*, brothers.

# ABOUT THE AUTHOR

A FTER GROWING UP in Buffalo, New York, the author (nickname: "Chipp") attended the United States Naval Academy and commissioned into the Marine Corps. In his nine years in the Marines, he served as an infantry officer in a variety of roles with a group of absolutely incredible people. Following his time in the service, he and his wife, Jenna, settled in Richmond, Virginia. Chipp currently works as an accountant, a job he acknowledges is just about as far from the content of this book as he could possibly travel.

www.hellgatepress.com

Made in the USA
Middletown, DE
03 June 2019